SON OF HARPO SPEAKS!

SON OF HARPO SPEAKS!

BILL MARX

APPLAUSE
THEATRE & CINEMA BOOKS
An Imprint of Hal Leonard Corporation

Applause Theatre & Cinema Books
An Imprint of Hal Leonard Corporation
7777 West Bluemound Road
Milwaukee, WI 53213

Trade Book Division Editorial Offices
33 Plymouth St., Montclair, NJ 07042

Published by Applause Theatre & Cinema Books in 2011

Originally published by BearManor Media in 2010

Printed in the United States of America

Book design by Valerie Thompson

The Library of Congress has cataloged the BearManor Media edition as follows:

Marx, Bill.
  Son of Harpo speaks! / by Bill Marx.
      p. cm.
  Includes bibliographical references and index.
  1. Marx, Harpo, 1888-1964. 2. Comedians--United States--Biography. 3.
Motion picture actors and actresses--United States--Biography. 4. Marx
Brothers. 5. Marx, Bill. 6. Musicians--United States--Biography. I. Title.

PN2287.M54M37 2007
791.4302'8092--dc22
[B]
                                           2006101540

Applause ISBN 978-1-55783-790-5

www.applausebooks.com

To Dad, Mom & Family

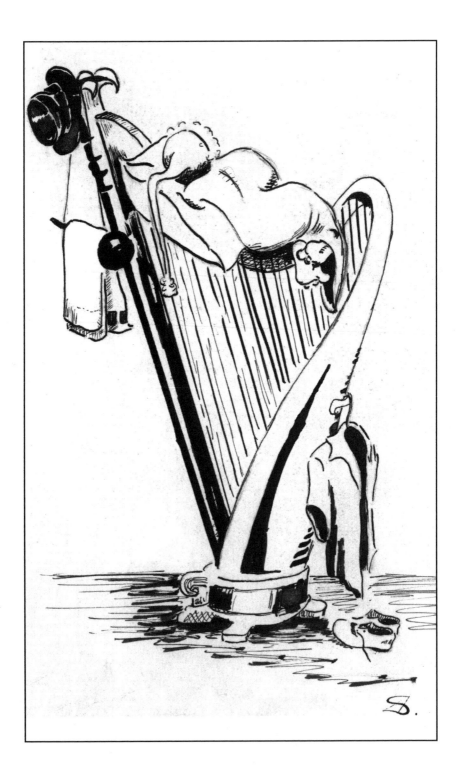

INTRODUCTION

For those of you, unfamiliar with one of America's most beloved comedy teams, permit me to introduce you to the Marx Brothers. My father, Harpo, was one of five brothers born to Minnie and Sam Marx. The Brothers' long, hard struggle to the top of the entertainment profession began not long after the turn of the twentieth century, and their humor remains as fresh and timeless today as it ever was. They may be the most aware group of any people ever, because when meeting with their uniqueness, they then realized it, lived it, and shared it with the world.

Mr. Green's Reception (pre 1915); Left to right: Leonard (Chico), Julius (Groucho), Milton (Gummo) & Arthur (Harpo).

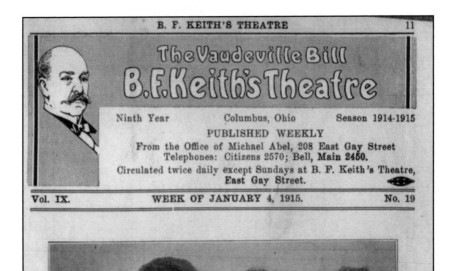

The Vaudeville Bill
B.F.Keith's Theatre

Ninth Year   Columbus, Ohio   Season 1914-1915

PUBLISHED WEEKLY

From the Office of Michael Abel, 208 East Gay Street
Telephones: Citizens 2570; Bell, Main 2450.
Circulated twice daily except Sundays at B. F. Keith's Theatre,
East Gay Street.

Vol. IX.   WEEK OF JANUARY 4, 1915.   No. 19

COMING NEXT WEEK

The four talented Marx Brothers in "Home Again,"
will headline the bill here next week. Julius, Milton, Leonard
and Arthur—count 'em— four of the nattiest, cleverest boys
in vaudeville. They are sure to please—they cannot help it
for they are natural comedians and born entertainers.

They began their career in Vaudeville (a stage variety show) and
spent twenty years on the various circuits, until they finally reached
the pinnacle of stage stardom on Broadway. They remained there
for seven smash years before winding up in Hollywood, California,
where they were to make thirteen classic movies for another twenty
years from 1929 to 1949.

When the Marx Brothers retired from the motion picture chapter
of their history, Groucho, with his cigar, mustache and acerbic
barbs, entered into the field of television for his fourteen-year-

VodeLife

August 15, 1915   Page Seven

The Four Marx Brothers

A Family of Entertainers Who Are Known the Length and Breadth of Vaudeville

FOUR of a kind—that aptly describes the Four Marx Brothers whose activities as entertainers are familiar to vaudeville fans from one end of the land to the other.

Leonard—
Arthur—
Julius—
Milton—

Starting from the oldest to the youngest, that's the way they run. And the odd part of their career is that the youngest member of the talented quartette—Milton—was the first to essay the perilous path of stage life. In co-partnership with Harry Sheehan, Milton delved into the mysteries of making a hit in vaudeville, and raising his wages from a salary to a competence. Seemingly, the courageous Milton had the right idea, for it was not long before he inveigled Julius and Arthur to join him in a family trio called "The Three Nightingales."

Following Milton's example, Julius had dived head foremost into a theatrical career, and when he came up for a breathing spell, he found himself installed as the leading man in "The Man of Her Choice." This was a traveling troupe designated to raise the theatrical standards of the natives of the "one-nighters," and Julius had progressed so far in the Thespian art, that he immediately jumped at the idea of a family trio. There was still one brother—Leonard—left at home. So without much more ado, he became a "Nightingale" and the trio welcomed the addition of

a fourth member. The boys discovered that among themselves they had the nucleus for an entire vaudeville show. Two were excellent comedians, essaying any character from "silly kid" to "Dago"; one was a fine harp player; another made a piano seemingly to talk; all were good singers and dancers.

Result: "The Four Marx Bros. and Company"—the "company" being four pretty girls, and the setting a schoolroom. From theatre to theatre the "Marx" combination traveled, piled up a huge success, and invariably were booked for return engagements. Their mother, Minnie Palmer, who has since acquired a wide reputation as a producer of vaudeville acts, was the manager of the "school" act. Soon the idea presented itself to Mrs. Palmer to incorporate the "school act" into a tabloid musical show. This was forthwith done, and the result was "Mr. Green's Reception." To say the musical show was a hit with the vaudeville patrons is but putting it mildly. Many were of the opinion that it had never been excelled. After two seasons on the "three-shows-a-day" circuits, the Four Marx Brothers produced a new piece called "At Home," and essayed the "big-time"— the Keith and Orpheum circuits.

Here their success was as instantaneous as it had been on the smaller circuits, and already they are regarded as "big-time" fixtures, having thousands of devotees amongst the vaudeville patrons of the larger cities.

The Four Marx Brothers are an excellent example of the success which is bound to come to vaudeville talent, if its efforts be kept clean, simple and up-to-date. They are unassuming, hard-working boys, who strive to entertain, and for that reason, always succeed.

Live Vaudeville Gossip

W. S. Butterfield, general manager of the Bijou Theatrical Enterprise Co., is arranging to transfer his general offices from Chicago to Battle Creek, where they were located until about a year ago. Battle Creek is the birthplace of the chain of houses known as the Butterfield circuit and as the bulk of the company's interests lie in Michigan, Mr. Butterfield believes they can best be administered from Battle Creek. The booking and publicity departments will still be maintained in Chicago.

Foster Ball and Ford West will not dissolve partnership, as has been reported, but have decided to stick together as a team. They will present their act, "Since the Days of '61," on the Orpheum circuit next season.

(Continued on page 8)

August 15, 1915

running and now in-perpetual-syndication-comedy-quiz show, *You Bet Your Life*.

Chico, with his Italian accent making mincemeat out of the English language and a unique style of playing the piano by "shooting the keys" with his right index finger, would occasionally show up as a guest on various television shows.

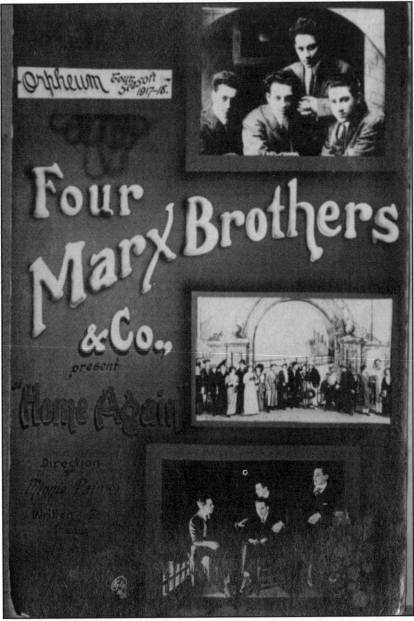

Orpheum circuit, 1917-1918; directed by Minnie (Marx) Palmer.

Harpo's character was that of an impish, impulsive, curly-haired mute. He wound up appearing on numerous television variety shows, as well as successfully tackling a straight dramatic role completely out of character.

Minnie, my grandmother.

But, because the Marx Brothers was an outgrowth of a musical act called The Four Nightingales, Harpo's love for music would continue throughout his career and help him to become an accomplished, world-renowned harpist, in spite of never having received any academic training or ever learning to read music. During this time period of his career, I became his musical arranger/conductor at the age of sixteen. We toured together and recorded two albums of music for Mercury Records. I was most fortunate to have both a father/son and professional relationship with him, and for me, something nothing could ever surpass. My autobiography chronicles some of our experiences in both relationships.

The Great Hennepin
Hennepin at Ninth Street

MARY HAYNES
IN
"Exclusive Songs"
WEEK OF OCTOBER 16 1918?
—1918—

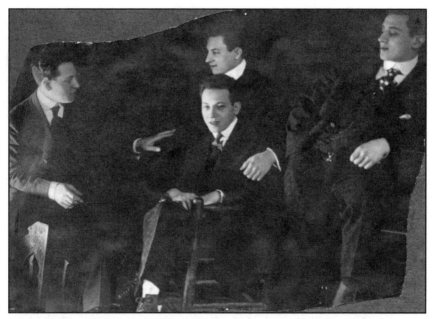

The Four Marx Brothers in *Home Again;* Left to right: Arthur, Leonard above Milton, and Julius.

There are a sizeable number of books on the Marx Brothers (including Dad's autobiography, ***Harpo Speaks!***) that reference their remarkably unique contribution to the American theater. All of their films have been digitally remastered and are available in the twenty-first century in DVD packages as well. The Marx Brothers live on . . .

WHY A BOOK?

For many years, friends and family have asked, "Bill, why don't you write a book about your life? You must have had quite a childhood growing up with your dad, Harpo, and those zany uncles of yours, the Marx Brothers. And what about those weird, maybe fatalistic, happenings you've experienced that can only be described as 'too-Hollywood-to-believe'?"

Having never written a book in my life, and already struggled to get through an Afterword for the paperback version of Dad's autobiography, only the help and expertise of the brilliant writer and co-author of Dad's book, Rowland Barber, saved me from the slings and arrows of outraged unfortunate readers the world over.

Frankly, I have always felt insecure, lacking self-confidence, and terrified at the thought of embarrassing myself forever by administering a below-the-belt blow to literature. Being and thinking as a musician, writing has always somehow seemed to be a much different creative process from composing. Perhaps, it's the tangible versus the intangible, the absolute of the written word as opposed to the abstract of the musical note.

However, upon the passing of my dear mother, Susan, and through more urging from sadistic friends, I decided to take on the awesome responsibility of writing something. But I needed some kind of support to squelch my anxiety about the whole idea of writing about myself. And, because Rowland wasn't available at the time to help, I had to look to other self-bolstering devices.

After careful consideration of all possible avenues, I thought I might take an intriguing course being offered at the university in normal and advanced megalomania. All that was required to pass the course was to read and then write a term paper on the book, *Egomania and I*. Why, maybe this could be the perfect tool in exacting the necessary reinforcement for my becoming confident enough in myself to finally and courageously take the plunge into the waters of my however-long-awaited autobiography! My curiosity leaped when I noticed there was one chapter that would be particularly helpful on developing a split personality, thus allowing one to objectively double the appreciation of one's self.

You have absolutely no idea of the feeling of pride that swelled through my chest just imagining them presenting me with my diploma, designating that I was now a full-fledged megalomaniac and graduating with honors as well. The course probably would even improve my posture. I'd now be ready to take them all on, Hemingway, Steinbeck, Proust, Joyce, Voltaire, Moliere, Shakespeare, Bacon, Barber. Merely the occasional thought of it made me so filled with myself that I knew there would be no stopping this author now. The feeling would then continue to encompass me as I pressed on during the writing of this most important book, one that no home or municipal library should be without.

Not only could I perceive the course giving me the inner strength and overwhelming pleasure of knowing me better than anyone else, it would allow me at last to talk freely about myself with great affection anywhere and to anyone. I'd be just wonderful at dinner parties, quickly bringing up the subject of me when necessary, thus eliminating the possibility of any lull in the conversation. And I'd always be there to give any person in need the benefit of my superb advice on any subject regarding the enigmas of just living life itself.

For weeks I so looked forward to beginning the new semester, until one morning I woke up feeling so good about myself that I realized I no longer felt I needed to take their dopey course. Right then and there, that day, I actually started my book, all by myself!

That having been said with boundless pride, I implore you to continue reading on. After all, it's all about I!!

I suppose some things I will never come to know. Some things I don't know I can ultimately learn. Other things I don't ever have to learn, because they are what I instinctively know. I have come to find all these possibilities as part of my life, with some unexpected improbabilities thrown in for good measure caused perhaps by fate.

CHAPTER ONE

"Oh, my God! Dad! Is it really you?"

"It is. Hi, Son."

"I've gotta be dreaming. Am I dreaming?"

"I'm not really the best person to ask. Does it really matter?"

"I guess not. What are you doing here?"

"I thought I'd visit with you."

"You did, huh? Why now? Why now, after forty years?"

"I thought it was time."

"Yeah, well . . . it's been forty years! You *died* forty years ago!"

"I know, Son. I was there. It's not like I abandoned you. It was time for me to go. Now it's time for me to come back."

"I wish you hadn't left in the first place."

"Yup. That's life, Bill. A lot of it hurts. I can't help that."

"It is *kind* of like you abandoned me. Me and Mom and the rest of us."

"I can't help that either. Why don't we talk about you and who you are now?"

"I'm Bill. I'm the same Bill you left in 1964. Only older."

"I sure hope that's not true, Son. I've got to believe you've learned a few things and matured a little since then."

"Yeah, me too. I guess *I'm* not the best person to ask that."

"Actually, you are. Well, I've got to go."

"Already?"

"I'll be back."

Hey, I was just sitting there in my playpen, minding my own business while focusing all attention on my latest effort. I knew something was up, so I had chosen to go on strike, a hunger strike. Being only eleven months old, and having yet to master the art of reading (or speaking), I didn't realize until I was much older that my new residence was an adoption agency, something called the Children's Home Society, located at a place somewhere in Los Angeles, California. As a result of my calculated refusal to eat anything, my little ploy rendered me a physical mess. I had contracted lung abscesses, ear abscesses and rickets. I had to get all this just because I wanted to attract a little attention? If I had only known those consequences would occur . . . maybe just crying a lot would have done the trick.

But how do you know about anything when you are only eleven months old?

CHAPTER TWO

Once upon a time, in the mid-1960s, there was a chic restaurant/nightclub called Dino's Lodge. Dean Martin lent his illustrious name to the establishment in return for a small percentage of an always-questionable profit. Dino's was located in the heart of West Hollywood, California, smack dab in the middle of the fabled Sunset Strip, adjacent to the building used as the façade for a popular television show of its day, *77 Sunset Strip*.

Dino's exterior

For purposes of historical vernacular, it was a time when the Strip was really swinging day and night and had its own groove going. The sidewalks were always teeming with people. Some wanted to "buzz the Strip" in cars of every conceivable make, model and/or remodel for "a little action," some were there to people watch, or still others showed up simply because it was absolutely "the place to be."

Dino's was a popular, well-run hangout for people of all professions; distinguished doctors, lawyers and Indian chiefs and, of course, the Hollywood celebrity set. On any given evening, you might see actors like Dick Van Dyke or Lee Marvin, or maybe comedians like Allan Sherman, Jackie Gayle and Joe E. Ross enjoying the atmosphere. If ever you needed a cultural icon that symbolized the pre-Woodstock, not-quite hard drugs yet, plush leather burgundy décor, blonde stewardesses in miniskirt uniforms, thick-clouds-of cigarette-smoke-floating-around-the-hanging lamps, Hugh Hefnery-Sunset Strip Sixties, it was Dino's Lodge. I worked there as a pianist of some note (often E-flat). There I was, in the thick of it, seated in front of a piano, noodling around night after night. It was my professional "home away from home," for five character-building years, six days a week, from 9:00 P.M. to 1:45 A.M. or even later. I fronted the house band, a jazz trio that played for dinner, dancing and shows for every singer in town who was on their way up or on their way down. Some singers were terrific but never made the big time. Some others who did make it really weren't very good. But on any given evening, I had the best rotation of bass players and drummers a pianist could ever have the pleasure of working with. No matter who came to play, I could be sure we would smoke the place that night. It was a part of the "Golden Years" for musicians in Los Angeles, as everything was swinging for everyone in both night clubs and the studios.

I was a very fortunate young man to have been a part of it, and the experience might have wound up yet just another time in my career to reflect upon. But an even more fortunate, unexpected event occurred over a glass of wine that led me to an amazing discovery that would transcend almost all probability. Little did I know what the Fates had in store. And so, Dino's Lodge would become the fulcrum of my life's strange odyssey.

That's me happily emceeing at Dino's.

Before I go any further, there are a few things you should know about me that make me slightly different from your average piano player, or even your above-average piano player. My dad is Arthur Harpo Marx, the silent member of the Marx Brothers' comedy team. My mom is Susan Fleming, a former Ziegfeld Girl and early film actress who longed to be a former film actress. She made the grade when she married my dad in 1936.

Oh, and one more thing: I am adopted.

If I were to list all the people who have influenced the Bill Marx who stands before you today, my father, Harpo, would surely be at the top of the list. I spent much of the first 26 years of my life within his delightful orbit. But I suspect that even people with only a brief or casual acquaintance with Dad might also include him high on their list of life influences. To use an overused but apt description, he was a force of nature. He was elemental. The guy just knew how to live.

How to be.

Arthur Marx, as a part of a vaudeville act with his brothers, Leonard, Julius, Milton and later Herbert, had been a very successful comedian and musician for many years, until he received a pivotal review of one of their shows. It was pointed out that his sight gags and pantomime work were exceptional, but his engaging persona was destroyed every time he opened his mouth. It was a crushing blow to his ego, so he vowed to become forever silent as an entertainer. As the Fates would have it, this seemingly negative review turned the Marx Brothers into the remarkable team that audiences the world over have come to know as those devilish anarchists of show business. (Dad was actually an extraordinary linguist. He could be silent in at least seven languages. At home, English was not one of them.)

As a result of Arthur's newfound silence, the Marx Brothers had tripped over, fallen into, stumbled upon, or just plain old accidentally discovered the time-honored formula of the legendary improvisational comic theater, *commedia dell'arte.* Created in the small-town, outdoor festivals of sixteenth-century Italy, its popularity quickly spread throughout Europe. It still exists today as a repertoire company whose triumvirate core remains the Authoritarian, the part Julius/Groucho assumed, the Idiot, the perfect role for Leonard/Chico, and finally the Mime that was to complete this enduringly successful concept.

As well read and knowledgeable as they were, all of the Brothers lived their whole lives without ever knowing the existence of *commedia dell'arte* in the history of theatre, nor its impact on their timeless success.

The Marx Brothers got their "o" names from a monologist by the name of Art Fisher. At that time, there was a very popular comic strip called **Sherlocko the Monk**, and a lot of the acts tried to cash in on its success by adding an "o" to the end of their names. Every playbill had a Wando, the magician, Shrimpo, the midget, or Clappo, the trained seal. One fine day, during their twenty-year tenure in vaudeville, the Brothers were involved in a backstage game of stud poker, and Fisher was dealing. Sending a card to Leonard, he renamed him Chico because of his reputation for chasing the chicks. The card to Julius came with the pronouncement of Groucho, because in the "grouch bag" that he wore around his

Dated April 23, 1816; seems like there always has been a "Harpo."

neck, he always had more money and assorted stuff than anyone else had. It was easy to choose a name for Arthur.

In ***Bulfinch's Mythology*** (which I often consult on matters concerning the Ancients), the Egyptian god, Osiris, is described as the god of the sun, the source of warmth, life, fruitfulness. In addition, he was also regarded as the god of the Nile, who once a year visited his wife, Isis (the Earth), by means of an inundation. (Now that's what I consider really overdoing it to prove one's ongoing commitment to a relationship.) Thus, they had a son, who is represented seating on a Lotus flower, with his finger on his lips, as the god of Silence. His name is Harpocrates.

Imagine the music of the harp and the sweet sound of silence working together in absolute harmony all those years. Ironically, Harpo lived his whole life without ever knowing the other significance of the name Art Fisher had given him. It has also occurred to me that Dad never knew the enduring significance of the name that he had given me. So often do I get something like this upon meeting someone new:

"Marx? Do you spell that with an 'x'? You do? You wouldn't happen to be related to . . ."

"That's right, you guessed it. Manifesto."

"No kidding! Karl?"

"No, just kidding. The Marx Brothers."

"No kidding! I love those guys. Who are you related to?"

"All of them."

"No, I mean, which one was your dad?"

"Harpo, and he still is my dad."

"You mean he's still living?"

"No, he passed away in 1964, but he's *still* my dad."

"Yeah, you're right; I guess he still would be, wouldn't he?"

"Yes, he would still be my dad."

"Gee, I never thought about that."

When Arthur Harpo Marx was a young child in the 1890s, he came to detest his given name, Adolph. Living on the Upper East Side of Manhattan, he was always called by his pals "Oddie" (pronounced Ahhdee with a New York accent), the nickname for Adolph.

One day he got the bright idea that he could change his name if he wanted to, but only if he could think of another one that would suit him. Aware that the New York accent would make "Oddie" sound very much like the nickname "Ahhtee," he decided to change his name to "Ahhthur."

With the later legal addition of Harpo, he now would have the rare distinction of becoming one of the chosen few in all of America, other than maybe fugitives from the law, to have had three different first names. Oh, yes, plus two separate but equal nicknames. He was obviously clairvoyant enough to change his name long before the Second World War, thus avoiding the terribly long wait he'd have to put up with until the rise of Nazism in Europe many years later.

Adolph had become Arthur who was to become Harpo who was to become Dad. That's a lot of names to keep track of, but he did a fine job of it and lived up to every one. I also have had two names—the one I was born with and the one I got when I joined up with Harpo and Susan to participate in their family. But being rather shiftless and lazy in my early years, I completely forgot my first "first name" and even my first "last name." Bill Marx was good enough for me and it was the only one I answered to as I went gallivanting through my boyhood, with its requisite slingshots, puppy dogs, apple pies and baseballs.

My new name wasn't all he gave me. When I was but twelve years old, he ordained me as his permanent personal prop man for all his subsequent stage and television appearances. Now being Dad's prop man was by no stretch a low-brainer job. Aside from making sure his magical coat was properly loaded up for the performance, it also always required my diligent checking to see that I would have all of his props returned to the prop trunk after the show, in place and ready to go his next time out of the chute.

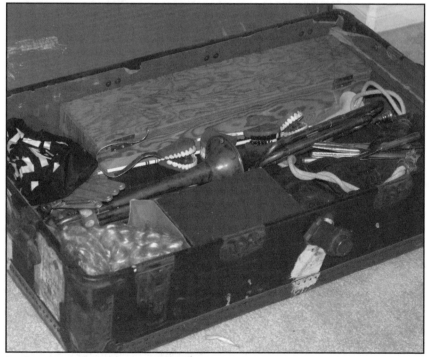
Dad's prop trunks, my responsibility.

The following is a list of props that served as my inventory: telescope; teeth; long black formal jacket w/tails; yellow and maroon flannel shirt with a sheriff badge that spins; two ladies black satin skirts; long horn; extendable box; bubble liquid; lots of fake money; several rubber hands; skirt-cutting scissors and powder bag; giant scissors; giant diamond ring; small diamond ring (with a jeweler's magnifying glass); tuners; piano ticker (metronome Seth Thomas); trunk that says name of the theater on top; knives that come out of the coat (and coat); two wigs and wig head in excellent shape; wardrobe trunk (empty) with Algonquin Hotel tags and Savoy Hotel stickers on it; long black box with more teeth; makeup; another bag of knives; rubber chicken; more wigs; two mechanical monkeys; large telescope in box; hatchet and table (for cutting cards); black top hat; wooden vase with flowers painted on and elastic attached to top; three shoes with skates on bottom; long metal tube with a string that pulls out-weighted; rubber carrot; three belts; rubber mallet; two short horns; tape measure; large cow bell; huge cigar; long rope (for opening); clarinet (with mechanical bubble machine and tube); four harmonicas; harp string case with tuning keys; orchestra music for act; signs for sewing on singer's rear end; marshmallows and garter belt. ("Prop list written by Dad.")

I carried this awesome responsibility with me for twelve wonderful years, and his props remain to this day exactly as I had packed them away after his final performance as Harpo Marx.

And when I was just sixteen years old, he also gave me my identity as a professional musician by making me his personal arranger/conductor. I was fortunate to have a dad who was willing to share his love for music with me. But that's the kind of guy he was. You can learn all about Dad, along with his wacky brothers, in his own words, from his autobiography, *Harpo Speaks!*, so I need not bother going into an extended biographical reverie. However, let me just share with you a snippet from another famed notable who felt compelled to rhapsodize about my dad. Ben Hecht, the brilliant American author and screenwriter, wrote in his book, *A Child of the Century,*

> "Harpo could fill a room with cheer by merely sitting in it. He could make you feel content as if some human sunlight were

warming you." Harpo's uniqueness attracted others of uniqueness, especially in the literary world. On the east coast, he was introduced in 1923 by Alexander Woollcott, the most powerful drama critic in New York, to the fabled Algonquin Round Table, and met the crème of that city's literary intelligencia.

Regular members that sat at lunch everyday trying to outwit their contemporaries included Robert Benchley, Mark Hellinger, Haywood Broun, Dorothy Parker, George S. Kaufman, and Moss Hart.

Harpo with close friends Moss Hart and George Kaufman.

Later, when my dad moved to Hollywood in the early 1930s, the regulars at Harpo's house every Sunday were also top novelists and playwrights of the day who came to Hollywood at the request of the studios. These writers agreed to dispense their talents not out of any burning desire to save the film industry, but rather because of the obscene amounts of money they were offered.

Dad and Ben Hecht

Among the transplants seen Sundays lunching about were Marc Connelly, Ring Lardner, F. Scott Fitzgerald, Lillian Hellman, H.G. Wells, Aldous Huxley and, of course, Ben Hecht.

Some of these literary legends were able to adapt to the studios and their commercial sights, while others refused to accept the critical castrations of their work by many egomaniacal types only in order to appease an accountant's bottom line. Academy Award-winning Hecht was one of the latter and even wrote a scathing bit of underground poetry reflecting his disdain for the studios. From a portion of his "Prayer to His Bosses," Hecht imparts . . .

GOOD GENTLEMEN WHO OVERPAY
ME FIFTY TIMES FOR EVERY FART,
WHO HAND ME STATUES WHEN I BRAY
AND HAIL MY WHINNYING AS ART—
I PICK YOUR POCKETS EVERY DAY
BUT HOW YOU BASTARDS BREAK MY HEART.

O MOLOCHS OF THE MOVIE SET
O GENIUSES WHOSE VIOLENCE
HAS TAMED THE LION FOR A PET,
O MIGHTY WIZARDS WHO DISPENSE
AMUSEMENT TO THE WORLD—PLEASE LET
ME WRITE A MOVIE THAT MAKES SENSE.

OH LET ME GROW ONE LEAF OF GRASS,
ONE BREATH OF TRUTH, ONE'S CRY OF MAN'S
TRAVAIL AND QUEST, ONE PEAL OF BRASS
TO DRIVE ART FROM ITS CRAPPING CANS—
ONE TALE THAT DOESN'T KISS THE ASS
OF NINETY MILLION FANS.

Susie flanked by Papa and Mamma Fleming

My mother, Susan Fleming, was also less than enthusiastic about the movie industry. Almost from the moment she found herself within it she looked for a way out. She was born in Brooklyn, New York, and because of her father's work as a mining engineer and stockbroker, her family was shuttled about all over the North American continent, from New Jersey to California to Long Island to Alaska to Connecticut, and finally landing in Forest Hills, New York. She was an only child, and while growing up never could solidify any lasting relationships with other children, what with all that nomadic moving about.

She got most of her early education through private tutoring, much of it from her father, William Lazear Fleming. "Bill" was a gentle soul with strong, artistic tendencies, thus making him thoroughly ill-equipped to deal with Gunhild "Bunny" Von Philp, whom he met while he was attending Lehigh University in Bethlehem, Pennsylvania. I've been asked why her nickname was Bunny, and I can only guess it was an improvement over Gunhild.

Bunny was a strong-willed, aggressive Swedish lady, whose discontent in life came from a promising singing career denied by her mother. She had lessons taken from Madam Divine, who taught the brilliant Italian soprano, Amelita Galli-Curci, and she had an opportunity to sing Wagner's music as a member of the New York Metropolitan Opera Company. However, nothing could overcome her mother's blue-blood heritage, which drove home the belief that it was beneath any upper-class family to be in the Arts as a professional. Leave Bethlehem to become a whore?

So became the source of a life of frustration for Bunny. Left with no option, she stayed at home in Bethlehem, did the upper-crust social scene, just marking time while waiting for her destiny to

arrive with the appearance of her charming Prince William of Fleming. Soon after he rode into her life on his white steed, they were married, moved to Brooklyn, and, soon after that, added Susan into their mix.

From there, the three of them would become globetrotters for the next several years, as Bill's occupations so dictated, until his stock brokering career had led his family full circle back to Brooklyn. This proximity to Manhattan by subway would lead Bunny to an alternative solution for having caved in to her mother's wishes. She decided it was time to counter her permanently ingrained frustration by vicariously living through her beautiful and talented daughter. Sixteen-year-old Susan started with commutes into the city for ballet lessons that she hated. But then came the well-respected Ned Wayburn's School of Dance, which was quite accessible from the Grace Court Subway Station.

At first, neither blossoming-stage-mother Bunny nor Susan knew that Wayburn put on all the dances for the lavish Florenz Ziegfeld revues. So Susan began with tap, was a natural, and shared her love for it with another beautiful little girl from the Bronx named Paulette Goddard. They became great friends during their dancing development at Wayburn, and their subsequent rise in the **Ziegfeld Follies**, from hoofers to the glamorous showgirls who were the real stars of his show. That upgrade happened for them when Ziegfeld put together a show called **Rio Rita**, and he decided that his beautiful young dancers should be stage decoration, sensuously clad in the most magnificent gowns the great couturiers of that time could fashion.

Susan was now seventeen and a part of the glamorous world of Broadway, and Bunny was finding some solace in her role as stage mother. One problem Susan had with her success was that she believed she had very little talent to support her good fortune. Also, she had always been very shy and had trouble handling the advances of all the rich Stage-Door Johnnies, including one that offered her a very pricey pearl necklace in exchange for something priceless that she wasn't yet willing to offer. (Though she did tell me that she thought about that one a lot.) Considering she already had acquired a gold mesh bag for just being a glamorous showgirl, she chose not

Susan and Paulette Goddard
to go commercial.

As Susan later looked back at that time of youthful naiveté, she realized that the only reason she survived the unreal world of Broadway was fate. Clotho, Lachesis, Atropos, better known as the Fates, were, according to the Greek poet Hesiod, three very old sisters who forever spin the threads of human destiny. From that time forward, Susan's view would be through the prism of a fatalist. The three sisters immediately began weaving on their loom of manipulation as Susan Fleming went from the Broadway stage, to the motion picture soundstage in Astoria (across the river from Manhattan) for Paramount Pictures. Eventually, she made a three-point cross-country landing in Hollywood with Columbia Pictures.

Susan as showgirl draped in an Adrian creation.

Harry Cohn was the head man at Columbia and was considered the most detested mogul in Hollywood, and not necessarily for cinematic reasons. Susan soon came to know why, as she figured her time with Columbia would be a short one, due to the fact her parents accompanied her everywhere. Still, she was given bit parts in three or four undistinguished movies, until they put her in a Buck Jones Western called ***Range Feud***, where she was cast as the love interest of another young contract player, John Wayne. She later claimed that she remembered little about the movie, in spite of it being her first leading role and the last one working with the Duke. With absolutely no malice toward him at all, she could only remember that she had to ride a horse.

Susan and the Duke unabashedly embracing in *Range Feud*.

After a couple more turkeys with Bunny looking over her shoulder, and Bill just going along for the ride, Susan was no longer enjoying her career in films at all. She also would not want to continue as an actress simply to satisfy her mother's neurosis. Then suddenly, without warning, Columbia decided to cancel her contract.

It was then that the Fates decided they had to crank it up a notch.

CHAPTER THREE

One curious evening at a dinner party thrown by Samuel Goldwyn honoring, of all people, Harry Cohn, the three sisters sat Susan next to Harpo Marx. There were sparks. Shortly thereafter she would receive a call from his secretary, Rachel Linden, inviting Susan to lunch at his place on the following Sunday. The Fates were

now in overdrive when that Sunday came, changing Susan's life forever when they opened the door to the wonderful world of Harpo Marx.

The Marx Brothers made only one movie a year for Paramount, so there was plenty of party time in between for Harpo. But Susan was back as a contract player and was working constantly with little time to herself other than weekends, much to the satisfaction of her mother. Herman Mankiewicz was also one of the Sunday lunch regulars at Harpo's and had just written a script called *Million Dollar Legs*. Mankiewicz, who later would become much more famous for the screenplay to *Citizen Kane*, decided to cast Susan, alongside W.C. Fields and Jack Oakie, in the picture.

W.C. Fields and Susan in *Million Dollar Legs*.

The movie also featured some of the great character actors of that time, such as Andy Clyde, Ben Turpin, Hugh Herbert, and Billy "the almost sneeze" Gilbert. The film has endured all these years as one of the great cult comedy classics of all time, and Susan always had felt that it was almost exclusively for her work in that one picture, that she would become somewhat known and somehow remembered. But during several more outings at Fox as a contract player, she became increasingly more than just unhappy with an industry she no longer cared to be in.

Susan Fleming was preparing to shift roles from the ongoing plot created by her mother to one of her own making.

People from all walks of life were drawn to Harpo. Here with him on the set of *Horsefeathers* is famed aviatrix Amelia Earhart.

Meanwhile, Harpo Marx was perfectly content being a confirmed bachelor.

Enjoying himself throwing a "Gookie" on the Riviera.

But as his relationship with Susan developed, his lifelong desire for independence was tested by Susan's new vision of her future. Because he was a free spirit, whose life was filled with a variety of worldly friends and varied experiences, he had no intention of settling down to such a permanent and conventional way of living as marriage. As long as that concept didn't enter into the picture, he could continue along his merry path with Susan at his side.

She and Harpo were now considered pretty much an item in Hollywood. Now it was time for Harpo to introduce his "better half" to his friends back east. His biggest friend (weighing in at over 300 pounds) was Alexander Woollcott, the critic for the *New York Sun*, who first brought the Marx Brothers to the attention of the public at large when he accidentally saw them perform on Broadway in 1924.

Susan and Harpo with Alexander Woollcott at his home in Lake Bomoseen.

Woollcott loved the brothers, and was entranced by Harpo's performance. They struck up a friendship that opened up an entirely new and exciting world to Harpo—the world of newspaper reporters, magazine owners, legitimate theater actresses, artists, politicians, models and the occasional hooker. Most of these folks were ensconced at the Algonquin Hotel, where Woollcott kept a running poker game (called The Thanatopsis Inside Straight Society) that lasted from one end of the 1920s through the other.

Harpo, his dear friend, author Alice Duer Miller, and Aleck.

Everybody liked Susan well enough, but they were more interested in hearing horror stories about gauche, infantile Hollywood. The card game at the Algonquin was still going and the witty repartee these clever people hurled at each other was still funny, but somehow Harpo didn't fit in anymore. Susan was the reason. I think he realized that Susan had been right. It was time to build a new home. He belonged out west. Hollywood may be gauche and infantile and lack the sophistication of the New York crowd, but it was also sunny and fun and Susan was there. And that was all Harpo needed. And it had Ben Hecht.

Thank you, Ben.

Harpo and Susan hightailed it back to sunny California as quickly as they could. They neither needed nor wanted anyone's approval or acceptance.

They had each other.

The cast of characters at Harpo's every Sunday would change from time to time, but the basic core was always there. As the days unfolded, Susan became part of Harpo's regular foursome that included the extraordinary neurotic, Oscar Levant. Harpo was never critical of troubled nonconformists, and because Oscar was the champ of them all, Harpo loved him. Levant was a man who coupled his enormous musical talent, wit and intelligence with hypersensitivity and insecurity that rendered him moody, surly and often subject to fits of despair. He had a desperate need for acceptance, and though Oscar's behavior was quirky, to say the least, he became Harpo's constant and most entertaining companion.

MGM brought Oscar to filmdom in Hollywood from New York, where he had already carved out a successful career as a pianist and the foremost interpreter of the works of his dear friend, George Gershwin.

Rare photo of both Ira and George Gershwin at work.

Living at a hotel without a piano, he usually could be found at Harpo's house, practicing his exercises on the Steinway with a *Time* magazine or some book propped up on the music stand. Once, years later, when his wife, June, kicked him out of their house, Oscar came to live with us for a while. I came home one day from elementary school to find him at the piano with tears streaming down his face.

"Why are you crying, Mr. Levant?" I asked.

"I can't play octaves!" he responded.

That didn't ring right with me. I had been told what a truly wonderful pianist he was, world famous for his performances of some of the most inspiring and difficult music any pianist could be asked to play.

"You can't play octaves?"

"Billy, it isn't that I can't play octaves. It's just that I can't play octaves the way I want to hear them played."

Much of Oscar's modus operandi was based on an obsession for his own successful personal failure. He would set forth for himself impossible standards of achievement that he could never meet, thus validating his inadequate self-image. Imagine what he could have been if he had *liked* himself. Then again, maybe he wouldn't have been the non-conforming Oscar Levant that Harpo and all of us came to know.

Rounding out the foursome was Levant's exact opposite, Charlie Lederer, a joyous, funny, idealistic, irrepressible and talented young screenwriter. The egomaniacs that ran the studios were the constant targets of Charlie's barbs, and his needling of them kept him in perpetual trouble. However, he was always able to avoid losing his job, maybe because his aunt was the popular actress, Marion Davies, and . . . the mistress of William Randolph Hearst. Studio execs certainly would never risk alienating the Hearst Empire. Marion's relationship with Hearst also made her quite a formidable force, and little would anyone know at that time how important a non-acting role she would ultimately be destined to play in the lives of Harpo and Susan.

And me.

CHAPTER FOUR

Strangely, Harpo had been always known for chasing blondes, but it was a brunette who would wind up chasing and catching *him*. Susan and Harpo finally got married in 1936. It wasn't easy, though, for Susan; Harpo enjoyed his bachelor ways and it took a four-year campaign, but Susan helped him understand how much more enjoyable the partnership of marriage would be for them both. Or maybe she helped him understand that she wasn't going to be his girlfriend forever and that either he was going to have to marry her or she was going to move on. Either way, she was right. And Harpo knew it. Thus, Susan Fleming joined the Marx family.

Susan & Harpo just married (whew, at last).

Right around the time Harpo and Susan were forging their lives together, Harpo's brothers, Chico and Groucho, were witnessing their marriages crumble. Chico's incorrigible gambling and womanizing doomed his marriage to Betty; Groucho's insecurities were largely responsible for the collapse of his marriage to Ruth.

Groucho loved Susan and was very envious of the successful marriage that she and his brother created, something that he would never have with any of his three marriages. Susan was the only woman Groucho knew that would not stand for any of his nonsense or his put-downs, and Groucho respected her for that. I know of one time, for example, when Susan and Harpo had a sit-down dinner party for twenty-six people, and the entrée was chicken. When Groucho was served his plate, he looked at it, got up from his chair and announced to everyone, "I'll be a happy man if the breast of this chicken is half as nice and big as the breasts on our hostess." That was vintage Groucho for you, but this time, it was Susan who was not amused, and in front of the entire gathering, boy, did she ever let him know it!

Well, it's mid to late February 1938, and we find Harpo and Susan at their home in Beverly Hills, and Susan has gone to Harpo with an idea that she feels warrants some discussion. She suggests, now that they have been married over a year, wouldn't it be a perfect time to start building a family. She points out that their close friends, George Burns and Gracie Allen, are so thrilled with their first child adoption that they are ready to do it again. (Incidentally, Susan and Harpo chose to adopt because Susan couldn't have children.) It is clear that Susan is now pretty much in command of their relationship, as she begins pushing the buttons that will dictate their future together.

They had been given sources for adopting a child, hoping to find a baby boy to start their family, and one day they showed up at a place called the Children's Home Society. One of the social workers took them to the room that had the available children for adoption. While looking for their prospective baby boy, they heard crying coming from a corner at the other end of the room. Susan, Harpo and the social worker went over to the noisy corner and, there they came across a frail, sickly little boy, sitting erect as could be while a nurse was failing in her attempt to feed him.

When the nurse explained that the little boy had been on a hunger strike for almost two months, Susan asked the nurse if she could try feeding him, maybe just the change might help. As Susan raised the spoon to the little boy's lips, he looked into her beautiful blue eyes and she looked into his big brown eyes, and his hunger strike became history. He ate and ate, and ate some more. And though he was older than the baby that they were originally looking for, Susan knew that this would be their little boy forever.

Susan and Harpo, using his name Arthur, were then ushered by the social worker into a room to discuss the serious details of adoption. At one point, they were asked if they were Catholic, because that was the wish of the birth mother, and under no circumstances could the child be given to any family other than a Catholic one. (Harpo, who was Jewish, and Susan, who was a borderline Episcopalian, had decided that their child would make its own religious choice if and when it came time to choose.) But without hesitation, Susan firmly said yes. So among the documents needed was their marriage license, which would confirm their having had a Catholic wedding. Armed with a list of other things that Susan and Harpo had to supply in order to qualify as the child's future parents, they went home and immediately made a phone call.

You also remember my mentioning earlier the name of Marion Davies, actress and mistress of William Randolph Hearst, the newspaper baron. Marion had recently given two million dollars to a Catholic parish right across the street from MGM Studios, where Harpo, Groucho and Chico were in the middle of making a movie. Susan explained to Marion the adoption situation and asked for her help. Marion said don't worry, just leave it to me.

The following day she arranged a mock wedding for Susan and Harpo, as the unrecognizable "Arthur," to take place at the parish across from MGM, a ceremony that the priest would perform without being told anything about the couple and the real story behind their marriage.

So Susan and "Arthur" showed up at the church, and as they were walking in, he noticed a table with a bowl of water on it. Curious about things as always, "Arthur" asked Susan, "What's this?"

Susan replied, "It's holy water and you're supposed to dip your fingers in it." Then she made the traditional sign of the cross. In a

Marion Davies

flash, "Arthur" became Harpo, shrugged his shoulders, picked up the sacred bowl, and drank from it. Refreshed, he turned to a stunned Susan and remarked, "Boy, was I thirsty!"

Inside the wedding chapel, Susan characterized herself to the priest as a Catholic gone astray, but one now ready to return to the church and its teachings. She explained that "Arthur" was planning to convert. The short ceremony went without a hitch, and the priest handed them their formal marriage license sanctioned by the Catholic Church, then they immediately drove downtown to the Home Society with all their papers in order. It was on March 7, 1938 that a young boy left abandoned at the Children's Home Society more than four months earlier, became ME, William Woollcott Marx.

Thank you forever, Marion.

Harpo and Susan brought me to their house in Beverly Hills, California, and though I was only fourteen months old, I will tell you that I remember what happened, and Mom filled me in on the details years later. I recall, almost as if it was yesterday, being plopped into a waiting highchair that was situated in a short hall, on one side of which was a door to the powder room, and the other side had a door leading to a storage closet. Mom brought me a dish of baby food, and when I saw it, my eyes lit up and I remember starting to rub my tummy. Goodbye, Children's Home Society. I was home at last, 701 North Canon Drive.

Unfortunately for my now Mom and Dad, they were on six months' probation as parents according to the Home Society regulations. This meant that once a week they would be visited by a nice social worker lady to see how little Willy was doing in his new Catholic surroundings. And to paraphrase Uncle Groucho's quip about the Irish podiatrist, "My fate was in her hands."

So every time she came to the house, they would haul out various representational items, such as crucifixes and the like, showing her what a nice environment they were providing for little Willy. The minute she left, Mom and Dad would hurriedly put away all the religious items, until they had to get them out again for the next time the nice social worker lady would come to visit. She had come to the house most dutifully about four or five times, when Dad decided that he'd had enough of her, no longer wishing to work his daily schedule around her obligatory visits. So the next time she arrived, all the religious items were in full view, as he opened the front door to greet her. When she went into shock upon seeing that he was stark-ass-naked, she gasped, turned and ran down the street, screaming at the top of her nice social worker lady's lungs.

No more crucifixes to haul out and holy water to sprinkle. From now on they'd never have a visit from her or any other nice social worker lady ever again. Dad called Woollcott and told him he was going to be my godfather. The three of us were now permanent.

Once again, thank you, Marion.

Back yard, 701 N. Canon Drive.

Harpo's defection to the west coast left Woollcott with a considerable void in his life, and he was especially bitter about losing his playmate to, uhg, Hollywood. In spite of both Woollcott's and his East Coast literary intellectuals' utter disdain for their West Coast contemporaries, about a year later, Aleck came out west to visit with Harpo, Susan and meet his new God-son, William. I honestly remember this huge man, looking much like an un-made king sized bed, bouncing me on his knee and perhaps reverting to his own childhood as he sang, "I'm dust a witto wabbit wunning awound in da sunshine." And this reluctant visit was to be the last time Aleck was to share his amazing relationship with his beloved Harpo. Not long after his return to his New York buddies and national radio show, Woollcott was to pass away.

But there was a piece of the puzzle of William Woollcott Marx that was missing. How did I manage to get to the Children's Home Society in the first place? Who brought me there, and why? What circumstances had conspired to produce me? I would find the first clue to this puzzle in, of all places, Dino's Lodge.

"Hey! Dad, you're back!"

"Toldya I'd be."

"Gotta ask you then. Why did you and Mom choose me out of all those other kids? I mean, I was nothin' but aggravation; sickly, didn't want to eat anything, always screaming my head off. Hell, they were all healthier and happier and would have offered you far less problems."

"It was your mom. She had good instincts and loved challenges. When she saw you, I don't think she just felt sorrier for you than the others. She knew there was something there between the two of you, period."

"Seems hard to believe that was it."

"Who knows? Maybe, Son, it was fate, whatever that is."

CHAPTER FIVE

There was this couple whom I never really knew much about that I met all too briefly. And for reasons that I rarely pondered at the time, they abandoned me in Los Angeles. I'm probably not the best person to ask regarding any latent or suppressed and unconscious issues I have regarding my being adopted. All I can tell you is that Harpo and Susan, contrary to 1938 contemporaneous practices, decided not to keep this news a secret from me. In fact, they made it seem as if I was somehow extra-specially theirs since they had gone to the trouble of picking me out from literally millions of children all over the world. Put that way, it makes adoption seem a lot better than getting stuck with the roulette wheel of genetics most poor parents and children are stuck contending with. (Sometimes the last thing you and your loved ones would want is for your baby to look or act like anyone in your family.) And I think I was reasonably happy, though somewhat uncurious about how it all worked out.

I suppose there was never any question that I would ultimately wind up being a professional musician, as my early attempts at other things certainly managed to foreshadow that eventuality. Like many young kids in the 1940s, I wanted to become a baseball player more than anything. More than even practicing the piano.

A great deal more.

I started lessons when I was four with Mrs. Cooper, who was the first to cultivate my disdain for discipline by introducing my fingers to the most dreadful of all musical concepts . . . scales! At that age, I had no understanding of how important these nonmusical-sounding exercises would be down the line for building a pianist's technique.

Billy getting started with his (ughh) scales.

Soon after came the despised Hanon and Czerny drudgeries, guaranteed to make my school homework really fun by comparison. Those two sadists must have been born with the musical talent of deaf bricklayers to conceive of and inflict such dastardly torture on my ears as well as my fingers. Somehow, through all of this boring and incessant cacophony, Mrs. Cooper finally did teach me the first piece I ever learned. It was called "March Slav," a rather tepid, droning Russian dirge that was easy enough for any four-year-old to negotiate. But it wasn't stimulating enough for this four-year-old to make me look forward to my next lesson. And besides, whenever I was resentfully practicing to develop my nonmusical repertoire, all of my friends were out having fun playing baseball. As none of them were musical, the only way I thought I could fit in and get some peer acceptance was by sharing their interests.

Dad got me interested in his love of baseball. Here he is with two Hall-of-Famers, Lou Boudreau & Bob Feller.

I was five years old when I saw my first ball game, and I remember only two things about it: the name Frenchy Uhalt, who was the Hollywood Stars' center-fielder, and the smell of cigar smoke wafting through the ever-present breeze. I didn't know at the time it was smoke from a cigar, but I soon came to find that for me it would become as much a part of the game as the organ music and the hot dogs and the Dr. Pepper. Today, the only time I can stand being around cigar smoke is if I'm at a ballpark.

From that first time to the last game played there in 1957, Dad always had the same season tickets at Gilmore Field, home of the Hollywood Stars of the eight-team, Triple-A Pacific Coast League. Today, that space is occupied by the parking lot of CBS Television City at Beverly Boulevard and Fairfax Avenue. Our seats were between home and first, right behind the bat rack. So when Frankie Kelleher or Butch Moran or Kenny Richardson or Babe Herman came to select their bat and wait in the on-deck circle, our close proximity allowed us to see their faces and even get to talk to them as if they were our pals. We got the intimate feeling that we were special and they were a part of our family. All of them were either on their way up to the "Bigs" or on their way down, but they all were playing for the same shared love of the game. For everyone, fans and players alike, there was a much different feeling about baseball back then. That feeling was far closer to the dreams a child might have, of simply participating in a game—one that was both an individual and a team sport—one that they could be playing in an Iowa cornfield or someone's backyard.

Everyone my dad and mom knew in Hollywood had season tickets as well and came to adopt the Stars for their very own, making Gilmore their home away from home. There were those who were genuine baseball fans, having originally come from cities with Major League teams, once again finding their childhood by having a team to passionately root for. The box directly behind us was that of Bob Cobb, the owner of the Hollywood Stars as well as the famous Brown Derby restaurant. I've thought of him often over the years whenever I can't decide what to order for lunch, because if I'm in any doubt, I usually wind up with a Cobb Salad, the one he created.

Whenever I went to the ballpark, I knew celebrities from all walks of life would visit our box. Some of them even liked baseball. Invariably, you would see the more recognizable ones of those days like Georgie Jessel, Jack Benny, the Ritz Brothers, Milton Berle, Danny Kaye, George Burns and all five Marx Brothers flitting about to schmooze with their pals at locations all over the grandstand, sometimes to make or collect on bets. My Uncle Zeppo's reason to be there was to bet on anything and everything. Forget who'd win the game. He would bet on the batter being out or safe, a ground ball or a pop up, what kind of pitch the next one will be; a strike, ball, fastball, curve, change up, and the number of foul balls that will be hit when the count is full. And sometimes the odds would change with every pitch. Double or nothing. Five to two for some serious moolah he gets a base hit! Raise you a hot dog! Call you

Harpo and Harry Ruby.

with a bag of peanuts! Don't think I'm kidding. And what's even more bizarre, Uncle Zeppo always had takers.

Harry Ruby, the great songwriter who wrote the music to many songs including Groucho's "Hooray for Captain Spaulding" for the hit Broadway show and film ***Animal Crackers***, was probably the most special fan of all Dad's and Mom's friends. Any ballpark was his second home. He told me more than once that he would gladly trade all of his hit songs, "Nevertheless," "Three Little Words," "Give Me the Simple Life," "Who's Sorry Now," "Thinking of You," naming a few, to have penned just one song, "Take Me Out to the Ball Game."

A true baseball fan, one might think. He rarely missed a game, happily comforted in the fresh air of his own personal heaven, yakking about everything with all of his cronies about whatever. But I must confess that he never seemed to be particularly interested in the game itself. Harry was a charming, funny, wonderful man, who I loved and who shared something in common with my Uncle Zeppo. The outcome of the game was incidental. Zeppo was about the gambling action, whereas Harry just liked being there. The only time I think that Harry and Uncle Zeppo ever really cared whether the Stars won or lost was during any series with our dreaded cross-town rival, the Los Angeles Angels. No matter where Hollywood was in the standings, we all knew that if we beat the Angels more games than they beat us, it would make our entire season. The Giants-Dodgers, Yankees-rest of the American League, had nothing on our rivalry with L.A.

I remember my mom keeping score of every game, recording all the plays, put-outs, strikeouts, hits and the like on her scorecard with the appropriate symbols, so that we could recreate that game anytime we wanted to. It was family fun for everyone as we pounded with our feet on the wooden floorboards beneath us hoping it would help to start a game-winning rally for the Stars.

My interest in baseball had pretty much taken over my life, even to the point that I could imitate any ballplayer's batting stance, left-handed or right-handed, and even the way they flailed their bat to and fro before the pitch. And sometimes if a bat wasn't available, I'd use a piece of Lincoln Log or a wooden ruler to practice my craft with. It didn't matter. I was busy being my heroes.

In case you'd forgotten what a Lincoln Log looked like.

As you might have guessed, my collaboration with Mrs. Cooper didn't last too long. My parents had been aware almost from the get-go that I instinctively already knew more about music than she did (frankly, her knowledge being quite an easily attainable standard). A month before I became three years old, they recorded me on our home device called a "Victrola" singing "Take Me Out to the Ball Game." Can I really remember that far back in time? Well, not that specific event. However, I know that it happened, because I still have the original recording. That was the very beginning of my parents' belief in my musical ability, and apparently they weren't particularly surprised by the revelation.

That "Victrola" was an integral part of our life, providing us with oodles of home entertainment. As long as its needle was sharp, we could enjoy our favorite 78 RPM acetate records. Eventually though, just the wear and tear on their surface would produce sounds like Kellogg's Pep, "snaps, crackles and pops," and the damaged grooves would cause exasperating skips in the music. We were also able to make our own recordings on a round, flat plastic substance, among them being a remarkable evening in 1939 when Groucho and Dad decided to send a birthday greeting to Irving Berlin. (And I still have that most cherished recording of Groucho singing with Dad accompanying him on the piano.)

Then, in the spring of 1944, our family of Harpo, Susan and me suddenly expanded to four, with the adoption of my new baby brother, Alexander, named of course, after Dad's close friend, Alexander Woollcott. I was told years later that the reason Mom and Dad decided to enlarge the family was that they had been spoiling me rotten, and it was perhaps time to spoil somebody else

Alex, Jimmy and Minnie.

rotten. They thought it would be a good thing for Willy, as Mom always called me, in the long run if they deflected some of their attention away from him for a while.

Alex had come to us via Salt Lake City, Utah, and from day one, we called him Sandy because of his shockingly beautiful white-blond hair. I must have wondered how I would adapt to Alex's presence after having been the center of attention all those years as a single child. But because I was almost seven years older than our new addition, I really felt no emotional competitiveness or territorial intervention. So for the next four or five months I dutifully played with Alex, who wanted mostly just to sit and stare at things.

All that was good with me until . . . what's this?

Another being was thrust into our midst. James Arthur Marx, also from Salt Lake City, had appeared on the scene and—voila!— I had a second baby brother to schedule into my daily activities. Jim was the easier of my two gigs, mainly because of his ability to amuse himself. He was blessed with a very round native boy's tummy, which, when lying on it and madly flailing his legs up and down like a swimmer, would rotate his entire body in a three-hundred-sixty-degree circle, as he laughed like hell. It was a rather amazing sight.

Not very long after Jim made us into five, number six showed up after a cross-country train ride from Peekskill, New York with

"Aunt" Gracie Allen to complete our family. Mom and Dad realized that a family wasn't a family without a little girl in it to stir things up. Minnie, named after her legendary paternal grandmother, was of pure Irish descent, and she had enough energy to supply all the wattage needed for a ten-story apartment building. So it wasn't long before she became the boss, mediator, arbitrator, referee and umpire of the very youthful trio. She ran the show completely. But always aware of that age difference between them and me, I thought of them moving about more as an entity, rather than three individuals separated only by their own marvelously unique personalities.

In Hollywood during the mid-to-late 1930s, adoption was becoming a very fashionable thing to do, and George and Gracie Burns had just adopted Ronnie and Sandra. Because of a close life-long friendship extending as far back as vaudeville, they became instrumental in helping Mom and Dad find their own complete family as well. We kids would always know them only as our Aunt Gracie and Uncle George.

We lived in a corner house on Canon Drive during the infancy of Beverly Hills, California. Then, it was a very quiet, unpretentious little town whose identity was marked by the presence of a quaint bridal path on Rodeo Drive. Businesses were pretty much "mom-and-pop" stores like Chapman's Ice Cream Parlor, Pioneer Hardware, Beverly Hills Camera Shop or Whelan's Drug Store. You might have even found me at Crawford's Music in one of their soundproof booths listening to records that I might buy if I liked them.

Residential was a blending of working-class and upper-middle-class, with a little bit of the very fancy-shmancy, much-more-well-to-do sprinkled in judiciously. There were nice public parks kids could be taken to by their parents or nannies for recreational purposes, such as skinning a knee, falling off a bicycle or accidentally tipping over into one of the inviting fish ponds while trying to catch, by hand, any one of the millions of tadpoles in residence.

We had a standard poodle named Charlie who once came home in a cab at four o'clock in the morning. He had jumped our backyard fence and ran all the way down to the park on Santa Monica Boulevard, because he enjoyed frolicking with fish in the pond. Some alert, early rising or late carousing citizen spotted him splashing

Christmastime was always very special to our family.

about, fished him out, looked at his identification tag, hailed a cab and sent him to us C.O.D.

Our house, the one that Charlie came home to, was a white-brick, two-story New England Colonial home with four windows facing the street, two on each floor, all tastefully accented with forest green shutters. There was a circular driveway that separated the house from what my friends and I christened our touch football field, though on rare occasions we grudgingly referred to it as the front lawn. "Uncle" George Burns once remarked that Dad designed those four windows purposely so that when he drove home at the end of a long day, he would see a smiling child looking out of each window. Not very long after we had become a complete family, one of those windows would be unavoidably vacant for a period of time.

Immediately after the Christmas holidays of 1945, Doctor Hirshfeld, our wonderful family doctor, (families actually had doctors that would come to their house in those days) recommended to my folks that the only way to control my chronic sinus condition and continuing asthma attacks was by sending me away from home to spend some time living in a very high altitude. That was sure to help clear up my physical problems. Before I knew it, I was celebrating my ninth birthday around seven-thousand feet above sea level in Nambe, New Mexico, just up the road from Santa Fe. Waring Ranch School for Boys was the first and only boarding school I ever had to attend, and not fully understanding the medical and medicinal facets that led me to my new environment, I felt abandoned once again.

However, during my stay at Waring, a seed was planted that would nurture me for the rest of my life. The school was in its first year at the Nambe location. It moved there, because its original site in Los Alamos had been taken over by the Atomic Energy Commission. Los Alamos would soon figure prominently and permanently in the history of the world when Robert Oppenheimer, Edward Teller and other scientists split the atom as part of the Manhattan Project.

My own experience at Nambe did not impact the earth and its inhabitants with quite the same force, but I found the whole process earthshaking, if only on a local level. I had been yanked from Bertha Lowe's fourth grade class at Hawthorne Grammar School to wind up at Waring in the fifth grade of History, the seventh grade of English, the third grade in Math and so on. I was considered intellectually all over the place. But that was how Waring believed all the students would learn more, by an evaluation of each student's skill levels in various subjects. The school was located on Smiling Serpent Ranch, which now exists today as an eight-bedroom/seven-bath private residence.

Each one of us was given a horse for which we would be responsible during the entire school year. I remember the second day I was there, Mr. Waring introduced me to "Blackie," a huge steed named appropriately for his not being a Palomino. I was asked if I had ever ridden before. With great assurance, I said, of course, harkening back to when I was three years old.

During the earlier parts of the 20th century the most popular place then to take young Los Angelenos, more for the parents' amusement than the kids', was Beverly Boulevard and La Cienega, home of the pony rides! Parents would buy the tickets, push their children through the turnstiles, then disappear. Meanwhile, us kids were screaming our heads off, apparently caught in some kidnapping and torture nightmare, as total strangers absconded with us and strapped us onto potential glue-factory nags. At this point our absentee parents would reappear, armed with cameras, to lie in wait for that Kodak moment. Soon, the whole macabre adventure would be preserved on silver nitrate as we terrified children sauntered by on our journey to nowhere, tethered to our beast of burden as we circled slavishly around the horse ring, monitored by another total stranger whose mind-numbing responsibility was to see that we didn't fall off. I can remember wondering when would it all be over, so I could at last be reunited with my parents, who, by then

Alex, Jimmy, Minnie & me, having loads of fun at Ponyland!

I was missing dreadfully. At least to the relief of the parents, the risk of our plummeting off a pony was, much like the ponies, not very high, considering that the owners were operating this absurd place with no insurance. This obstacle was offset by the three speeds of the horses. They walked very slowly, very, very slowly and even slower than that. If there had been a match race between any one of these horses and a turtle, the turtle would have won. By eight lengths.

But I digress. Back to Waring School. So the next thing I knew, Mr. Waring was helping me mount Blackie. After checking the saddle cinch, adjusting my stirrups, he handed me the reins and led me to where the rest of the students were waiting to go on the first ride of the school year. I was somewhere in the middle of the pack when we took off galloping toward the horizon. No sooner than we were out of the corral, I found myself on the ground being trampled by a couple of the horses from behind me. I didn't know what caused me to fall, but strangely enough when I got up, I felt virtually no pain. Fortunately, one of the counselors behind me saw what happened and did for me what they say you're supposed to do. He helped me back into my saddle, returned me to the waiting group, and from that time on, Blackie and I were pals.

In the weeks that followed, the more I was with him, the more he became both an antidote and an enigma for my lingering homesickness. His presence eased my pain, just knowing he was there anytime for me, and I liked my feeling of being there for him. But whenever I projected thoughts about the day that I would eventually return home, I wondered how Blackie would feel when he noticed that I was gone.

Then, one day in early February, Mr. Waring notified me that a huge, heavy box along with a smaller one had arrived for me from back home. Inside these two boxes I found the seed of a lifelong enchantment. When I opened the larger of the two, out popped Harry James. Then came, not necessarily in this order, Tommy Dorsey, Stan Kenton, Artie Shaw, Duke Ellington, Glenn Miller, Benny Goodman, Claude Thornhill, Count Basie, Les Brown, and yes, Spike Jones, along with many more.

There were vocalists as well: Ella Fitzgerald, Doris Day, Helen Forrest, June Christy, Perry Como, Herb Jeffries, Nat "King" Cole,

Dick Haymes, Bing Crosby and Satchmo to name a few. My folks had sent me more than one hundred 78-speed records with the hope that the music would make me feel better about being away. The smaller box produced the record player that would bring all my newfound friends to life. Minus some breakage over the last half-century, I still have most of those recordings today. These discs were the beginning of the musical foundation that would serve me throughout my professional career. By the time the school year ended, I would know every record by heart. So, there I was, my days filled to the brim with schoolwork, Blackie and my music to keep me well occupied. But what about when evening came? When I went to bed and turned out the lights at day's end, I was left with nothing to keep my mind off the prevalent loneliness.

It took a while for the answer to surface.

Then one day during class, I saw out of the corner of my eye, Chuck Higgins surreptitiously writing stuff down with his Parker fountain pen on a bunch of index cards, which he was then placing in a certain order into a box. Later, when I asked him what he was doing, he told me that each index card contained the name of an imaginary baseball player, his fielding position and current batting average. He was some years older than I, and because I thought that what he was doing was really great, he became kind of a role model for me. Also, because I saw that he was a pretty good first baseman during our Physical Ed classes, I decided to incorporate his idea into my lonely life after dark.

Before long, I had created my very own team of my very own players in my very own league. I was beginning to feel more comfortable in that dreaded vacuum just before sleep. I was soothed by the knowledge that Walt Gill and Porky Oliver were now my catchers. There was lefty Mel Jacobs over on first. Wiley Sandler at second and Joey Morrill at short comprised my flossy fielding double-play combination, and Nels Martenson held down the hot corner at third. Sam Blickett was my complete package ballplayer in center, chasing down whatever Murray Grodin in left or Russ Haversal in right couldn't get to. Grizzled veteran George Brockman was the ace of the pitching staff, and with an ever-present toothpick constantly darting to and fro across his mouth, Dutch Leonard was my inspirational manager. From having read and loved *The Kid from Thompkinsville*, the first in a series of baseball books for young people by John R. Tunis, I used Dutch's name because I needed someone of substance I could trust with my special ball club.

All of my players had first names, because I felt it sounded more realistic than just the impersonal last names you see in a box score. I was the owner of the team and treated everyone like they were my adopted family. I then hired myself to be the play-by-play commentator. It was to become a lifetime position, I might add. I also provided all the crowd noises.

Usually my games would start somewhere in the middle innings, and my team would be losing by a couple of runs just so I could orchestrate a come-from-behind rally. Before that inning was over, I was asleep, and when I awakened the next morning, I could never remember the account of last night's game. But I now knew that I had all the artillery I needed to fight off my homesickness twenty-four hours a day and all seven days of the week.

Just like the people in the comics have never aged, looking exactly the same today as they first did, my team is still intact, the players appearing just as young and fit as when I created them. Also, the guys are always at the ready to play whenever my schedule or weather permits. I must admit that with some reluctance, I pay them more now than I used to, but that keeps them happy and motivated. And the reason I can still financially afford to retain ownership of my team is that thank God our league doesn't have free agency.

I have always felt too embarrassed to divulge this very intimate, secret behavior of mine to anyone, as I believe that others would think it childish and immature. Still, why was I fighting a curious desire to include this episode in the book? I called my trusted friend, Joe Lubell, to ask him what I should do. (Joe is a retired businessman I've known for years since we met in Palm Springs.) When I told him I was writing a section about my homesickness as a nine-year-old boy in New Mexico, how scared I was every night, and what I finally did to counteract those feelings, his astonished reply was, "Bill, I want you to know that when I was a kid I did the very same thing. And I'd almost bet the farm that there probably have been many other leagues and teams in America that have existed without our knowledge."

My God! That was it! Having chosen these lifelong partners to share my evenings with, I had found a mature way to overcome my demons of the dark. I had become a part of a team from which I could never be separated, released or traded. Then Joe, who is as Jewish as Sandy Koufax, revealed to me *his* All-Star infield starting with good hit, no field Lenny Goldstein at third base. For future historians to note, the fabled double-play combination of Tinkers-to-Evers-to-Chance couldn't compare to his own crack double-play combination of Ackerman-to-Weinstein-to-Moskowitz. (They were also his team's law firm.)

Then one day, months into my stay, a married couple came to visit the school. Their appearance came as a surprise to everyone, including me. Everyone, that is, with the exception Mr. and Mrs. Waring. They had been aware of the couple's pending arrival for some time and somehow managed to keep it a secret. It was Mom and Dad, coming from a personal appearance in Florida by Dad's other self, Harpo, and on their drive home cross-country made a plan to drop in and see how their little Willy was doing. I was shocked to see them at first, and quite embarrassed by their presence, because the thought that I might be made fun of for being just a little baby boy who needed his mommy and daddy was making me very uncomfortable. After all, nobody else's parents came to visit their children. But Dad brought with him one of the Marx Brothers' movies, and that very evening wound up filled with laughter from kids and grownups alike. Just sitting there watching and listening to what Dad had done for everyone made me feel so proud to be his son and my self-conscious feelings of the day suddenly vanished. He was a hit once again, this time in Nambe! As Mom and Dad left the next day, I realized that Dad had made me important in the eyes of all the other kids because I was his son. He made me feel special. I didn't realize at the time that Dad made his living making people all over the world feel special. Even people who'd never met him in the flesh.

As I reflect back upon my school year stay at Waring School, aside from the initial sense of abandonment, the impact my experience there became much more than I would have ever imagined. It seems all of my life I have been drawn back to New

Mexico over the years for some important reason or other, including several world premieres of my symphonic works. The spiritual understanding of the earth and the architectural beauty of its topography have been forever ingrained in me.

And now, I was on my way home, praying that Blackie wouldn't become aware of my sudden departure from his life. Mom and Dad at the train station in Los Angeles met me most enthusiastically. Though I was still nine years old, it would be the second very important time in my life that Union Station was my destination.

The first one I have no memory of.

CHAPTER SIX

It was post-World War II, and I was back home in our sleepy little town with Mom and Dad. They thought that it would be a good time to prepare little Willy with life-broadening experiences. So, between 1946 and 1948, I spent most of my time taking lessons. Every kind of lesson. Yes, piano lessons, dancing lessons, painting lessons, swimming lessons, etc. We had a huge jacaranda tree in our backyard, and because it was nearing the Christmas holidays, my folks had hired a professional handyman to string electric lights onto and through every branch of this tall, massive, arboreal specimen. When I saw him that day, he was way up at the top, and I was pretty impressed with his prowess. So, as naturally curious as I could be, I inquired, "Who do you take your climbing lessons from?"

Talk about maybe being inundated with stuff to learn? But at least I was happy to be home with my very own toys, games and things that were so meaningful to me. I used to treat my inanimate objects as if they were actually alive, with feelings just like mine. Even to this day, whatever room in the house, I always try to have all inanimate objects that are on shelves or in cabinets facing the room. That way they can see what's going on and participate as if they are part of my family. I want them to feel comfortable in their surroundings, and I don't want to hurt any object's feelings by excluding them from any activity in the room. Yes, I just might be as crazy as you think, but they are family and I would never have it any other way.

So, after more trying times at the piano, my parents stopped trying and temporarily backed me off from my lessons and into the newly-developed Cub Scout softball league, created by my mom and a wonderful man named Jack Gilbert. In the particular community where I grew up, the schools were not crowded, and nobody needed to be concerned about our neighborhood being unsafe. There was really only one villain for our parents to deal with—a possible epidemic of an insidious thing called Boredom. Boredom could break out anywhere, easily infecting children, causing unstable behavior which could negatively affect school grades, and perhaps subsequently lead to a life of crime, like clandestinely smoking in the parking lot or stealing hubcaps. This was the reason that my very first girlfriend's father became a positive influence on all of us in Beverly Hills' Cub Scout Pack 77.

Jack Gilbert

Mr. Gilbert had been crippled by polio at twenty-one and confined to a wheelchair. But his mind, spirit and love for baseball sidestepped that horrid disease. From what we learned through his three years of guidance, including his subtle ways of keeping me away from his daughter, we won the league championship every season. More importantly, this experience Jack afforded us was without today's Little League 'win, or you're a loser' mentality. Also missing were parents constantly demanding more playing time for their children or dictating to the manager what the starting line up and batting order should be. For all of us kids, this was a learning process that taught respect for authority, teamwork and the ability to overcome little personal failures, like making an out your last time at bat or booting a double-play ball.

I look back on those times, as I neglected the development and nurturing of my musical talent, comforted to have found as our captain and league's all-star catcher, the peer acceptance and feelings of belonging I always seemed to be looking for. Jack Gilbert imparted a memorable positive view of life while teaching us to understand the mental aspect to the game he loved so much but physically never would be able to play again.

Thank you, Coach G.

And along with my mother's support in her crusade against dreaded Boredom, my dad was there every game rooting like hell for our team, their total commitment instilled in us kids the concept of what sport should really be all about. I was eleven years old when my Cub Scout era sadly came to an end, but I did continue on with my interest in sports, and sometimes, even music.

Another broadening experience chosen for Willy was spending two summers at Camp Troy for boys in the beautiful surroundings of Lake Arrowhead, California. A famous former University of Southern California football player named Harry Edelson ran the camp. During the school year, Harry was the football coach for Fremont High School in Los Angeles. He and his wife, Ruth, provided all the right stuff for all of us, thus giving our parents an eight-week respite to regenerate their own batteries before our next school year began. Water skiing, aquaplaning, baseball games, archery, nights around the campfire, the telling of scary stories that frightened the hell out of us, like "Where's My Liver?," and the ever popular game of "Capture the Flag."

"Capture the Flag" must be at the top of the list of pointless childhood games. Take my flag . . . please! We usually played this exciting game with flashlights in the dark in some available forest. The skills required for anyone to be considered qualified to play up to the game's standards basically consisted of being really good at taunting and shrieking hysterically. Exhaustive efforts are made by both sides for someone to infiltrate into enemy territory (going beyond an imaginary line separating them from us, or us from them) without being detected by the other guys, captured and taken prisoner. Hours later, a hero would finally emerge safely from the enemy's clutches, having absconded, while no one was looking, with their flag, (usually an old towel) waving it high over his head, thus producing the ensuing ear-piercing screams of great convulsive cheering from his teammates. Just great stuff.

It was at Camp Troy that I met my lifelong friend, Norman Ross, he, too, a victim of these silly games. I was eight years old and he was nine. Over the years, Norman and I have played every conceivable kind of game imaginable to "win." No matter the outcome, we have never had a cross word with one another. Our friendship has always transcended the final score. I remember my Uncle Chico being competitive through his astounding grasp of mathematics. His satisfaction from gambling came from his ego-driven desire to show off his God-given abilities in front of any kibitzers on hand. He could remember every hand of cards he was ever dealt, and he would tell you the serial number from a dollar bill you gave him to memorize twenty years ago. On the other hand, my Uncle Zeppo wasn't into the action to "win" the contest. He just wanted to beat the crap out of you.

Playing catch with someone who enjoys it as much as you do can create one of the highest forms of communication. Whenever Norman and I have gotten together throughout the years, one of us is always armed with a tennis ball to set into motion our catching up with each others' latest life's events. Our therapy includes pop-ups, grounders, as well as fast balls, curves and change-ups.

Norm and me at Camp Troy.

I can recall only one time he ever let me down. It was the day he left the comfortable guy thing we had together to get married. For a while I felt abandoned once again, without my buddy. I had to learn that it was not his intent to imply that our relationship had become dispensable now that he had a "new best-buddy," but that things were simply going to be a different kind of okay. It has been just that since Camp Troy.

Two years later after Camp Troy, much to my parents' surprise, I had graduated to the seventh grade in spite of my general indifference to anything not having to do with sports, like say homework. During our Physical Education class the first day, I was one of two captains named to choose up teams that would play a bunch of sports games against each other throughout the school year. That day I couldn't have been more surprised or delighted!

There was Norman Ross, who was equally astounded to see me. His folks had moved into the Beverly Hills school district and

Yours truly with Norm during our high school years.

enrolled Norman at Hawthorne. We had not been in contact since Camp Troy, and he had thought that I went to El Rodeo, another school in the district. After the captain of the other team made his first choice of the best player available, it was my turn to pick my top gun. I surprised everyone when I pointed to Norman, the new kid no one knew. But I knew of his athletic abilities from Camp Troy, and I was sure that I had made the best choice (maybe just like every player I chose for my fantasy team).

It was many years later that Norman told me how apprehensive he was that day about going to a new school, meeting new kids and wondering whether he would be accepted or rejected in a strange new environment. He said, when I made him my choice, it changed his whole perspective from that day forward. For my selfish needs, I guess I picked Norman because I thought he would be the best guy to help my team win. At least, that's what I thought I felt at the time.

Maybe however, there was a far more deep-seeded reason than that.

CHAPTER SEVEN

I was eleven years old when my dad was making the last of the Marx Brothers' films, *Love Happy*. It was not originally intended to be a Marx Brother film, nor their last, but because of a series of nasty little deceptions, it wound up that way. Dad had written a story with Ben Hecht that was to be the vehicle for his own movie without the Brothers. He also worked with another superb writer, Frank Tashlin. Tashlin polished their very cute idea, built around Harpo, who played a happy-go-lucky resident of New York's Central Park.

Not long after Dad signed his contract, he found out that, without his knowledge, certain parts of the script were being rewritten to include Chico. This disturbing news would thereby alter the whole concept of the original script. But Chico needed the money, and, well, Chico always needed the money, so Dad acquiesced to the story changes, and the producer told him that it would be written just as a cameo role.

It wasn't much later when Dad got another jolt. They were rewriting the script once again, this time to include a cameo role for Groucho, who, incidentally, did *not* need the money. Dad saw his whole story slipping away into something he, Hecht and Tashlin had not envisioned, and he was both furious and hurt. He went to the producer and asked for an explanation, and it had turned out that Dad had been lied to all along. Taking it from the top, the producer had never been able to fully finance the movie, and as time went on, the only possible way to get the money to finish it was to turn it into a Marx Brothers movie. Because of the continuous premeditated deceptions by the producer, Dad told me that it was one of the very rare times in his entire professional career that he felt and expressed hatred toward anyone. Finishing the picture was probably the most difficult time he ever endured all his years in show business. I know, because Mom and I were often there on the set at Eagle-Lion Studios to give him support throughout the remaining ordeal.

Dad and me on the set of *Love Happy.*

The underlying reason why I have brought this particular episode up, is because one of my life's pivotal incidents occurred during this time while on a visit to see Dad at the studio. It was during summer, so I was out of school and had just come from (you guessed it) another lesson; this one in art, to show him a picture of a palomino horse I had just drawn with pastels and decided to be very proud of it, if for no other reason than I had done it. I arrived at a time that everyone was breaking for dinner. It was six o'clock and Daylight-Savings-Time with still plenty of sunshine, so on one of the studio's streets, we all assembled at series of long tables and benches to break bread. Another picture was being shot at the same time as **Love Happy**. It was called **One Touch of Venus**, and they conveniently broke for dinner at the same time we did.

As I sat patiently waiting to be served, a defining moment in my life suddenly sneaked up on me, slamming me right in the heart. It arrived in the form of the staggering beauty of the woman who sat down next to me. For the first time I became aware that there was a real difference between boys and girls. I had never seen in real life anyone more strikingly feminine than Ava Gardner. And when she was nice enough to speak to me from time to time, I just sat there staring at her, tongue-tied and consumed by a feeling of both awkward embarrassment and youthful vulnerability. In recalling this revelation, it occurs to me that, even though by that time Mickey Rooney and Artie Shaw had already beaten me to Ava, it was still a thrill to know that I had been able to play a part in her life, and hers in mine at an earlier age (I was only eleven) than Frank Sinatra. So there!

Dad finished the picture just after the New Year and soon his agent at the William Morris Theatrical Agency was contacted about a tour through the British Music Halls that they were arranging for Dad and Chico. Dad agreed to go when the deal included taking Mom and me. He also considered the fact that, of course, Chico needed the money. So on Monday, May 16, 1949, Dad, Mom and I were on our way to England, stopping on the way for three days in New York City. It was there that Mom and I went to the old Yankee Stadium and where I saw my first Major League baseball game—New York versus the Cleveland Indians.

The Yanks were a perennial powerhouse in those days with Joltin' Joe Dimaggio patrolling center for them. But Larry Doby, the first African American to play in the American League, was the story that afternoon, leading the Indians to a three-to-two win by knocking in all three runs with a bases-loaded single and a booming four-hundred-and-thirty-foot home run. Yogi Berra also hit one out of sight, but it wasn't enough, as Steve Gromek picked up the win. Despite the excitement of my first Major League experience, I still preferred the family intimacy Gilmore Field provided, and even though they weren't in the Majors, I would always remain loyal to my true heroes, the Hollywood Stars.

My next amazing first occurred the following evening when we went to the Majestic Theater to see the new Broadway show, Rodgers and Hammerstein's blockbuster hit, **South Pacific.** Imagine seeing the original cast with Ezio Pinza and Mary Martin as my initial exposure to the wonderful world of Musical Comedy. How fortunate was that?! Well, I shall tell you. In looking into the diary I kept throughout our trip, my review of the show was as follows: "The music was good, the performance was good, the singing was good. The show was good at that also."

It's probably also good that I wasn't the reviewer for the **New York Times**, or the show wouldn't have become nearly as successful as it did. Good God! Godfather Woollcott would have never forgiven me. Just for the record, over the years more exposure to the show and its music has upgraded that review considerably.

Our third day in New York was the day we boarded the **Queen Mary** to cross the Atlantic for England. It was another first in my life, having never been on a cruise ship before. Three firsts, three days in a row. However, we did have a serious problem confronting us. A month before we were to leave, I came down with a bad case of the mumps, which lasted for a whole painful week. And now, Mom had suddenly been stricken, I guess having gotten it from me, and we had to conceal the untimely problem from everyone, or the whole ship would have gone into quarantine. So Mom spent the whole trip in our stateroom with a scarf wrapped around her face to hide the swelling. Dad and I played a lot of ping pong in the five days we were at sea.

When we weren't playing ping pong, Dad would go down to the

baggage room to practice the harp. Harpists need to play every day in order to keep up the calluses on their fingers. It's an absolute must for them to do so in order to avoid raw and bloody fingertips. But Dad also practiced because he actually loved to practice. He was one of the few musicians I ever knew that looked forward to it. It didn't matter whether he was preparing for a job or not, he liked to practice almost three hours every day. He would sit at the harp in his own private heaven, reveling in the musical vibrations from the strings that were sent from the harp's sounding board, absorbed through his shoulder as the harp rested upon him, and on into the rest of his body, resonating throughout. One couldn't help but notice the metamorphosis in him, drawn to the sensuality of the music as he became 'at one' with the beauty of the instrument.

About the fourth day, the swelling in Mom's face began to subside, and she was on her way to recovery. By then we all were all thinking that four days on a cruise ship was a day too long. Finally, on the fifth day, we landed in Southampton, and not a moment too soon. From there we were on our way to London, trading our sea legs for some pretty shaky train legs. Our arrival signaled the end to a six-thousand-mile journey, and we celebrated our exhaustion by going right to bed.

The next day, we hooked up with Chico and his companion, Mary Dee, to coordinate their schedule with ours. The next nine days would be spent sightseeing, shopping, and rehearsing their material for the highlight of the tour, four weeks at the London Palladium. We hit all the tourist hot spots (the forced continuing education of Willy); the clammy Tower of London; the magnificent Hampton Court palace built by Cardinal Wolsey, of course constructed just in time before King Henry the Eighth's unfriendly act of beheading him; the requisite changing of the guard at Buckingham Palace; the Parliament in session with its mumbling approvals; the beautiful old paintings and exquisite armor of the Wallace Collection; the National Gallery's comprehensive exhibit of the Dutch masters, of course, the spooky Madame Tausaud's Wax Museum and the indescribable architectural complexity of Westminster Abbey.

Mom and Mary also carefully planned for shopping and antiquing without interfering with the rehearsal times that were set in concrete. Dad and Chico would work on the routines they did, as well as sketches they did together with Alga and Evelyn, two lovely gals who would act as foils for them. It was now to be my first responsible job as his personal prop man. I had to see to it that the coat he wore was properly prepared for all of his sight gags; the carrot goes into the upper right inside pocket, the telescope must be in the lower left inside pocket, the scissors for immediate availability in the small middle right inside pocket, the rubber chicken accessible in the large left inside pocket, and on and on.

Dad had a bit that he did in **Animal Crackers** on Broadway and in its subsequent movie that was always a showstopper. He would be apprehended by a police officer or house detective for stealing silverware. Chico would insist on Dad's innocence, proclaiming to the officer what an upstanding citizen Dad was. The apprehender would then apologize for the mistake and shake Dad's hand in a gesture of friendliness. As he did this, knives would start to fall from Dad's sleeve. They would continue to fall as the audience howled. He could easily milk the gag for a good four minutes. Every night in our dressing room, it would take ten minutes for me to load some four hundred knives up his sleeve, and I did this while his arm was in it! (Wide sleeve.)

I was in show business. I was in vaudeville! Dad had given me an important role to play in his act. And that was just another one of my many jobs. My biggest responsibility was seeing to it that when it was time for his musical solo spot in the show, I would bring his harp onto the stage, making sure it was placed perfectly for the spotlight.

Dad also had me dressed as an angel. When I had completed my task, he thanked me in pantomime, and while shaking my hand and turning me toward the exit, the audience would see the sign on my wings: "Eat at Olivelli's." That one laugh that I always got from the audience was my salary as Dad's prop man, and I have forever felt that I was grossly overpaid.

It was also my job to time each sketch, making sure that we would not run over our allotted thirty-five or forty minutes. On the last day in London, we left to go out on a tour of the British Isles for the next two weeks, polishing the stuff we had been rehearsing, in preparation for our return to London for our four-week engagement

The "dropping the knives" bit.

at the Palladium. We were booked separately, with Chico and Mary
Dee going off in one direction to work his material as the featured
headliner, while Dad, Mom and I went with Alga and Evelyn to
headline at our first week stop in Leeds.

The bill had six or seven of the usual vaudeville acts; comic acrobats, magician, ventriloquist, juggler, high-wire walker, tap dancer, stand-up comedian, and so on. All were first-rate, as the circuit always had the best possible attractions. There was a lot less to do in Leeds than London, not surprisingly, but I do remember one occasion we had during the day to visit a charming little town. This was the original York that "New" was probably named after. It was also without a doubt the birthplace of the word "quaint." Charles Dickens had to have been the developer of the place: cobblestone streets meandering everywhere, lined by three-hundred-year-old buildings, and a main street right out of a Sherlock Holmes movie. It was afternoon when our tour led us to an astoundingly beautiful church with exquisite stained-glass windows, and fabulous antique rugs everywhere covering all the floors and walls. Suddenly, Mom, having forgotten to wear her watch, and realizing we may have to leave soon to get back for that night's show, turned to Dad to ask him what time it was. He looked up at the walls of the church and said, "tap-es-try." I looked at my watch and it was actually twenty-five minutes past three. Astonishingly, Dad was only five minutes fast, and close enough to real time that we decided that we wouldn't have to buy him a watch for his next birthday.

Dad's show in Leeds was booked for five days, and like everywhere in the British Isles in the years immediately following the Second World War, we always played to appreciative audiences and never juries. They were there to be entertained, and entertained they were. Our five-day stay at the Moss Empire in Glasgow, Scotland was equally gratifying, as the show was tightening up beautifully. By then, I even knew where the exact spot for the harp was on stage without looking. Then, it was finally time to head back to London to combine our act with Chico's, and we were as ready for the Palladium as we were ever going to be.

The show always got off to a good start with a terrific sight gag. In front of the curtain, Harpo and Chico appeared from the stage right wing with their backs to the audience, tugging away at a rope and struggling from the resistance at the other end while crossing the stage. As they disappeared into the stage left wing, who should emerge from the stage right wing at the other end of the rope facing the audience but, that's right, the real Harpo and Chico. From then

Self explanatory.

on it was clear sailing for their act.

They did the mock bridge game sketch, where upon Evelyn's having completed her turn to shuffle, Alga asked Dad to cut the cards, which he did, with a hatchet. To blackout!

Chico did his monologue, talking about how the Brothers got their names, and that Julius was named because of the "grouch bag" he had around his neck that was always bigger and fuller than anyone else's.

"Harpo also had a bag, but he got rid of her in a hurry."

Then came the cutting of the skirt sketch. Evelyn would come out in a long evening gown and proceed to sing an operatic aria with elegance and grace. A minute later, Dad would appear from the wings, walking toward her, mesmerized by her beautiful voice and elegant attire. But, alas, he notices a glaring thread sticking out at the bottom of her gown. He tries to inform her of this little embarrassment, but, not noticing him, she just keeps on singing. To solve the problem, he takes out a pair of scissors from his coat, and proceeds to snip off the thread. Unfortunately, in his zeal to perform this well-intentioned deed, he accidentally cuts off a piece of her gown as well, thus making the hemline uneven. In an effort to right his wrong, he goes to the other side of her and cuts some off there, trying to make everything even. But he over cuts and the problem persists. She continues to sing, unaware of Dad's presence and what is occurring beneath her.

She's *really* into this aria.

For the rest of the bit, he vainly attempts to cut evenly around the entire dress, but he manages instead to steal her huge diamond ring and bejeweled necklace, and stops along the way to eat the decorations off of her garter belt. She keeps on singing, still oblivious to it all, until at last, she comes to the end of the aria.

By that time, Dad has cut off her entire skirt to her waist. During the great applause that was to follow, Dad shakes Evelyn's hand, congratulating her for an aria well sung, and then he turns her around to reveal to the audience a sign on the back of her black panties, "MEN AT WORK," or some other popular phrase of the time. Evelyn reacts to the audience's response, looks down, sees that she is without the bottom of her gown, screams and runs off stage, leaving Dad alone on stage, with such an impish look of innocence, as the laughter continues to blackout!

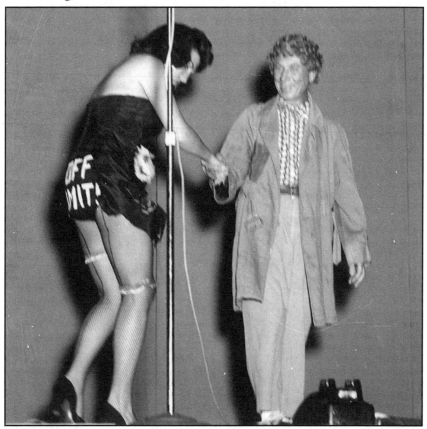

Oh, my God!!

I must add a curious footnote about the origin of the cutting of the skirt sketch. Dad told me that in the early days of American vaudeville, there was a very fine comedian by the name of "Doc" Rockwell. One night Dad saw him do a bit where he cut the skirt off an attractive woman. Dad liked the idea so much, and had ideas of his own on how to expand on the bit, that he asked Rockwell if he could buy the bit from him and also pay a royalty every time he used it. Rockwell agreed to the deal, so Dad took it and transformed it into his very own, with an operatic setting, which spawned its own special kind of gags. It wasn't until years later and many royalty checks that Dad found out that this great vaudevillian had died penniless, and of a broken heart, having felt disgraced and humiliated by the fact that his son, George Lincoln, had become founder and leader of the American Neo-Nazi Party.

One of my responsibilities as Dad's prop man as far back as my beginnings in British Music Hall was to see to it that the bubble machine worked. Yes, Dad had a bubble machine. However, it was like no other bubble machine in that it, along with some of his other props, was made especially for him by a company that was world renown for making the finest illusions for most of the top magicians of the time. No, this bubble machine didn't at some point in Dad's act disappear. It was just that you didn't know it was there because it was hidden from view by, could you have guessed, a clarinet. It was a contraption that fit inside the bell of the clarinet, and it would be activated by him blowing into a tube that was attached to the side of the clarinet. It was always my job to see to it that the bubble machine was filled with liquid bubble stuff and then test the mechanism, so that at a most strategic moment during his playing the song, "I'm Forever Blowing Bubbles," little round objects would appear from the bell of the clarinet, filling the entire stage with bubbles, those as if by magic. I had to make absolutely sure that nothing went wrong, because if the bubble machine didn't work, the bit would simply become having to listen to him play a less than sparkling clarinet solo. Fortunately for Dad (and me), the bubble machine worked like a dream when he did the bit years later on Milton Berle's TV show.

Incidentally, this ultimately became a staple for Dad whenever he gave concerts as fund raisers for always financially needy symphony orchestras. One day, out of the year 1963, he decided that he wanted to do "Bubbles" with his good friend, artistic director and conductor, Thomas Facey, and the Riverside Symphony Orchestra. So as I then had become Dad's musical arranger/conductor, he asked me to write an impressive but also considerably ponderous-sounding symphonic arrangement for the orchestra to accompany him, his clarinet and his bubble machine.

The sketch would begin with Dad (introduced as noted guest conductor, Arturo Harponini), leading the orchestra.

Maestro Arturo Harponini!

Yay, team!

But he was soon to become disturbed, because the orchestra's clarinetist kept goofing up on his solos so much that Dad, in frustration, shoots him and becomes the new clarinet soloist. Dad would then have the real conductor take over leading the orchestra. However, his conducting would always have the orchestra finishing their musical phrase before Dad would finish his part of the melody. This lack of musical communication would exasperate the hell out of Dad, until he would finally ask the guest female vocalist to help keep everyone together by singing the melody. This solved the problem, and he was now free to play along with the orchestra until the bubble machine was put into action. Then, at the end of "Bubbles," Dad would wind up the bit with the seventy-five-piece orchestra going into an ear-splitting Dixieland rendition of "Hold That Tiger" as he built a shrieking crescendo of high notes never before heard being played on the clarinet, and doing so while waving a stuffed tiger at the audience he had somehow magically produced from one of his secret pockets. The audience went crazy. So did Thomas Facey, and so did the entire symphony orchestra. It was what my working with Dad was all about. He would always give me the important responsibility of solving any musical problem he had. He believed in me. We were a team.

Continuing with their fast paced act, both Chico, shooting the piano keys, and Dad, with his sweeping glissandos, had their separate musical solos to break up the comedy. Dad had recently experienced some heart troubles and would take a little nitroglycerin pill whenever he felt palpitations. He prepared for that possibility by inconspicuously gluing to the harp a small box filled with the pills, availing himself of quick and easy access. He rarely had occasion to take one, but it comforted him to know that they were there for him.

He also had a habitual ritual that he once told me about. It came into play whenever he performed harp solos before an audience. It all stemmed from a concern about the fact that he was a self-taught harpist and had no real academic musical training. Sitting on his harp stool just before beginning to play, he looked out at the audience and then did a silent dialogue with himself.

"I'm up here, and they're down there. I really should be down there, and someone from down there who is a much more qualified harpist should be up here. But I'm here, and they aren't, or they'd be up here, and I'd be down there. But I'm not down there, because I'm up here. I must be here, because they want me to be here, so I guess I'll start playing."

This entire mental machination took no more than five seconds, but it sure worked to set his confidence in motion.

On occasion, I was permitted to sit in the orchestra pit during the show. Those were the days when you had a full orchestra playing all kinds of different music for all kinds of different acts. Recordings of orchestras were my only previous connection with music until then. I was now in the middle of a performing orchestra and feeling the power and precision of all the instruments playing. It added a dimension to my appreciation of music, and provided an all-consuming euphoria from the immediacy of it all. It was something that I had never experienced before, and

I would never again feel from recordings the magic that live performance conjures up for me.

We broke the record set by Danny Kaye during our four-week stint at the Palladium, while having had command performances before the Queen and Princess Margaret. I had been given a remarkably diverse education by Mom and Dad that few would ever be privileged to have in an entire lifetime. I had already experienced exposure to all kinds of lessons, plus Broadway, Yankee Stadium, the Arts and their masters, British history and its Music Hall vaudeville, and I was still only twelve years old.

But some nights, Mom and I sat in the audience to carefully critique the act, and now and then Dad would stop the show between sketches. The spotlight swung over to us as in pantomime, he proudly introduced Mom, who stood up smiling and waving as she acknowledged the applause. Then, he proudly introduced me, and all I could do was raise myself up to a half standing position, as I shyly responded to the moment at hand. Embarrassed by the ovation, I then quickly sat down, feeling that the only reason they were applauding was that I was Harpo's kid, and that I had done nothing on my own to warrant any recognition, other than placing the harp on stage in an angel outfit. So, fearing that there might be someone behind me so jealous of my being lucky enough to be a part of Dad's family, I avoided standing straight up to keep from presenting anyone with unreasonable envy, a perfect target to shoot at.

I was no different from anyone else in wanting to be acknowledged by others. But I found it discomforting to know that the audience was recognizing my worth to them before I was recognizing my worth to myself.

It was back home and back to the normal routine. Dad was happy to be playing golf and hanging out with his pals at the Hillcrest Country Club. Mom was carrying out the endlessly responsible job of running the household and seeing to it that we all did our homework. I would complete my final year of elementary/grammar school, while taking another grueling stab at piano lessons. While I was practicing my dreaded Czerny and Hanon exercises, Mom would often stand on the other side of the closed door, just waiting for that moment of silence when I stopped playing. Then she would peek in at me to see what I was doing during that moment of silence, and I would look up and find some lame excuse like "I was just getting out the music to the Beethoven Sonata that I'm working on."

She would then close the door and wait for my next moment of silence, which I'm sure she assumed was induced by boredom. Incidentally, it was. I really couldn't make an emotional connection with the classical piano music I was learning. I was not getting to play some of the music I emotionally related to, like the Gershwin, Ravel, Debussy, and Berlin I always heard Dad practicing. It was explained to me that I needed to learn the fundamentals of technique before I could venture into further musical exploration. I never quite figured out why he got to play all that great stuff without ever having to have any formal training, while I was getting formal training without getting to play all that great stuff.

I have always thought it ironic that Dad was envious of the formal education I got, something he never had. And I was envious of him being able to play whatever music he chose that made him

I really just wanted to look at the picture on the wall.

feel good and not have to deal with all the academia that I had to go through. Why did I have to learn to read all this classical literature? (I was to find out some time later.)

Dad never learned how to read music, so instead he learned those complicated pieces by ear. Yet, he was the disciplined one, and I was not. You need discipline to play the great classical music, and for years I wasn't mature enough to understand the value of practice. If I had chosen the harp instead, maybe it would have been a lot more fun. But Dad said that one harpist in a family is enough. Because he told me this when I was three years old, I wasn't particularly convinced of his reasoning until many years later.

He knew I was fascinated with the harp. So he decided that if I took up the piano, which is the closest thing to a harp, I'd still, in a sense, be able to play the harp, because the musical sound of a piano comes from the strings of the harp that exists inside every piano. However, this does not happen with a harp. No matter how hard you may look, you will never find a piano in any harp. There's just not enough room in there, not even for a spinet.

If you ever have seen the movie *A Day at the Races*, you may recall a wild scene where my dad was in a tuxedo playing this majestic grand piano. He comes to a loud musical passage, and as he starts pounding away, the keys start flying off in all directions. Then the piano begins to fall apart, and soon Dad is dismantling the rest of it as he continues to pound the hell out of it. In the rubble, he discovers a harp, for him a far nobler instrument, then pulls it out of the mess and proceeds to play a beautiful solo on it. Whether or not he ever knew there was a harp in there somewhere, he always did feel that the instrument was just made for him.

The Brothers' act was originally a musical act, and Minnie, who booked them, soon found out that an act with a harp in it got five dollars more a week than an act without one. So because Julius had his mandolin, and Leonard was already the piano player, she sent Arthur an old harp to add to accompanying all the singing numbers. As the need became more evident for the harp to be incorporated into the act as a solo instrument, Dad's musical survival instincts had only to be fueled by his natural curiosity about anything and everything in general. Being self-taught from the moment he received the harp and with no time or money for any academic training, he had to become a tinkerer, hopefully discovering what the harp was capable or not capable of doing. As a result of his bizarre experimentations, he ultimately developed his unique dramatically visual style of performance, in a way no other harpists had ever performed before, including his dazzling display of those flashy glissandos that would end many of his solos.

Years later and by then known as Harpo, he befriended two of the most distinguished concert harpists in the world, Marcel Granjany and Mildred Dilling, trading tricks of the trade with each of them. One of his more significant and peculiar musical devices that he shared could have almost even challenged the laws of physics. Harp strings when struck produce a pure non-vibrating tone, but in one of his more inventive moments he produced an ingenious way of his getting vibrato out of a harp string, something that astonished Granjany and Dilling, as neither had ever seen it introduced in any previous harp literature. Marcel and Mildred were to immediately inject Dad's new gift to them into their respective recital repertoires. I kind of feel that if it hadn't already been invented, given enough time through his dabblings, Dad would have probably also brought to the world in all its glorious, living incandescence, the light bulb. It sure was always on, shining brightly over his head.

Dilling and Dad

It wasn't till I was sixteen years old, and became his arranger and conductor, that I fully understood the complexities inherent to the harp. He explained it to me this way. It's got forty-seven strings, representing all the notes on the harp, seven pedals at the base of the frame, each one controlling the string for each note in the scale, and three pedal positions that create all the necessary sharps, naturals and flats by lengthening or shortening the string in order to produce the note desired. Now get this. There is only one possible way to play any intended single note correctly, let alone a cluster of them at the same time. To begin with, you have to pluck the right string for the right note you want. While you are doing that, you have to find the right pedal that corresponds to the string for that specific note, and then pray that you chose the correct foot, so that it can push that particular pedal into the appropriate position to get the note you hoped to play in the first place. All this goes on at the same time, in a split second.

When it's presented to you this way as Dad presented it to me, it really does sound pretty "iffy," doesn't it? The odds are stacked against your ever playing the right note. He said that if you multiply the forty-seven strings times the seven pedals times the three pedal positions, you will find that for every single note that you want to play correctly, there are nine-hundred and eighty-six ways to screw it up! The lottery has better odds than nine-hundred and eighty-six to one. And that's just per one note! Once again Dad had given me some invaluable guidance (that is, if you are not heavy into public ridicule).Why risk it? Play the favorite. I figured right then and there that it would always be a much safer bet to write for the harp than to play it. Besides all that, I've come to learn that most harpists spend fifty-percent of their time tuning the harp and the remaining fifty-percent of their time playing out of tune.

I was thirteen years old my first year at Beverly Hills High School, and I certainly wasn't ready to try out for a baseball team mainly consisting of juniors and seniors. Besides, it was quite the mental and physical jump from Hawthorne Elementary to being a freshman with thoughts of how to deal with the four years ahead of me. So I did everything I thought you should do to fit in with my peers. I got plenty of white tee shirts, a couple of pairs of blue jeans to wear low, and long enough in the legs to be able to roll up to show the white socks and the penny loafers. Sometimes, just for variety, we all would sport fluorescent-colored socks. That was hip, for a while, until the day you found out that they had gone out of fashion, and you were the only one still wearing them.

I wasn't yet ready for or interested in the girls my age and/or in my class. The vision of Ava Gardner was not only still with me, but it also was helping me to temporarily push aside having to awkwardly communicate with them, thus sparing me the ultimate humiliation of their outright rejection. Yikes! So I was more or less left with having to, oh my god, *study*, while trying to adapt to the new routine of things, again acting just like every other freshman in any school, anywhere, ever. Oh, for the day I would finally become a sophomore! I remember absolutely nothing else about my freshman year, and probably for very good reason. I guess absolutely nothing of any importance was what happened.

Just us all growing up was what happened.

But that summer I decided to go out for junior varsity basketball, and I met Steve Miletich, who coached both the junior varsity and varsity teams. He was my high school "Jack Gilbert."

Coach Miletich was first and foremost a teacher of sportsmanship. His no-nonsense attitude about commitment was exemplified by his position on school activities. You must choose carefully between being on the hill in campus politics and being on the field in sports.

With Coach Miletich.

He wanted total focus on either choice, so as to get the best possible out of every student. You would not be able to play on his teams if you had less than a B-minus scholastic average, yes, even if you were an all-league forward. He also was very capable of suspending an athlete or kicking him off the team permanently for insubordination. Coach was so highly respected by faculty and parents that subsequently he became Dean of Boys and later, Principal of the school. Once again, another positive influence had been added to my life. Thank you, Coach M.

I wondered if Mom might just be right about her instinctive belief in the Fates.

CHAPTER NINE

One day when I was about fourteen, I came home from high school and heard Dad practicing a tune he was learning from one of his piano lessons. It sounded like the kind of music that I would be jazzed about playing. The tune was an old standard, "Sweet Lorraine," and Dad was having the best time with it. I asked him who was teaching it to him. He said that if he told me, would I like to take a lesson or two from his teacher?

For the next couple of years, I would bicycle twice a week seven or eight miles to a little house on Melrose Avenue. There, I took lessons from the man who I credit with being pivotal in making me excited about playing the piano, Charles Crenshaw. Crenshaw was an extremely mild-mannered man, who never seemed to have a concern in the world, beyond seeing to it that the ever-present pipe that he talked to me through, was constantly filled, packed and lit.

Charlie was considered somewhat of a black sheep in his family because of his insistence on becoming simply a typical starving musician and not a successful businessman like his father. This decision was bittersweet, for while it made Charlie all the stronger for choosing the life he truly wished to live, it also created a mammoth breach between him and his father. Charlie's father had been a renowned and well-respected developer in Los Angeles, so prestigious a man was he that, for his contributions to the city, a major thoroughfare, Crenshaw Boulevard, is named in his honor. Fortunately, his father came to recognize Charlie's successful career, and the breach closed for good.

Charlie's choice seemed to suit him just fine. He taught many of Hollywood's movie stars and executives, and became socially

Charles Crenshaw.

accepted into their world and, yes, quite the ladies man. He also was one hell of a player, especially when he was demonstrating his complete mastery of the "stride piano" style, made famous by people like Teddy Wilson, Jelly Roll Morton, and the genius, Art Tatum. I never came to know whether it was just for demonstration purposes to get my attention, or whether that was all of the tune that he knew, but I must say that I never heard him ever play any more than four bars of anything. But what great four bars they always were!

Charlie also introduced my ears to George Shearing and the mellow sound of his quintet. Through the years Shearing has been high on my list as one of the all-time greats of the keyboard, wielding his musical masterstrokes in jazz as well as the classical repertoire. (Years later, George and Dad appeared together in the television special, *Swingin' at the Summit*.) But I think that of all the pianists who influenced Charles Crenshaw, Art Tatum, with whom he became close friends, would be the stand out. Charlie had the same kind of fullness to his playing and a similar harmonic sense. Soon after our being introduced to Tatum, Dad and I were out looking for and listening to every record of his available.

Many musicians eventually become teachers, because sooner or later, they objectively, and maybe even painfully, recognize that their limited abilities have hindered them in their pursuit of making it professionally. However, in Charlie's case, there was none of that. Teaching was definitely made for Charlie, he knew it, and he loved it. Whenever I see a piano or a pipe, it always brings to mind Charles Crenshaw. Thank you, Charlie.

But other careers still beckoned, so music would have to take a backseat in my teenage mind while I explored, however delusional, my options. I finally decided to give baseball a go in my senior year. Hardly fleet afoot, but having had very good reflexes, I settled in at third base. I was doing a decent job there as the season started, and during infield practice prior to one game, I leaped high for an errant throw from the first baseman. After catching it, I came down on the side of the bag and fell to the ground, writhing in pain. A heavily sprained ankle, which took ten to twelve weeks to heal, put an end to my baseball playing days.

Disconsolate that I now wasn't able to be some kind of campus jock, I turned my attention to the piano. I continued to mix lessons from Charles Crenshaw with the classical academia taught by either Ignace Hilsberg, Natalie Lemonic or Ted Saidenberg, three remarkably distinguished pianists, as well as very highly-credentialed teachers.

What time I had left after that and my schoolwork was devoted to the wonderful world of hormones. The notion of relating to girls had started very slowly in my sophomore year, gathered some steam as my junior year came to a close, and was now in full force. I never really had a girlfriend for any length of time that could wear my YMCA pin. (That irrational concept of the times was to show everyone we were "going steady.")

On one occasion when I was dating a girl by the name of Margie Thomas, she asked me to be her escort to the First Annual Emmy Awards Gala. I told her that I didn't have a tuxedo for the formal event, so her dad arranged for me to wear one of his for the evening's festivities. As it turned out, her father walked away with just about every award they handed out that night. It was very special for me to be a part of history in the making, and to have been Margie's escort. Our relationship never got serious, but over the years, through a variety of unrelated circumstances, we have accidentally and sporadically had telephone contact. Upon her slam-dunk decision to leave me in the lurch, she wisely opted instead to have a very successful career in show business, and the girl I would never be able to call "My Little Margie" changed her name to Marlo. And Danny, wherever you are, thank you so very much once again for your kind attention to and gracious resolution of my formal sartorial inadequacies.

Looking back upon my junior year, I made the decision, with the advice of Mom and Dad, of course, to join the U.S. Coast Guard Reserve. We chose this particular service because that's where my cousin Arthur, Groucho's son, and my cousin Bob, Gummo's son, had served. Since I was only sixteen, we all thought it would be a good idea for me to start my obligation early on, getting it out of the way before continuing on to higher education. I must say that I was never cut out to be in the service, not because I didn't want to be, but because I approached everything they asked me to do with sincere ineptitude. You would have thought I had looked up the answer to everything they tried to teach me in the "How *Not* To" manual. When we marched, I always started off on the wrong foot. In learning how to tie various knots, I managed to create ones never before seen in any branch of our armed forces. I could easily take a gun apart, but putting it back together required someone else doing it for me.

It wasn't until two years later that I actually got to fire one. It was at boot camp in Alameda, California. I took my M1 rifle, aimed it carefully at whatever I was supposed to hit, and pulled the trigger. The sound was so deafening, with everyone firing away at the same time, I thought that I was hearing some kind of horrible drum solo. Well, I got so scared that I panicked, and immediately pointed my rifle skyward. As swiftly as possible, I, terrified, emptied the remaining bullets in my clip into the air, and they landed I know not where. Except for one. When they went to check out our scores, they found I had shot only one bullet that hit the target, and that one was a bull's eye. It turned out that my very first shot heralded my arrival as a true marxman.

Nothing was happening in great quantities for me to remember about my junior year, except for an occurrence out of school. Art

Linkletter's son, Jack, had a radio show and asked me to be on it. I was billed as his school pal and Harpo's kid, meaning that because Harpo didn't speak, I could only communicate by whistling.

Fine. So, I called my cousin Bob and asked him if he would come to the show and whistle the answers to Jack's questions for me, since I wasn't much of a whistler myself. We did the show to a studio audience and I would put my fingers in my mouth and Bob would whistle from his position in the wings. I must admit it was pretty embarrassing standing there in front of everyone as they all listened to Bob bailing me out. To Bob's everlasting credit, he whistled so well, that I wouldn't have been surprised a bit if Lauren Bacall suddenly had emerged from the wings. I'm sure my whistler's mother, Helen, was proud of him that day for helping me out.

The rest of my high school days as a senior were spent preparing for our classes' graduation exercises. I'll never know who recommended me; it was probably an avenging conspiracy, but I was asked to write and perform the music that would reflect our four years at Beverly High. Before I knew it, I found myself having to write additional music for a choral group that was unilaterally added to accompany my piano performance. Then I came to find that Rita Seiler, one of my more brilliant classmates, was recruited to write a libretto that my music had to fit.

Soon after that, Alan Reed, Jr. was selected to deliver Rita's illuminating and poignant work. The selection of Alan turned out to be the right choice, what with his having a father who was then immensely successful doing "voice-overs" for many television shows, including, a few years later, the voice of Fred Flintstone. So Alan Jr. definitely had the right genes for the job as our narrator. But because it required a considerable amount of rehearsal time for everyone in order to coordinate all the elements, there wasn't much time left for me to indulge myself in much of anything else, other than making sure that I, too, would graduate.

Finally came the big day when flipping the tassels on our hat to the other side was supposed to send the signal to our parents that all of a sudden, we were all grown up! Before that questionable revelation occurred, and in spite of my having to endure a serious case of butterflyitis, *The Best Years* was performed all the way from beginning to end without a hitch. My pride swelled, not from the sudden explosion of applause from the audience, but from the fact that I got myself through the whole thing without an attack from my heart. That accomplishment let me know I was able to start and finish something I had never done before. Surprisingly enough, I still have the recording of that work, because as gratifying as the experience was, I've always been very grateful that the music critics from the **New York, London** and **Los Angeles Times** were not in attendance.

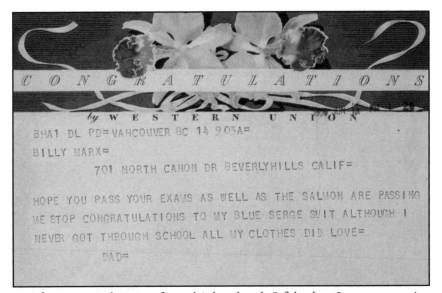

CONGRATULATIONS

by WESTERN UNION

BHA1 DL PD=VANCOUVER BC 14 903A=

BILLY MARX=

701 NORTH CANON DR BEVERLYHILLS CALIF=

HOPE YOU PASS YOUR EXAMS AS WELL AS THE SALMON ARE PASSING
ME STOP CONGRATULATIONS TO MY BLUE SERGE SUIT ALTHOUGH I
NEVER GOT THROUGH SCHOOL ALL MY CLOTHES DID LOVE=

DAD=

After my graduation from high school, I felt that I was not quite ready enough mentally to go into active duty, so I chose to enroll at UCLA to begin my higher education. But after my first semester, I felt that I was not quite ready mentally for higher education, so I chose to activate myself for my two-year obligation in the Coast Guard. I went for my physical in downtown Los Angeles, and the first orders we had to obey were to strip to our shorts and then stand in line for our shots. One of them was to be administered with a much larger-than-life needle, affectionately called "the Skyhook," and we all trembled with fear every time the line moved up a notch.

Then came the turn of the guy who was two places ahead of me. He was the only one I saw with no sense of fear. Small wonder. His skin was so thick that on three attempts, it broke three Skyhooks. During this unusual demonstration, the guy immediately in front of me fainted. This behavior gave me a pause, especially while watching two guys pick him up and haul him off to the infirmary. Now it was my turn to have what by all rights should have become an everlasting memory. However, I guess for purposes of emotional self-preservation, I have conveniently managed to block out all recollection of the results of my participation in "Operation Skyhook."

My next orders were to report to San Pedro for duty on the **USS Minnetonka** Coast Guard cutter. The idea of my being on

At least my uniform fit.

something with the name Minnetonka amused me. But it hardly seemed like a name that would strike fear into the hearts of enemy pirate ships. "Ship ahoy! But wait! Good God! It can't be! It is! Just as I feared! Trouble, hearties! We've got to turn tail and get out of here, and fast. There's no way we have any chance to withstand the power and force of everyone's dreaded nemesis, the scourge of the seas, the mighty . . . *MINNETONKA!!*"

My amusement didn't last too long. For some inexplicable reason, other than there was nothing else for us to do because it was eleven years since World War II ended, we rookie seamen were assigned to the deck, where our job was first to chip the paint off, then sand it down, and then paint it. This entire, carefully thought-out procedure started all over again the minute the paint dried. Oh what fun active duty was! The second day I was aboard, an ensign came up to me and said that I had been ordained as the lucky one to raise the flag at muster. I obeyed his order and took the flag from him. Then I proceeded to the pole as he went off to cue the trumpet for the call to colors. The wind was blowing fiercely, which made it very difficult to fasten the flag to the rope. Muster was already in progress, and I had not yet completed the raising of the flag. Just as I saw the irate ensign coming back to see what the delay was all about, with great relief, I felt the flag and rope come to the end of their destination. The ensign looked up and inquired, "Who died?"

I then looked up to discover that due to one of my unintended "creative" knots, the flag got stuck half way up the pole. And what was worse, it was upside down. The ensign made me take the flag down and raise it again, or however many times it might take until I got it right. Fortunately for everyone, they exercised prudent judgment in never recommending me for that job ever again. Though my tour of duty on the mighty **Minnetonka** wound up lasting only four weeks, I was proud to be able to garner overseas pay when we were assigned the ever dangerous mission of being the sole escort for the . . . . Ensenada Yacht Races!

I suppose that I was never cut out to be in the service for any another reason besides ineptitude. My screw-ups were making my Coast Guard motto more like "Semper Paralysis," but having had rickets stemming from my hunger strike at The Children's Home Society created a history of nagging foot problems. Standing on them, ten to fourteen hours a day aboard ship, caused me considerable pain, which was getting worse with each passing day. I asked to have a thorough examination of my aching feet. They agreed that my feet couldn't stand up to the punishing grind, so I was granted my request for a medical discharge. I was then sent for assignment to the Coast Guard Base in San Pedro, California while the processing of my papers was attended to.

While I was marking time there in anticipation of my release, they made me a steward's mate. I was given the job of serving lunch and dinner to the commissioned officers in their private dining room, and also had to make sure that there was always a fresh pot of coffee available sixteen hours a day. I got the hang of it fairly soon, and the weeks seem to be passing quickly enough. Then one day at lunch, and I don't recall how it happened, but somehow, I managed to spill a piping-hot bowl of "cream of something" soup right into the lap of the Commander of the Base. He leaped to his feet in shock and distress from my unexpected mishap, and for one split second I was reminded of the line Groucho had in **Night in Casablanca** when he spilled a bowl of tomato soup into Count Pfefferman's lap. Groucho tried to assuage him with, "Don't worry, no one will ever notice, unless they happen to be looking for a bowl of tomato soup."

My instincts told me that now was not the time to use that line. I knew I was already in enough trouble. Wiping the coagulating mess from his pants, he boomed, "Marx! You're the one who is pending medical discharge, aren't you?"

Shaking like a leaf, I was able to respond with a barely audible, "Yes, Sir."

"Well, I'm going to do everything in my power to see that your release be expedited as swiftly as is humanly possible."

The Commander of the Base was a man of his word, and a good judge of military character. I received my discharge shortly thereafter. I knew the Coast Guard was thrilled to get rid of me, but maybe not as thrilled as I was to get rid of the Coast Guard.

"Dad, I always wondered—why were you and Mom constantly sending me off to different places? It was tough, dealing with that every single time."

"I'm sorry you felt that way. We thought you could handle it. We didn't mean to hurt you. Sometimes parents hurt their kids, even when they love them very much. It happens."

"Yeah, this kid sure felt that way."

"Well, maybe we didn't think it out enough, I don't know. But we did it, and I've been dead for over forty years, so all I can say to you at this point is you need to get over it."

"I just always wondered."

CHAPTER TEN

After I returned home and got re-acclimated to civilian life, I felt that I was not quite ready enough mentally to decide what I was going to do with myself. So my folks decided to decide for me. Mom spoke to Dad, and they discussed at length what to do with the kid who didn't know what to do. Their plan for me unfolded the very next day, when Mom and Norm Ross drove me to Los Angeles International Airport, where my mom presented me with a one-way ticket to New York City. They both could see that from the suddenness of the decision, I was numb from the shock of what was happening to me. Then as if it was all a dream, through the layer of light lachrymal fog that had formed over my eyes, I saw them waving goodbye to me as I boarded the plane that would spirit me onto a new adventure. My folks were of the opinion that it was time to really kick me out of the nest to get some street smarts. What seemed odd was that they thought that at the age of seventeen, I would be able to handle their confidence in me. I was in too much of a funk to wonder.

I arrived in Manhattan with one suitcase, an overcoat and a typewriter. My cousin Bob had belonged to a fraternity, and he made arrangements for me to stay in their frat house across from Columbia University until I found permanent digs. It was there that I met Bernie Speyer, who immediately took me under his wing. Bernie was from Columbus, Ohio, so aside from him having to be in New York to do whatever he was there to do, his real love in life and main topic of conversation was always, of course, Ohio State football. Coach Woody Hayes and his "three yards and a cloud of dust" had deity status with Bernie and everyone else in the state of

Ohio. I had found a friend my second uneasy day away from home.

That second night in the city I spent having dinner with my folks' dear friends, Mr. and Mrs. Oscar Hammerstein, II, who quickly made themselves available when they were alerted to my arrival. I remember only two things about the evening; feeling uncomfortable as hell in their formal dining room, and then after dinner feeling even more uncomfortable as hell when I was asked to play something for them on their piano. I do recall them being most encouraging and very gracious in acknowledging my talent, in spite of my glaring self-consciousness. They were there for my folks, to see to it that Willy got off to a good start in the really big city. I had yet to shake off the shock I was in, but clear headed enough to understand why Mom and Dad had been friends with them for some twenty years. And then there was the irony of my first and only Broadway musical, **South Pacific**, being the work of Mr. Hammerstein. I went back home to the fraternity house, walking through Central Park to the subway on the West Side, wondering what in the world was going on.

Though I felt that I was not quite ready enough mentally to cope with the awesome specter of New York, in order to do something, I made the half-hearted choice to study music at NYU. Not long after I enrolled, Bernie and I found a place in Woodside, Queens that we thought would be convenient enough to Manhattan by subway. Within three weeks, I conveniently got mononucleosis and dropped out of NYU. During the next three weeks of my recovery, Bernie discovered that our place wasn't convenient enough for either of us. So we both decided to find are own apartments right in Manhattan that would suit our individual needs best. Bernie would still continue to act as my big brother.

It was October twelfth, Columbus Day. I was standing on Fifth Avenue watching the parade go by. It was my first day out since my illness, and the whole picture was New York beautiful. It briefly took my mind off the problem confronting me. I had to find something to do until the new semester began in January. So I applied for enrollment at Gimbel's department store as a salesperson for the holiday season. They assigned me to the musical toy section, and they asked me please, if necessary, to demonstrate the various instruments as well. I was a cheerful enough salesperson, and I put in my eight to ten hours, six days a week. But another first in my life was to occur, and it was not one that I knew how to deal with.

Over the years, I have had the spooky intrusion of several "stalkers." Curiously, my first one was a male. On my way to work one day, some guy at the bus stop started chatting with me and he seemed to be a rather friendly sort. He told me that he would be most happy to show me around to help me get familiar with the city. We exchanged phone numbers, and I thought maybe I had found another New York friend to pal around with. I'm sure you have now gotten the picture. Soon after, something was beginning to tell me that his picture was not mine. And he would call me every day, asking me when we could get together. But one day he said he would like to come over and see my place, and I began to be even more suspicious of his persistent requests. It wasn't the city he wanted me to get familiar with. So I told him that my job at Gimbel's kept me so busy that I just had no time to spend with him. I said it in a very naive and pleasant manner, and he assured me that he understood completely.

In retrospect, it was one of those times that you already instinctively knew what was happening. Every day from that day on, he would come to Gimbel's and just stare at me, like from behind some plant or peer around a pillar, sometimes even glaring at me from the top of the escalator. He would do this at different times of the day for a half an hour or so and then disappear. But like an old boomerang, he would come back. The next day he'd be there to haunt me once again. When I realized it was becoming a daily habit with him, I told Rachel, a very nice saleslady who insisted on calling me Rory, because she thought that I looked like a young Rory Calhoun, the actor (not the tailor or deli owner). She had noticed this guy as well and advanced my concern to security, and they apparently dealt with the problem, because suddenly he stopped showing up in the store, much to my relief. However, from time to time, I would see him standing outside the store entrance, waiting to get a fleeting glimpse of me. I always made sure that he never followed me home, and my eerie experience came to an end when he finally disappeared from my life as instantly as he had entered it. I learned at an early age that it takes some people longer than others to recognize and then accept a hint.

I continued on at Gimbel's as Rory Calhoun's younger brother in the musical toys section, until the day they came to tell me that I had been transferred to another part of the toy department. It seems that management was getting complaints from both salespeople and customers who said they were being driven crazy from hearing me play the same damn Bach cantata over and over all day long on all of the different toy pianos, kazoos and other dopey instruments. So they exiled me to another section that was called "Cowboy Suits, Guns, Holsters and Rifles." For a passionate musician and a true pacifist, this was a real comedown. But I pressed on dutifully in my new environment, meeting the everyday challenges that were to confront me with monotonous regularity.

One day, my instincts were tested again. I was subbing for Rachel in her section during her lunch break, when a heavyset lady walked up to the counter. She was very fair complexioned, her hair was pulled straight back, she wore a black muumuu, and on her head was a black scarf with a whole bunch of gold stars on it. I immediately and mysteriously sensed what she wanted and was already in the process of directing her to the location of her request even before she was to ask me where she could find our collection of Ouija boards.

This was to be the first Christmas holiday season I would spend away from home. My work at Gimbel's kept me from thinking about how homesick I really was. Intellectually, I understood that my folks sent me away to expose me to their beloved New York in their continuing pursuit of my education. But I couldn't help feeling a little abandoned, an emotion I realized that was fully ingrained in me.

Then something curious began occurring on a regular basis. Almost every day I would receive a Christmas card with a handwritten addition wishing me well in my pursuits during the coming year. What made it peculiar was, though I knew who the senders were, none of them were friends of mine, and somehow they knew my address in New York. I was getting cards from people like Eleanor Roosevelt, Adlai Stevenson, Dwight Eisenhower and Dr. Ralph Bunche. I didn't know why all these famous people were so interested in my well being, but at least the cards served to ease my thoughts of not being with my family during the holiday season.

It took till two days before Christmas when it finally seeped through my skull and hit me. These were cards originally sent to my Mom and Dad, and they in turn wrote on them words of love and encouragement, put them in new envelopes, and then forwarded the cards to me. I called Mom and Dad to confirm my suspicion, and all they said was that since I've been away, they hadn't any idea of how popular I had become with so many in such a short period of time. They also knew that I was being well looked after, checking from time to time with a fabulous lady who was my "Designated New York Mom."

Margaret Hamilton was one of the wonderfully special people to grace our planet, in spite of us all knowing her as the dreaded "Wicked Witch of the West" in *The Wizard of Oz*. She was as good in real life as she was evil in that movie. We had known her from her years living in Beverly Hills raising her son, Tony. His full legal name was Hamilton T. Meserve, the Hamilton from his mother's maiden name, and Meserve from his father's last name. The times being what they were, Maggie was left with the unusual responsibility as a single parent of guiding Tony's life while continuing her career in acting. He had gone through elementary school at Hawthorne with me, and just like my mom, Maggie managed to schedule in tenure as a Cub Scout den mother when nobody else wanted to be one.

Upon our graduation from Hawthorne, Tony went with Maggie to relocate in New York, so she could redirect her acting career toward her love of the stage. Tony went from high school onto graduating from Princeton University with honors. The only thing I ever disliked about him was that he was so damn much smarter than everybody else. Straight-laced, forthright and dripping with Ivy League, you couldn't help but figure then

Hamilton T. "Tony" Meserve.

that he would be odds-on favorite to become a model citizen, which of course, he became. However, whenever I think of Tony now, a sad and heartwarming event in his life comes to mind.

Pandro S. Berman, the producer of many classic films including *The Blackboard Jungle, Ivanhoe, Top Hat, Gunga Din,* and yes, even *Room Service* with the Marx Brothers, gave a party one afternoon for his son Michael's eighth birthday. Pandro had a projection room in his house to run pictures at his leisure. Oftentimes, a bunch of us kids would be invited over on a Friday night to sit in his big living room and see some musical starring someone like Kathryn Grayson or Mario Lanza or Howard Keel. Occasionally we'd see maybe a Martin and Lewis film or some innocent family comedy. So, for Michael's birthday, Pandro had carefully chosen *The Wizard of Oz* for all us kids in his class.

Well, everything was going smoothly, and all of us were having a great time watching Judy Garland as Dorothy, Ray Bolger as the Scarecrow, Jack Haley as the Tin Woodsman, Bert Lahr as the Cowardly Lion, Billie Burke as the Good Witch of the East, Frank Morgan as the Wizard, and all of those cute Munchkins. Then, all at once, all hell broke loose for Tony. He didn't seem to mind that, for the entire picture, his mother was the villain out to make Dorothy's life absolutely miserable. But when Dorothy poured the water all over her evil nemesis, and Tony saw the "Wicked Witch of the West" start shriveling up and deteriorating into nothingness, he ran out of the room crying and screaming, "They've killed my mother! They've killed my mother!"

All the consoling by Pandro, Mrs. Berman and the rest of us, trying to explain to Tony that it was only a make-believe movie, was a futile effort. Finally, they called Tony's mother on the phone to assure Tony that his mother was still alive and kicking and dry. But Tony still didn't think it was his mom he was talking to. So she jumped in her car and came dashing over to show Tony that she was just fine, and he hadn't really lost his mom at all. When she arrived, Tony immediately went from tears into the greatest smile of relief. Not long after, the two of them said their thank you's for a rather unique afternoon and thankfully drove off. Yes, Tony, there's no place like home.

Since my arrival in New York, I had been to visit Maggie and

Tony on occasion for dinner and conversation in the cutest little phone booth of an apartment you would ever want to see. Their home was filled with personally meaningful antiques, show posters and playbills all over the walls, a slew of old-world needlepoint pillows, and this itty-bitty kitchen that confirmed that "no matter where she'd have a guest, they always liked her kitchen best." Frankly, there wasn't much room for her guests. But that never discouraged Maggie or the constant flow of friends that were invited into her welcoming environs. It was here that I spent my first Christmas without my parents.

My tenure in "Cowboy Suits, Guns, Holsters and Rifles" continued through to the end of the year, in spite of an incident in which, while demonstrating the latest in water pistols, I inadvertently shot the floor manager. I was sure that my departure was in order just before Christmas Day, but surprisingly, they asked me to stay on as a permanent employee, but only if I promised to avoid squirting anyone again. I thanked them for the reprieve and told them I would consider their employment offer, but very soon after, there were other plans in the works for Willy in the really big city.

Though I felt that I was not quite ready enough mentally, just before the New Year came, I chose to do what had been in the back of my mind for a long time. I decided that about the only thing that was natural to me was music, and it was time that I made some sort of real commitment to develop whatever talent I had. So I showed up for work at Gimbel's the next day and thanked them for their offer of full-time employment, but I was moving on.

I went to my apartment, and for the next couple of days, I wrote a four-minute piece of music for the harp and then submitted it for my possible enrollment at the Juilliard School of Music as a composition major. I waited nervously for the day of my review by the faculty. I was even more nervous when I appeared before them in a large and sterile room. There was the prestigious group of composers including Professors Menin, Wagenaar, Persichetti and Giannini sitting on folding chairs arranged in a crescent shape. I stood about twenty feet from their imposing cluster as they asked me very studious-sounding questions about my musical background. My having studied the piano was of no major importance to being accepted as a composer, and the only original compositions I had written were the harp piece I just submitted and the music for my high school graduation. Soon it became evident that I didn't have the body of work or experience in composition that would meet with their entrance standards.

Just as they were at the point of concluding my interview, Professor Giannini jumped to his feet and ran to the piano. He took his left arm from his wrist up to his elbow, and placed it indiscriminately onto the keyboard. From across the room, he asked me to name the notes that were sounding from bottom to top. I complied. Three days later, I received notice of my acceptance as a composition major at Juilliard. Though I was not born with perfect pitch, my acute relative pitch, the magical gift that gives me the ability to tell any note being played, was my ticket into the hallowed halls of their storied music school. Professor Giannini's instincts were responsible for helping to catapult me into the next part of my life by allowing me to pursue becoming a "serious" composer at the age of eighteen. Thank you, Mr. Giannini.

I moved into my new apartment on 83rd and West End, which was so small, that I could step out of the shower right into the living room without touching the bathroom floor. However, I was pleased by its proximity to Juilliard, which was also on the West Side at 123rd, and easily accessible by the IRT subway.

The first weeks of my first semester were spent getting used to the new conservatory environment. Some of my classes were repeats of private music theory lessons I had taken in the past, solfege, or sight-reading classes, and a few general obligatory classes including history and chorale singing. The private composition teacher I was assigned to for my entire time at Juilliard was Bernard Wagenaar. He was up there in age, always impeccably dressed, topped off with his trademark bow tie, and looked ever the elegant and prideful internationally distinguished modern composer. His early years in Europe were manifest in his mannered way, and he always disseminated positive criticism, doing it in a very kind and gentle way.

In the theory class that he taught, he would sit at the piano and play certain musical passages to demonstrate a point he wanted to instill in all of us. As he played, his fingers trembled on the keys. Yet, the few bars you heard were so exquisite, that you just sat there mesmerized by the music coming out of those quivering hands.

Like Charlie Crenshaw, he was never without his pipe and always acknowledged the very minute that it went out. While continuing his lecture without dropping a beat, he would search everywhere through his coat and pants pockets for his box of matches. He usually went to five or six pockets before he found where he had placed them last. And because he never put the matches back in the same place after he finished lighting his pipe, when it went out again, only a moment later, he would then go through the same exercise for his matches, mercifully discovering their whereabouts in . . . . another surprising place! Often, I would go to his home for my private lessons, and his wife always offered me tea and something to eat while I listened to him dissect my orchestration of some piece of musical homework. Through the years I came to realize that I had in fact absorbed everything he taught me, but for a very long time, drew on very little of it. As a composer, I'd spent a lot of time just half-heartedly improving the craft aspect of my music, because I only really ever cared about the creative part. And besides, craft required discipline. And that never was for me, for sure.

Toward the end of my first year at Juilliard, I learned that my dad had cooked up a surprise for me during my summer vacation. It was a musical surprise, and one that we could share together, which was the best part of the whole event for him. But for me, it would mark my first venture into professional musicianship.

It was the summer after my first year studying composition at the Juilliard School of Music in New York that Dad hit me with a surprise business proposition. He had gotten a recording contract, and he wanted me to arrange all of the harp music and some of the band charts for the album. He said that I had better get started right away, because we were to record before I returned to Juilliard at the end of summer vacation. So, at the age of eighteen, I would become a bona fide professional musician. For the first time in my life as a composer/arranger, I would get paid actual money!

My dad was a man with a voracious musical appetite. He was open to anything new in any kind of music. He would listen with an open mind and then decide whether or not it was for him. I remember him coming into my room one day while I was listening to the rather innovative orchestra of Eddie Sauter and Bill Finnegan.

The arrangements were unique, different and very fresh. The avant-garde of music seemed to appeal to the avant-garde in him. Back during my high school years, I had already been busy discovering West Coast jazz. I had records of Dave Brubeck, Shorty Rogers, Shelly Manne, Pete Rugulo, Zoot Sims, Stan Getz, and the Chet Baker/Gerry Mulligan Quartet, to name just a few of the talented beboppers whose music I grew to love. One day I played for Dad a record featuring the unusual instrumentation of the Chico Hamilton Quintet. He was so taken by their special sound that, even though it was not his bag to be an improvisational jazz player, Dad decided that he absolutely had to make an album with them. The highly sophisticated-sounding group included Carson Smith, bass, Jim Hall, guitar; Buddy Collette and later Paul Horn, all the wind instruments; Chico on drums, and the amazing composer/arranger Fred Katz playing the cello, an instrument not usually considered being found swinging in jazz circles. Of all the musicians I have ever come to know, Fred was as total a composite of the

Clockwise from bottom: Fred Katz, Chico Hamilton, Carson Smith, John Pisano and Paul Horn.

classical academician with the avant-garde mind. I had already gotten to know these guys in the band, having heard them in a few jazz clubs, so when Dad and I approached them about doing an album, they jumped all over the thought of adding a harp to their sound. And with Fred Katz's expertise and experience leading the way, *Harpo* was created. It was the first of two albums Dad and I would do for Mercury Records.

Twenty-five years later, I received an unexpected telephone call from Carson Smith, who was living and working in Las Vegas. As he had been the bass player on the album, he called just to touch "bass" as it were. But his real reason was to tell me that of all the record dates he'd ever been on, *Harpo* was the favorite and most memorable experience of his entire musical life. I still get wonderfully kind remembrances like that from people who had worked with Dad over the years.

A real "dream come true" for Dad and me.

Recently, I reunited with Fred Katz, whom I hadn't seen or talked to in over forty years. I had come to find that he has also been a Professor of Anthropology for the last twenty-five years. It was like we just saw each other last week. No sooner had we finished hugging each other, he was quick to tell me about the time we were recording **Harpo**, and Dad was practicing a difficult passage over and over. Fred went up to him and said, "Isn't music sometimes a real bitch?"

Dad replied, "It sure as hell is better than digging ditches."

As a composer, Dad recorded his most important work on *Harpo*.

Other artists as well as even I have recorded it, including Mario Lanza, and pictured above, Mahalia Jackson.

Fred and Dad became very close acquaintances during this time, and on several occasions he was invited down to Dad's desert home. Fred told me how impressed he was with another facet of Dad's personality—his paintings, some of which were surprisingly traditional and some just as surprisingly avant-garde.

As thrilled as Dad was to be performing on the albums with these talented musicians, he must have realized he might have been in just a little bit over his head. Not that Dad wasn't equally talented himself, but his skills as a harpist were rather specialized, and Fred Katz and his band mates were as varied, versatile and improvisational as any musicians performing at the time. Dad wasn't used to playing with an orchestra and the strict adherence to rhythmic discipline, which that entailed. And we were throwing him into the deep end of some very modern rhythms and harmonies with nothing but a very heavy and complicated harp.

Fred Katz conducting.

On the first day, I frankly felt that his performance was lacking. He wasn't nailing my arrangements the way I'd anticipated he would. After the session we drove to Uncle Groucho's for dinner, and on the way I told him matter-of-factly that I was a little disappointed in his performance and that he needed to get it together better for our second session. I don't recall that evening's dinner, or our drive home. I do know that on our second day, Dad's harpistic skill had improved sufficiently to where we went back and fixed some mistakes from the first session. Problem solved.

It was only much later that Mom told me how much I'd hurt my father when I told him he wasn't performing well enough. He'd kept it to himself all through dinner at Groucho's, and only shared it with my mother that evening as they were going to bed. It wasn't that I was wrong, or that I shouldn't have told him. Or even that I had done it tactlessly, maybe I had. It was simply that he was hurt. I realize now that Dad must have been intimidated not only by the sophisticated jazz musicians on his album, but also, for the first time, by me. In that bittersweet dance of fathers and sons, I was moving beyond his knowledge of music, though never his fame. Of course, I was too young and immature to see any of this at the time. And my father was too mature and compassionate to let me know.

Most of the rest of whatever went on during the making of the album is a blur to me now, but another particular problem that occurred during one of our three recording sessions stands out in my mind. Of course, Dad solved it with a "typically Harpo" solution. The dilemma began because he wanted to include a song by his dear friend, Harry Ruby, the ultimate baseball fan. He chose "Thinking of You," but when it was time to record it, he hadn't had sufficient time to learn my arrangement to be really comfortable enough to record. Dad was okay with most of it, but he just couldn't get the rhythm of the melody right. After several exasperating tries, he thought to himself that there had to be a way to solve this rhythmic dilemma. He then motioned me over to the harp and asked me to lie down on my back so that he could see me through his harp strings as he played. The tape rolled and he followed me as I conducted the rhythm of the melody with my hands and arms flailing about, as if I was a capsized turtle, upside down on its shell, desperately struggling to turn over. Harpo's ingenuity had struck again, and we got the take beautifully.

I also recall from the gauzy past, another occasion during our rehearsals in which Uncle Groucho played a role. Groucho was by this time the most professionally ubiquitous of the brothers, appearing weekly on NBC's long-running radio and TV quiz show, **You Bet Your Life**. Despite his professional responsibilities, he and Dad kept in touch, either electronically or in person. The phone rang and it was the daily call from Uncle Groucho. Dad started to speak and suddenly he said, "Grouch, can you hang on for a moment? Susan wants to ask me about something." He put the phone down and motioned me to come with him. We got in the car and drove over to Groucho's house, which was only about five minutes away from ours. We bolted out of the car and went up to the window adjacent to the front door. Through the window we could see Groucho pacing back and forth like an impatient caged lion while still holding on to the telephone. Finally, we rang the doorbell, and when Groucho opened the front door, Dad matter-of-factly said to him, "As you were saying?" Living up to his name, Groucho was not amused.

My dad's uncanny ability to accept the new and different manifested itself through his innate musical instinct. For example, in 1964, when he was then seventy-five years old, we were having dinner at the Cock and Bull restaurant on the Sunset Strip, when we got into a pretty good argument. Dad had just seen the Beatles on some television show, and he loved them. I was under contract to the all-jazz and blues label, VeeJay Records, and so I thought very little of the Beatles' idea of music. He predicted that they would become the biggest musical act ever. I thought his musical taste had gone south and told him he was nuts.

Several years later at Dino's Lodge, I found myself playing some of their songs like "Yesterday," "Hey Jude," "Come Together," "Something," "Here, There and Everywhere," to name only a few. I was doing them with a jazz approach, which helped me to realize that it wasn't their music that I didn't like, but it was the instrumentation and rock 'n' roll concept of the Beatles that had turned me off. Dad had the marvelous ability to keep up with the times. He was able to assimilate into the present like no one I have ever known. Music and the Arts were among the many facets of the always-changing world in which he lived.

Another aspect that nurtured his musical appetite was his learning how to play other musical instruments. The first film in which he was seen tooting away on the clarinet was **The Cocoanuts**, the very first Marx Brothers film. For some mysterious reason, he seemed to really enjoy the instrument more than any other, other than the harp, of course. He was an average player, but that never bothered him.

One night, Dad had a jam session at our house. One of the guests was Benny Goodman, as good a clarinetist as there ever was. Dad asked Benny to try a clarinet that he had just purchased, so he could tell him what he thought of it. Benny played a tune on the instrument, and liked the sound it produced so much that he offered to trade his brand-new LeBlanc for Dad's, straight up. The swap was agreed to, and everyone was happy. Benny was thrilled with his new find, and Dad was overjoyed that he had just received a brand-new seven-hundred-dollar clarinet for an instrument that he bought at a pawn shop for five dollars. Incidentally, Dad's clarinet was soon immortalized, as Goodman wound up using it on a number of his recordings.

Dad also fooled around a lot with the harmonica. He took it with him wherever he traveled, and he also used it in his act. He learned to play the tricky chromatic harmonica, but the one he used in the act to play "Turkey in the Straw" was only an inch long. It always brought the house down. As a matter of fact, thinking about it now, Dad had structured his act in a very peculiar and unorthodox way. He would start his musical spot with his harp solo. Then he would do "Turkey in the Straw" on the harmonica and would close on the clarinet playing a rousing version of "Tiger Rag" with the band, which would whip the audience into an absolute frenzy. You would have thought the sequence would be just the opposite, knowing the way he played the clarinet compared to his prowess on the harp. But it worked, because they always waited for his mesmerizing harp solo, but then he would surprise them with his completely unexpected abilities on the harmonica and clarinet. His act had a perfect build.

Incidentally, he passed on this very important observation about performance that has stayed with me throughout the years. He noted how many times have you seen an entertainer allow their ego to transcend the climax of a satisfying show by continuing to stay on too long? Sadly, this is a huge mistake that happens all too often. He told me, "If you've got twenty-five really good minutes to do, just do twenty and get off. Always leave your audience wanting a little bit more. That way, you'll know they will be looking forward to your next show."

I plodded through my first two years at Juilliard in New York, and each summer I flew home to make an album with Dad. While I was in school I would send him arrangements of songs to learn, so that we would be ready to record when I returned. Yes, Dad couldn't read music, so I devised a system of musical notation that would allow him to learn all these new tunes. When trying to explain my system to someone, I feel sometimes that talking about music is like listening to someone paint. But as simply as I am able to put it, I will. I would substitute all the notes of the melody and the chords with their corresponding letters of the alphabet. The melody would be written horizontally with the chord structures written vertically underneath the melody, changing when the melody so dictated. Is that clear? I didn't think so. Well, it worked for Dad, and thank God for that.

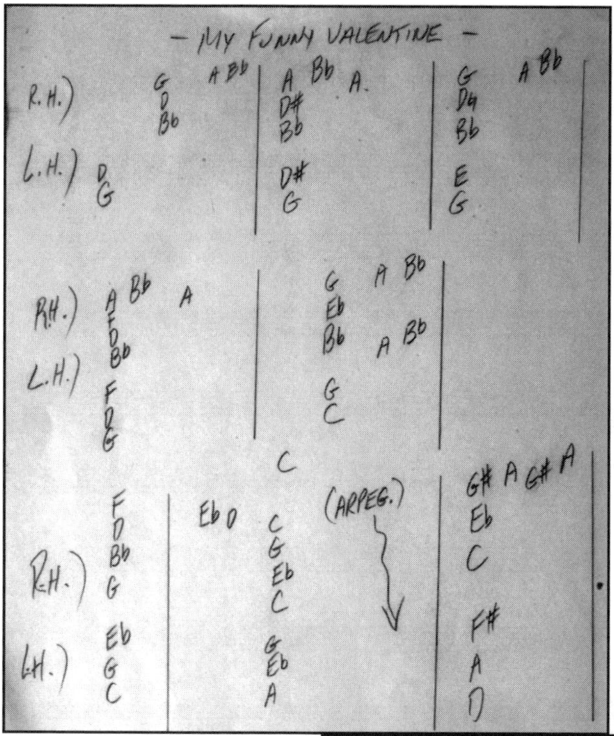

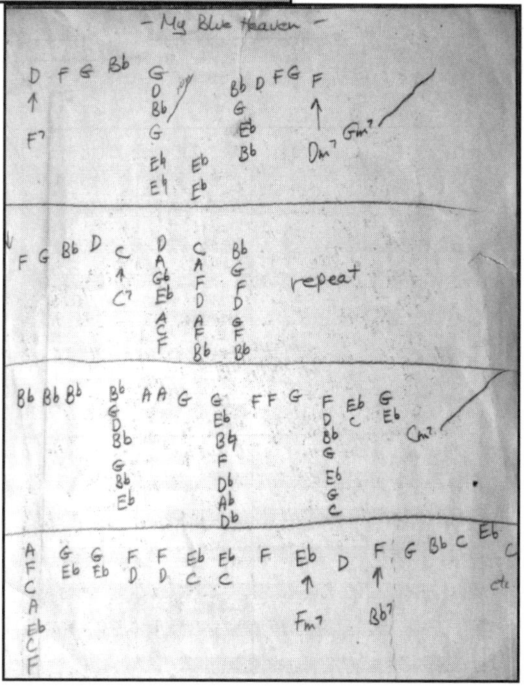

My music charts for Dad.

I told you so.

The cover of the second album that we did, ***Harpo at Work***, was a photo of Dad fast asleep on the sounding board of the harp. While he was in dreamland, I was given the responsibility of doing all the arrangements for the orchestra. So I wound up doing far more work and getting a lot less sleep than he did. But it was more than worth the fatigue and sleep deprivation.

We finally got to the recording session, and what a thrill it was for me to stand in front of the finest of all professional studio musicians, and hear them play back all my arrangements. When that red recording light went on, the band would pay no attention to me at all, as they could see right away that I had no real conducting experience. But I flapped my arms with reckless abandon anyway, thinking that I really was making some kind of important contribution that would motivate their musical interpretation. Yet, nobody would ever make a mistake! They were being paid to avoid the playing of wrong notes, and they always got paid, and always quite well. I do shudder to think what might have occurred had they chose to follow me instead.

Then the summer came to an end and I was back to Juilliard.

"Isn't it amazing, Dad, that we're so connected by music? I mean, was it . . . Well, what do you think?"

"It was meant to be."

"Simple as that, eh?"

"Nothing else. And why is it necessary for it to be anything else?"

"It just seems like such a lucky crap shoot for it to have happened."

"It is."

My years at Juilliard were pretty much lumped into one overall feeling. It came from the blending of the silence of my room, while I studied the sterile academics of composition, mixed with the cacophony of sound throughout the school's halls emanating from the instrumentalists diligently practicing their fundamentals in the rehearsal rooms. I was also now twenty years old and coping with the really big city, negotiating my survival with a sort of naive numbness and blind faith. I had moved into a brownstone with a very large studio apartment on West 75th Street that could accommodate an upright piano that I used when composing. The rent was a little high, so I took on a roommate to cut my obligation in half. This was to be the first in my life of several "cries for help" I have been a witness to.

Eddie was twenty years older than I was, a recovering alcoholic, and working daily at a men's store that sold tailor-made custom suits, simply marking time until his ship would come in as a successful Broadway singer. His favorite song was the Broadway show tune, "There But for You Go I," and he had a very nice voice and a good understanding of any lyric's story. Now if your ship hasn't yet come in over the years and becomes a major source of frustration for you, it could cause radical behavior, maybe even similar to Eddie's. One day he asked me when I'd be coming home later, and I said about three o'clock. Based on that knowledge of my schedule, he put into effect his master "cry for help" plan. He would slit his wrists about five minutes before my arrival at three, and I would then find him in plenty of time to get him to the hospital before he lost too much blood. It was to be his way of getting some desperately needed attention, much too hard a way, if you ask me.

His plan would have worked better if I hadn't been about fifteen minutes late. I found him in our bathroom lying in a pool of blood that was crawling all over the cold tiled floor. I raced down stairs to alert Lennie, who I guess you could say was our beacon of aid and the responsible decision-maker for all of us in our brownstone. He quickly called the paramedics, and an ashened Eddie was spirited post haste to their choice of Bellevue Hospital. He pulled through somehow, but because of his enormous loss of blood, he remained there for five days under observation. During that time, Eddie rifled off a scathing letter to the Gillette Company, demanding his money back, complaining that their razor blades were a bitter disappointment and grossly inadequate when he employed them for his recent attempted suicide. He threatened that if they don't give him his money back, he would become a Schick man for life. Now, he continued, if from a public relations standpoint, maybe they could at least respond by sending him an entire lifetime supply of their product, in his case, one blade. He never heard from them. Eddie and I didn't stay roommates, and I sincerely hope he got the help he cried out for, but I was not emotionally mature enough to take on his demons.

Incidentally, years later, I was faced with a similar "cry for help" from a gal I met and became good friends with from the time she did a TV commercial with Dad. She was a sweet, beautiful, big busted, sexy blonde named Joi Lansing, who worked a lot in the industry as an actress, but she always thought *only* because of her looks. She did have reasonable objectivity. One day I followed a trail of blood from her living room into the bathroom. Fortunately, I got to her just in time, just like Eddie. Unfortunately, whether it was true, only her imagination, or both, never was she to overcome the insecurity that plagued her.

My love for West Coast jazz had been challenged by many students at Juilliard, their railing about how it was too intellectual and without the passion and soul of East Coast jazz. Many of my colleagues were jazz freaks, especially one guy in particular. He was a black tenor player who wore dark glasses morning, noon and night. He told me he even slept with them on. One day, I finally had to ask him why he wore shades all the time. His answer was,

Joi Lansing and Dad.

"I just don't dig gettin' dug diggin'." This guy's knowledge of East Coast jazz and my curiosity about it led me to a number of nightclubs that featured such jazz giants as Miles Davis, John Coltrane, Max Roach, Clifford Brown et al. It was a definite difference. The music was less arranged and played with a far more aggressive and energetic style of improvisational interpretation. As a composer hearing from an orchestrally broader aural pallet, I never cared much for the traditional texture of trumpet, tenor sax, piano, bass and drums. And I also noticed that with so much of East Coast music, the tunes were performed from beginning to end at the same volume. I tired of its monotone sameness, and for me, it lacked the subtleties in variations of volume and instrumentation that the West Coast scene offered.

Throughout the years of my listening to jazz or rock 'n' roll, I have always been puzzled by the musician's belief that increasing the volume is what you have to do to display musical intensity and excitement in a performance. Oh, yes, for sure it works, and it's the technique most often used, but simply because it is easy doesn't mean it's the best or only way to accomplish that goal. The harder, more difficult choice employed is to keep your inner intensity as you bring the volume of your music down to a very soft "triple pianissimo." If your intent is to be intense, forceful or aggressive when communicating with another person verbally, even at a whisper, you can still make them feel your extraordinary inner energy, believe me. The same thing holds true in music, and it is one of the things I am drawn to. For example, intensity can come from a drummer artfully playing brushes. Or, how about the breeziness of Brazilian Bossa Nova. It doesn't have to hammer you senseless with volume for you to feel its urgency. It does that instead with the grace and subtlety of its intensely rhythmic undercurrent. The same can be said for "serious" concert works that can produce astounding energy at a barely audible volume. Just for example, I can refer to some of the works composed not by our second American president, John Adams, but our great contemporary American composer, John Adams.

But my soapbox and I have jumped track and wish to pursue my indoctrination in East Coast jazz. I have given my reasons why I was not as thrilled with it as much as West Coast jazz, and maybe that's just because West Coast jazz got to me first. However, and for the record, I became deeply immersed in it because of the remarkable musicians who played it when I was hearing it back in the late 1950s. All of them were virtuosos, and my personal respect for their musicianship never waned. Talking about the true sophistication of Bebop jazz seems like an oxymoron, but it's not. Only God-given talent can produce the intricate improvisation that its artistry requires and demands. My perception of East Coast jazz did improve dramatically not very long after I finished Juilliard when I heard the unique collaboration between the plaintive interplay of Miles Davis' trumpet combined with the refreshing orchestral textures of the arranger, Gil Evans. I had finally found what had been missing for me, a satisfying connection to my sense of composition. The trilogy of *Miles Ahead, Porgy and Bess* and *Sketches of Spain* is acknowledged as a classic musical marriage of extraordinary proportions, and they remain high on my personal list of all-time favorite albums.

My exposure to bi-coastal jazz helped to broaden my understanding of what would become an important part of my life's profession. It was some years later, when I signed a recording contract with VeeJay Records, based in Chicago, that I was introduced to another geographical home for jazz. For the record, Vee-Jay Records was the first large independent record company to be solely (souly) owned by blacks, and it was the most successful black record company before Detroit's Motown. The label specialized in Blues, Rhythm and Blues, Soul, Gospel, Pop and Jazz. Curiously, I became the first white jazz artist signed by Vee-Jay. And in the Pop field, the first signed was The Beatles. Though I never heard anyone refer to it as such, I guess you could call it the first musical home of Midwest Jazz.

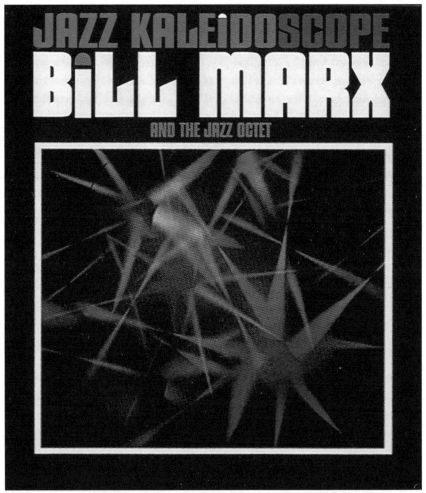

Yet my first album for Vee-Jay would feature all West Coast musicians: Jack Sheldon & Ray Linn, Trumpets; Dick Nash, Trombone; Paul Horn & Roger Benioff, Wood Winds; Larry Bunker, Vibes & Percussion; Jimmy Bond, Bass; Lawrence Marable, Drums.

Just before I finished up at Juilliard, Mr. Wagenaar had me come over to his house for a lesson. He spent half the time discussing my orchestration of something, and the other half encouraging me to continue studying composition upon my return to the West Coast. Because he knew of my love for the harp, he recommended that I look up a contemporary of his, the wonderful composer and excellent teacher, Mario Castelnueve-Tedesco. Tedesco was a Spanish Jew who fled to the United States during World War II, ultimately landing in Hollywood. In order to make financial ends meet in those days, often a well-known "serious" composer would be assigned by some studio to do the score for one of their upcoming movies. Tedesco accepted the job of scoring the music to a Marx Brothers movie, **The Big Store**. He immediately went home and wrote for three weeks, producing a beautiful harp concerto and proudly presented it to Dad to play in the film. The only trouble was that nobody had bothered telling him that Dad couldn't read a note of music, and there wasn't enough time for him to learn the entire concerto and commit it to memory. When Tedesco found this out from Dad, he decided that film scoring wasn't really for him, and he could do just fine directing full-focus on his teaching abilities.

Other remarkable "serious" composers have had their trouble adapting to the tricky job of film scoring.

Igor Stravinsky was once asked to score a film, and just before he signed the contract, they wanted to know how long it would take for him to complete the score. "I should have it ready for you in about two years."

Citing another example, Dad told me a story that is found in his autobiography, **Harpo Speaks!**, about Arnold Schoenberg, the composer of the "twelve-tone technique" of composition. I chose to repeat this anecdote here because of two strange coincidences I share with him that I shall explain later. Schoenberg was another internationally renowned composer leaving Europe, coming to the States to avoid the persecution in Nazi Germany during World War II. Dad found out that Schoenberg had come to Hollywood and was looking for work. After contacting him, Dad went to Irving Thalberg, production supervisor at MGM, the studio for whom the Brothers then toiled. He told Thalberg about this famous composer from Europe, and so on his recommendation, Thalberg arranged a meeting with Schoenberg.

Thalberg explained the audition process that composers had to go through at the studio. For his audition piece, Schoenberg was to write music for a scene in a movie that was near completion called **The Good Earth**, starring Paul Muni and Luise Rainer. Thalberg explained that setting was a rice field somewhere in China at time of harvest. As they are working the fields, all of a sudden, Luise Rainer is overcome with intense labor pains and is about ready to give birth. Then, out of nowhere, comes a massive swarm of locusts to ravage the harvest, and people are frantically running in all directions to get away from the onslaught. Paul Muni sees Luise Rainer writhing in pain and runs to her side to help in the delivery. This was the audition scene that Thalberg wanted him to score.

Schoenberg stood up and said, "Meester Taulbeig, vit all dat goink on, you dun't neet moosic!" And Schoenberg walked right out of the office and MGM forever. Post Script: When the movie was released, that scene appeared with no music. Double Post Script: Rather obliquely, I have two things in common with Arnold Shoenberg. One, my paternal grandmother's name is Minnie Shoenberg. Two, Schoenberg and I chose the same soloist, the famed violinist, Israel Baker to perform the World Premieres of both of our violin concertos.

My years at Juilliard and New York wound down, and when I returned to Hollywood, I took Mr. Wagenaar's advice and studied with Mr. Tedesco for the next year or two. He was getting up in years, extremely soft-spoken, and he was as gentle a soul as the music he wrote. Whenever he wanted to impart a criticism, he would take my hand and always start it off with an almost inaudible, "Beelee . . ." During the time I studied with him he was really slowing down, and not long after I stopped seeing him, I remember reading in the newspaper that he had passed away. I often listen to his magnificent guitar concerto, which reminds me of what a gentleman he was.

Dad had ordained me as a professional musician with the two albums we did together, and I continued to arrange music for him for his "guest star" appearances on television. So it was now time to dive into the music industry to see if I could make a living.

But first, a pointless detour.

At the age of twenty-one, I was definitely not quite ready enough mentally to know which direction to take in my blind pursuit of becoming a truly professional musician. So naturally the logical progression was to enroll in acting class at 20th Century-Fox studios. Yes, I couldn't stand being without yet another lesson that would impart more dribs and drabs to my overall limited knowledge. It was my mother who suggested this folly, convincing me that anyone with a cute face like mine (spoken like a true mother), should try acting, and besides, it would help to instill some much needed self-confidence in me. This class was taught by Ben Bard, an older man who had some Shakespearian background that he foisted on all of us. The first and only thing I remember remembering was the beginning of some speech he made us memorize that was to improve our elocution. "In promulgating your esoteric cogitations . . . .," began this forgettable malaise of baffling words, hardly the kind of dialogue that would be given in any movie of that time to Tab Hunter, Rock Hudson, Sandra Dee or Frankie Avalon.

The highlight of my most inadequate actors' tour of duty at 20th was an advertising campaign that the publicity department had concocted for their new horror film release, *The Fly*. All of the aspiring actors in our class, with the aid of the wardrobe and makeup departments, were to be dressed up like various famous ghoulish personalities. In full costume, The Mummy, Frankenstein's Monster, The Werewolf, Mr. Hyde, The Hunchback and others, including myself as Dracula, all boarded a plane and flew to San Francisco to participate in the world premiere that evening at the Fox Theater.

We arrived in San Francisco early afternoon in time for a photo-op of us riding on a cable car, waving at and blowing kisses to all the pedestrians. From there, we went on a TV show, where, because most monsters have real trouble forming words, being Dracula, I was chosen to be their spokesperson. Translating from perfect Transylvanianese into perfect English, I answered with the cheapest shot I could, "We are here today because, this evening, *The Fly* is opening in theaters and drive-ins all over the city."

Well, I thought it was just brilliant repartee, but then again I was only twenty-two.

When we arrived at the theater about seven in the evening, all of

A rare, heart warming candid of drunken monsters. The PR guy is in the middle. (Yes, without a disguise, just him.)

us monsters already had dinner and "a few" drinks—maybe a few too many—while disturbing the restaurant clientele. During the break before the screening of **The Fly**, we were supposed to run up and down the aisles trying to scare the crap out of the terrified theatergoers. That part went pretty much according to form. But Ted Markland, who later went on to be a successful character actor, decided to give the patrons a real charge when he, as Frankenstein's Monster, climbed onto the huge stage and proceeded to grope at the audience with outstretched arms while growling unintelligibly. The audience loved it. However! I was pulled aside by one of the publicity guys, who told me to get Ted the hell off the stage as fast as I could, because we were running overtime and the movie was to start in five minutes. So, as only Dracula could do, I dutifully materialized from the wings, and, like one of those absurd movies with Boris Karloff and Bela Lugosi as dueling dreadfuls, I went to stage center and put a stranglehold on Ted as I began to bite him on the neck.

As I made him slowly succumb to my faux force, I whispered to him to get his ass off the stage with me as soon as possible, or we may never be invited back again. While the two of us were trying to conceal our hysterical laughter, he fell to the stage floor in a huge clump, and the audience burst into cheers and howls of approval. I then dragged him off into the wings hearing the accolades afforded me for subduing Terrifying Ted as Frightening Frankenstein's Menacing Monster. Without biting anyone at all, I had won the hearts of the audience, and also more importantly, the publicity guy.

There was one other actor that was supposed to go with us and portray The Invisible Man, but none of us ever knew whether or not he showed up.

I lasted about a year in acting class at 20th, leaving Ben to his fondness for the Bard, when one day, and purely by accident, I briefly came to my senses in a moment of reflection. I realized that I could never have become a baseball player, retail was certainly not for me, and I was a lousy actor. Those three outs ended the inning as far as pursuits of my peripheral aspirations. But the ball game wasn't over. It had definitely become time to stop sidestepping a career in music and start doing about the only thing that I had any talent for. All I needed was some self-confidence, the lack of which was probably the reason for my experimentation into other areas. I had been marking time to the inevitable. And the inevitable would lead to even further opportunities for self-discovery.

CHAPTER TWELVE

I don't know which I was more in fear of, failure or success. After all, it was just fine to be validated by my dad as a professional musician, but could I measure up to the same criteria all other professional musicians were required to? I always had a conflicted attitude about my musical talent. At the North Pole, I knew deep down that I had been blessed with an extraordinary birth gift, and I had complete confidence in its uniqueness and creative depth. (Though where it came from I knew not.) At the South Pole, there was this feeling that I might not ever be quite ready enough mentally to handle the pressures and stresses of any of the industry's expectations of my work, like you're only as good as your last time at bat. If you don't live up to that standard, you may not get your next time at bat. While you are waiting to see if you get that next job, you will experience a liberal amount of anxiety. Then finally there will come the day of reckoning, when you either *get* that next job, or you come to realize, sometimes during heavy medication, that there will no longer ever be *that* next job.

My first steady and salaried job in the record industry was at Liberty Records, a nice little easygoing label at the time. Easygoing until it suddenly shot into prominence because of Julie London's ultra-sultry recording of Arthur Hamilton's "Cry Me a River." Or perhaps it achieved public awareness because of a then provocative album cover, featuring a bust shot of Julie in a dress that was revealing her bust almost as much as if she wasn't wearing the dress. Whichever the reason, and it certainly became a topic for spirited speculation, that album really put Liberty on the map.

During my six-month stay there, among things like writing songs for certain artists they had under contract, I was assigned to record surreptitiously as one of their more prominent artists, Martin Denny. Because it was often difficult for Denny and his quintet to get to the mainland from his home in Hawaii to record, I would ghost for him on piano. Denny's popularity was centered on his music of the islands being coupled with the incessant sounds of exotic birds chirping away in the background throughout the entire record. If I hadn't known that all the bird sounds were prerecorded, I would have envisioned Denny's recording studio with wall-to-wall newspaper on the floor. Among some of the things I did for him was a commercially successful single called "The Enchanted Sea." I made the record, and Martin Denny made the royalties. Hey, what did I know? I was still only twenty-two. Oh, and that's still the record biz.

It was also at Liberty that I met my first professional collaborator, Joe Lubin, and the two of us wound up moving over to Arvin Records, owned by Marty Melcher, who was married to Doris Day. Lubin was a genuinely bizarre, fun-to-work-with-British-loony, a pal of Marty's and responsible for my getting to arrange and orchestrate the record version of the title tune he wrote for the movie of the best-selling book, ***Please Don't Eat the Daisies***. It was an important moment in my budding career, because it was for the very great big Columbia Records, and they had the exclusive recording contract at that time with Doris.

During the time I was writing away and preparing for the recording session, I had heard through the grapevine that Doris could be difficult to work with. By the day of the session, I was emotionally on edge. There would be the Columbia Artists and Repertoire people in the booth producing the date that I would have to contend with. There would be the rehearsal of the twenty-six-piece orchestra, the rehearsal of the twelve hyper kid singers, then the rehearsal of the orchestra together with the hyper kid singers, and after that the rehearsal of the orchestra with the hyper kid singers *and* Doris.

Somehow, as frazzled and nervous as I was, I still had the courage to show up that day ready to rehearse and record, all the while concerned about the stories I had heard about the possibly persnickety Miss Day. I walked in and, sure enough, the cast of characters was assembled, ready to get started. From my vantage point at the conductor's podium, even with the chaos of so many people in one place doing so many different things at the same time, it looked to me like everything was going smoothly enough, and most importantly, we were on schedule time-wise. And then it happened.

Coming toward me from across the room with a face projecting a look of firm resolve and deep apparent concern was Miss Day. With every step she took, under my breath I uttered an "uh-oh." When she finally reached me at the conductor's podium, I took a deep breath and tried to steady myself. Then, in a very business-like voice, staring straight ahead with her piercingly beautiful eyes, she asked, "Excuse me, Bill, but is this note right here in bar seventy-four an E natural or an E flat?" I looked at my score and told her it was an E flat, and she said thank you, smiled and walked off. That was the extent of my communication with her for the entire three-hour

My day with Doris Day.

session. I never had any problem with Doris Day, and I guess she had no problem with me.

Oh, incidentally the record became a big hit. I made the arrangements and conducted, and Joe Lubin made the royalties. I told you that was always the record biz.

My early developmental years playing in clubs all over Los Angeles were also to be one of the most curious of times for my dad. In the mid- to late 1950s he had suffered a series of mild to moderate heart attacks, which sent him into a seemingly endless series of retirements, semi-retirements and enthusiastic "coming out of retirements." He no longer made movies with his brothers—

Continuing to do charity events, Dad is pictured here with, clockwise: Georgie Jessel, Errol Flynn, Betty Hutton and Van Johnson.

Love Happy took all the fun out of that for them, and he kept busy professionally with rare but regular appearances on television. Once or twice a year, he and Chico would play a club date in Reno or Las Vegas, or Dad would play the date alone, or he'd make a charity appearance for the United Jewish Appeal, some symphony orchestra or the Policeman's Retirement Association. He had earned the right, after all those years in vaudeville and on Broadway, to not have to work unless he felt like it.

Some of Dad's television appearances are undiscovered classics, others still turn up on sitcom reruns at all hours all over the world, and still others are simply memorable to me because I was there and something funny or wonderful happened behind the scenes. One of the latter memories concerns the very distinguished *Playhouse 90* series, in which Dad appeared in 1957. This particular presentation featured a story about a racehorse named "Snowshoes," and it starred Barry Sullivan, John Carradine, Hillary Brooke, Stu Erwin and a live stallion perfectly cast as the lead.

These being the earlier days of television and editing so limited, the director would shoot an entire scene in as few takes as possible, preferably one. Then the edit would simply be butting it up to the previous scene. There was one particular take that was a very long one, and this caused the horse some discomfort. When the horse was overcome by the need to relieve himself, the horse's owner put a very large pail under the nag, which had been cleverly trained to let fly right into the waiting container. So, all production had to stop, until this happening stopped happening.

Then another amazing happening happened. A minute-and-a-half is not usually considered a very long time, unless you are, with great fascination, watching and listening to a horse peeing into a bucket. Put your trust in me! I was there. When the horse finally completed this seemingly endless trick, through power of suggestion, seventy-five-percent of the cast and crew had left for a potty break. Naturally, this delighted Dad as he watched them and me all head for the head.

The show emanated from a sound studio at Gilmore Field, (er, just kidding,) CBS Television City, which has that one big "eye" for its logo. The location is on Fairfax Avenue, which is in the heart of the Jewish section and deli heaven. It's really easy to find. Just look for a building not having a "tongue" hanging in its window. I remember many of Dad's other television appearances emanating from Los Angeles and New York; **The Colgate Comedy Hour** with Donald O'Connor; **The Martha Raye Show** (with the great prizefighter, Rocky Graziano); **The Spike Jones Show; The Red Mill**, with Evelyn Rudie, Mike Nichols and Elaine May, and Shirley Jones; **Mr. Smith Goes to Washington**, with Fess Parker; **The Ed Sullivan Show**, with you know who; **The Kraft Music Hall**, with Milton Berle, and **The Wonderful World of Toys**, with Carol Burnett and Merv Griffin.

The show with Carol and Merv was a poignant one for Dad because it was shot back in his old stomping ground—New York

Carol Burnett with Dad.

City, in Central Park, where he had spent so many childhood hours stomping.

It was just days before he left for the taping, in October 1961, that Uncle Chico died of a heart attack. It was truly the end on an era. Nevertheless, Dad managed to keep his sense of humor. During the taping, a woman from the Philadelphia Symphony Orchestra kept calling Dad at the hotel where he and Mom were staying in order to arrange for him to appear at the Symphony's 105th anniversary show. This woman was remarkably persistent, calling ceaselessly over the week or so that Dad was in town. Each time she called he explained to her that the tight television shooting schedule prevented him from making time to meet her. But her persistence finally wore him down and he agreed to have dinner with her one night. She arrived at Mom and Dad's room and after introducing one another, the three of them headed for the door and their dinner reservation at a local restaurant. But before they could leave, the phone rang. Dad made no effort to answer it, and the woman from the symphony finally blurted out,

"Aren't you going to pick that up?"

"Why?" said Dad, calmly. "It's undoubtedly you again."

Needless to say, in January of 1962, Dad, Mom and I went to Philadelphia, PA, for the 105th Anniversary of the founding of the Philadelphia Symphony Orchestra. It was quite an honor for Dad to be asked to concertize and then conduct the Philadelphia Symphony Orchestra in an epic performance of Handel's "Toy Symphony in C." Dad had carved out a comedic character based quite loosely on the fabled conductor of the New York Philharmonic Orchestra, Arturo Toscanini; that maestro being none other than the world renown conducting genius, once again, Arturo Harponini. Incidentally, Toscanini's limited knowledge of the English language and his fierce temper were the cause of many true but unfortunate stories that occurred during his orchestra rehearsals. They too, were comical, but not intended to be. One such story stemmed from his love for the cello. Because it was the instrument he played and therefore most familiar with, he was always overly critical and demanding of that section of the orchestra. Once in the middle of some passage of a Beethoven Symphony, he stopped everyone abruptly, furious over what he was hearing. Scowling and fuming uncontrollably, he turned his frustration onto the lady who was the first cellist and blurted out, "Lady, you've got God's greatest gift between your legs, and all you do is scratch!" Imagine the self-control that's necessary from an entire orchestra after an outburst like that.

It was so surreal for me to watch the orchestra performing, this time not under the direction of its superb resident conductor, Leopold Stokowski, but responding instead to the deeply sensitive and flawless musical interpretation from the revered baton of Maestro Harponini.

And speaking of things surreal, for the record, Dad was the only entertainer to ever sit for the ultimate Surrealist artist, Salvador Dali, because he felt that Harpo Marx, in both the visual and visceral sense, was the ultimate depiction of Surrealism.

Dad sitting for Salvador Dali.

But however much Harpo's surrealistic nature was the engine for his free-spirited behavior, as Harpo was to Dali, one day my dad was to become every bit as surreal to me through an enlightening and preposterously poignant dream.

I was there with Dad, as I was at most of his guest shots. (I even appeared and quickly disappeared in two of those television shows, ***Mr. Smith Goes to Washington*** and ***Silent Panic***.)

The Berle show was particularly interesting as it gave me a special insight to Uncle Miltie. This came at dress rehearsal, his behavior being quite the opposite of Red Skelton's goof-off approach. I was to find out why he was dubbed "Mr. Television." It was not just because his show was so highly rated for so many years. I watched

Fess and Clem Marx calling a spade a spade.

Dad is trying to "tell" me something in *Silent Panic*.

him work at that rehearsal, and to my amazement, he knew every directorial nuance, every camera angle, every close-up, every line of dialogue. His and everybody else's as well. He would hum along every arrangement of bandleader Billy May's, and even knew to tell the drummer when he should give the good ol' rim-shot accents. His years of experience were not lost, as he darted through rehearsal, an omnipotent, all-knowing dictator.

The vision of Berle doing his TV thing clicked off my image of an earlier total package of entertainment experience, Desi Arnaz and Lucille Ball. Dad's 1955 appearance on *I Love Lucy* has become one of the very highest-rated and requested of all the one-hundred seventy-eight shows in the series. Desi and Lucy were an unparalleled duo that was able, for a while anyway, to overcome whatever problems they may have had in their private lives. They also stayed pretty much with a doggone good director, Bill Asher, who did over one-hundred-twenty episodes for them, including the time when we first met during Dad's appearance on the show. Recently we have become good friends, all from that show he directed. But now, fifty years later, I can reveal another reason the show was so successful, and it has a lot to do with *me*—I was working for CBS, ushering people to their seats!

Several things happened on that show, which are indelibly etched in my mind's eye. I was eighteen years old and working as a page, or usher, during summer vacation from school. Along with Four Star Studios where other Bill Asher shows such as *December Bride* and *Make Room For Daddy* were being launched into success, the *Lucy* show was being done at Desilu and also being shot before a live studio audience. After I escorted the people to their appropriate seats, I quickly ran backstage to assume my other job, continuing the longtime career I was to have as Dad's prop man.

Again, it was the time when they filmed each scene in its entirety. It was indeed strange for me to watch Lucy and Dad at one point mimicking each other as two "Harpos" choreographed in perfect unison, while reprising the "mirror scene" I knew so well from *Duck Soup* with Dad and Groucho. This epic sketch was to become quite an acting stretch for Dad, and required a great deal of rehearsal, because the script's storyline called for a role reversal for him. As opposed to the bit in **Duck Soup**, Dad played Groucho's part, and Lucy took Dad's. Then he serenaded Lucy's nearsighted friend, "Caroline Appleby," with my arrangement of "Take Me Out to the Ball Game." (He reprised it the following year as well on **The Martha Raye Show**.)

But the one thing that has struck me whenever I see the show was that he, as all good actors do, always lived in the moment. The scene called for him to chase Lucy's friend around the couch, capture her, pick her up, hoist her over his shoulder, grab his harp stool and then leave through the front door. However, in the process, his hat accidentally fell off. He put down the harp stool, and without missing a beat, bent over with the woman still on his shoulder, picked up his hat, put it on while straightening himself up, grabbed the harp stool again and sauntered merrily out the door with his female "catch of the day."

To me, this was a perfect example of acting through a problem. He didn't ask the director to "cut" and do another take in front of a live studio audience. His experience taught him to "make it work" by going with the situation as it presented itself, and making natural, spontaneous acting choices along the way. Though by today's standards of longevity, sixty-seven may not appear to be very old, when you were sixty-seven as was my dad in 1955 and already having mounting heart problems, I found this a defining moment in his professionalism and his love of and dedication for his work.

Thinking of Dad as a professional actor rather than just a well-known surrealistic clown, **Silent Panic** jumps right out at me.

The show gave him an opportunity to do a serious acting performance about a mute who is a witness to a murder and tries to communicate to the police who he knows to be the perpetrator. With different clothes and different makeup, he was a very different Dad to me, but his portrayal displayed the fountain of creativity that was ever present in him. Interestingly, **Silent Panic** was one of the few performances in which he did not play the harp or engage in any musical interludes. Another favorite of my dad's TV performances allowed me to witness an historic, though relatively private celestial conjunction of 20th-century superstars.

Swingin' at the Summit, with Tony Bennett, Louis "Satchmo" Armstrong, George Shearing and Kay Starr, was a fantastic musical treat, "brought to you in living color by NBC" in January of 1961. But as good as it was on television's broad stage, what went on backstage was more memorable for me and the singer's singer, Tony Bennett. "Satchmo," my dad and I were in Dad's dressing room, where aside from dressing in it, he would practice the number he was to play on the show. But as Tony was in the hall walking to his dressing room, he heard more than just harp music coming from Dad's dressing room. Brimming with curiosity, he cracked open the door and peeked in to see Dad and Satchmo havin' a ball jammin' a tune, and immediately while still playing, Dad motioned for Tony to come in.

Harp and Satch jammin'.

About six years ago, Tony came into a club where I was playing, and on my break, he pulled me aside. He then reminisced about that very surrealistic incident, and how I was there, shouting out the tune's chord changes to Dad as they played and played and played on for ten or fifteen minutes. Tony told me that it was then and always will be the most memorable jam session of his entire life. I was then to remind him of the time I was working at Dino's, and after the gig, he asked me to come back to his place and listen to a group whose music he had just discovered and fallen in love with. As I left his home an hour later, having been blown away by what I heard, he presented me with that remarkable "reel to reel" tape that he claimed, through his recent exposure to this most unusual musical group, was to have changed his approach to singing and elevated it to another level, forever. I still have that tape of The Abyssinian Choir.

"Dad! You just surprised the hell out of me. I thought I was alone. When did you get back here?"

"Just a short while ago. Sorry if I gave you a start, but I've been somewhat curious."

"As long as I can remember, you were always curious about everything. What's it about this time?"

"Your book. How's it coming along?"

"I'll let you know how, if I ever know. Come on, Dad. You've been through this with yours. It's real hard to say."

"When you're done, I want to be the first to read it."

"Oh, of course. I see. My proofreader, eh?"

"Could be."

El Rancho Harpo

Harpo, Susan and the family no longer lived in Beverly Hills, having moved to their weekend vacation retreat in 1956, where Dad spent the 300 or so days he wasn't working, playing golf, painting and practicing the harp. He was an early riser and enjoyed getting his three hours in with the harp first thing in the morning. On one occasion, Helen Perrin, an old family friend and the wife of the Marx Brothers' great screenwriter, Nat Perrin, spent the night at El Rancho Harpo, which was what we called Mom and Dad's place in the desert. There was Dad at the harp at his usual time, sending heavenly glissandos and arpeggios wafting through the house, when Helen walked out of her bedroom with a slightly panicked look on her face that relaxed the moment she saw Dad.

"Oh, thank God," she said, relieved. "I heard the harp and for a moment I thought I was dead."

It was in Rancho Mirage that our family had what in my mind was *its* defining moment. It was also one of Dad's most memorably delightful television appearances. Back in 1958, we got to be on a segment of the prestigious show, **Person to Person**, hosted by Edward R. Murrow. We watched in amazement one morning as a camera crew came in and immediately took over our house in a bloodless coup. Soon there were people running about carrying out their appointed duties—audio and video lines carefully strewn all over the place, preparation for all the camera angles, the strategic placing of the overhead microphones for the best possible sound pickup, and all the other necessary technical stuff that was being done. All part of putting on a seamless twenty minutes that the following day would be shot live and beamed to the entire world. El Rancho Harpo had become a soundstage.

The director had the job of coordinating the interview by Murrow, who was on a remote from New York, with all the action going on at El Rancho Harpo. Remember, that was pretty tricky stuff in 1958. It really was a remarkable accomplishment when you consider the whole thing was done in such a short time. And that it was the first show ever done live from the Coachella Valley, because up until then, though they had gotten video out of the area before, this was the first time they were able to transmit audio out as well. Murrow went one by one, asking questions and getting answers from Mom, who would constantly apologize for Dad's wonderfully childlike behavior, then me, Alex, Minnie, and Jimmy. But nary a word was out of Dad, as he deftly guided the viewers through the house, then circling the outside premises in his golf cart, and finally running back into the house to land squarely behind his precious harp.

I was seated off to the side at an organ, and then introduced the song, "My Blue Heaven," from our forthcoming album. Dad and I played it together, did some shtick afterward, and then, on behalf of the family, by way of a harp glissando, Dad bade a very good evening to Mr. Murrow. We were all there, together, a glowing justification for what Dad and Mom had chosen for all of us. They had brought to everyone the sense and joy of family to make our lives more complete.

Mom was busy taking good care of Dad, which alone would have been a full-time job, what with his fragile health after a number of heart attacks. But he became despondent about the physical restrictions he had to live with until recovery, so much so that Mom finally had enough of his negative attitude. She arranged that I get Dad an apartment for the summer up in L.A., so he could visit with his Hillcrest Country Club cronies, hang out with me now and then, and do some painting, all hopefully to get his mind off himself. She then gathered up Alex, Jimmy and Minnie, who had finished that year in high school, and they all took off on a National Park sightseeing tour for six weeks.

Occasionally, Dad would invite me to Hillcrest for lunch, and we sat at the table called "Round Table West," listening to all the comedians trying to top one another. It was always *quite* an education, with no holds barred, and no profanity spared. But of all the crazy stuff I ever heard that came out of Hillcrest, this true story, *not* emanating from the "Round Table West," may just have topped them all.

First, a bit of history.

Hillcrest Country Club in West Los Angeles was the daytime home for so many of the show business stars that relocated to Hollywood from the east coast to continue their careers in radio and motion pictures. Dad, along with his stage and vaudeville pals, all became members and felt the need to create their own version of the Algonquin Hotel's illustrious literary lunch gathering by establishing Hillcrest's "Round Table West." Any day of the week at lunch time, you would surely see an array of celebrity crazies such as George Burns, Danny Kaye, the Ritz Brothers, George Jessel, Buddy Hackett, Lou Holtz, Milton Berle, Jack Benny, Groucho, Gummo, Zeppo, Chico, and, of course, Dad, all trying to top one another with hilarious showbiz stories of times gone by.

Now, in the early 1940s, before the organization of the Professional Golfer's Association, most country clubs employed pros as caddies for their golf-playing members. At Hillcrest, many of their members had achieved celebrity status. However, there was one fella who *became* a celebrity while working at Hillcrest as a caddy. Within its confines, Shorty was as respected as all those other aforementioned celebrity members. And speaking of

The Round Table West celebrates a Harry Ritz Birthday.

members, Shorty was so named because he was reputed to be endowed with the longest member anyone could possibly ever imagine. As it was more affectionately referred to by Dad and his cronies as a "shvontz," Shorty's was to be the stuff from which legends are made.

Then, without warning, on one fortuitous day, a new caddy sauntered into town and went to work at Hillcrest. He, too, had a reputation that preceded him, and he immediately challenged Shorty to a high-stakes-winner-take-all "shvontz-off" to see whose was the longest. Hillcrest had never been rocking with such excitement as everyone anteed-up for the following day's show-down, as it were.

Due to a most unfortunate scheduling problem, Dad was unable to attend the big event. So the following day, he ran into his pal, screenwriter and producer, Harry Tugend, who had been there, and asked him who won.

"No contest. Shorty won hands down. Wasn't even close."

Dad then asked what the length of Shorty's turned out to be.

"No one knows for sure. He just pulled out enough to win."

This story has been attributed over the years to Milton Berle's measurements. However, Dad told me its true genesis was Shorty, indeed. Who will ever know for sure?

Speaking of Hillcrest, I am reminded of the time when Dad was a conformist and nonconformist at the very same time. This amazing accomplishment occurred one day when after he and George Burns had finished a round of golf, they were told that a new rule had just been implemented by the club ordering everyone to wear shirts both at the first tee and the eighteenth green. It seems that the members' wives, while having lunch at the outside tables overlooking the course, were tired of having to watch a constant parade of men's silly and sweaty bodies. Rushing to the aid of the ladies' digestion, the club's Board of Directors acted swiftly with a stern edict.

July 28, 1941

Mr. Harpo Marx,
701 North Camden Drive,
Beverly Hills, California.

Dear Mr. Marx:

At the last meeting of the Board of Directors it was reported that within the last thirty days you played golf with your shirt removed and stripped to the waist.

I was instructed by the Board of Directors to write you directly, informing you that there is in effect a rule adopted by the Board of Directors that no men shall play golf on the course with their shirts removed and stripped to the waist.

I am sure that if you had known about this rule you would have fully complied with the same.

Will you please govern yourself ac cordingly in the future?

Sincerely yours,

HILLCREST COUNTRY CLUB

By_____
　　　　　Secretary

So, the next day, George and Dad wore their appropriate shirts at the first tee box, then permissibly discarding them at the first green, way out of view of the luncheoning ladies. They continued the round shirtless until they were on the eighteenth fairway approaching the green. Now, at one point that fairway slopes downward into a small ravine where the golfers disappear from view and can put their shirts back on, only to reappear in view as they ascend to the green. Dutifully complying with the new rule, George and Dad emerged from the ravine, each wearing their shirt as ordered. However, that was the only thing that Dad had on. For the record, the board members slapped him with a merciless one-day suspension and added a pair of pants to the new rule.

When everyone returned to the normalcy of the desert at the end of summer, Mom went back to entrenching herself into a distinguished career with the Palm Springs Unified School District that would earn her a position as a long-standing incumbent member of the School Board. Dad went back to his routine of retirement, un-retirement and heart attacks. Not too long after,

He even started dancing again, as Fred Astaire's partner.

he was hit with another attack, and with it, the awareness of an existing aortic aneurysm. But the second heart attack seemed to change his attitude about living. He decided to hell with feeling sorry for himself and his physical condition. It had kept him from participating in life, which was quite contrary to his nature.

Dad then proceeded to embrace every day, immersing himself in one of the busiest and most productive times of his life. He described his new outlook on life being like "living on velvet." He managed to finish his autobiography, do an extensive book tour all over the country, and learn new harp arrangements for his guest shots on the Ed Sullivan and Art Linkletter shows.

Dad actually getting Ed Sullivan to crack a smile? You saw it here!

Dad also appeared in that TV special with Carol Burnett and starred in a 90-minute spectacular Ford Car Company 90-minute color film with Mickey Rooney, introducing Ford's 1962 line of cars. (This film has miraculously and completely disappeared.)

Alex, Jimmy and Minnie also appeared on Linkletter's *Kids Say the Darndest Things* **show.**

Later, he went with Mom and a handpicked group of distinguished Americans, including James Michener, on a goodwill tour to Israel on behalf of our State Department, and (gasp) still had the time to get in a lot of golf and plenty of painting.

Dad loved to paint and had a remarkable output over the years. He really got into it seriously when the doctors informed him after his first attack that he needed to give his heart a rest and temporarily put a cap on performing until he fully recovered.

So the uniqueness of Dad went to work by creating a scheme only he could come up with. Dad decided that *he*, the artist, would select the people that he wanted to have commissioning and buying *his* art work. He would paint a picture, usually oils on casonite, and then invite one of his rich friends over to see what he had done. I was there to vouch for the perfection of his madness. Al Hart, who created and was CEO of then City National Bank, came over to the house one day, and Dad showed him his latest effort. He then asked

Mom and Dad in Israel.

Al what he thought it was worth in relation to the art community's standards. Al thought this particular piece maybe could go for about five hundred dollars. Dad said ok. You give me a check made out to your favorite charity for three thousand dollars and the painting is yours.

Dad would lose himself creatively while painting in his studio.

Dad has Al Hart right where he wants him. My father, the extortionist.

Dad always got his man, and in all the distributions of his artwork, he never took a penny for himself. He also donated much of his work to hospitals around the country, and strangely, the more he painted toward the end of his life, the more he came to look very much like a double for Pablo Picasso.

Dad had the ability to adapt to any situation, making it all work for him by taking any reality and making it surreal. Painting had become the outlet for Dad's creative thirst that was in his nature until he was given the go-ahead to return to the world of entertainment.

Dad as I knew him best.

CHAPTER THIRTEEN

I've Got a Secret Left to right: Heinz Romholz (Academy Award for score to *Ruby,*) Melody Condos (daughter of Martha Raye), Garry Moore (Emcee), Jim Kelly (brother of Gene Kelly) and me.

Little would I know that my appearance in 1956 on the TV show, *I've Got a Secret* would eventually lead to a milestone in entertainment history. No, I know I was good, but not that good. I'm not talking about that at all. And besides, the milestone wasn't to occur until January 19, 1963. Though I never met the man when I did the show, I later received a very nice thank-you note for being a participant from the producer of the show, Allan Sherman.

Yes, *that* Allan Sherman.

As successful a producer as he was, he felt that he didn't fit right with Madison Avenue and his bosses, Mark Goodson and Bill Todman. So, in the summer of 1961, he pulled up his eastern stakes and moved his family way out west to the little prairie town of Yee Haa, Hollywood! The Fates had to be at it once again, this time masquerading as real estate brokers, because they saw to it that two houses next to one another on North Saltair Drive in Brentwood were to be rented for the summer. They were really up to their old tricks when they serendipitously convinced Allan to rent one of them and my dad the other. Directly behind both of them, on the next street over, lived Steve Allen and Jayne Meadows. This geographically desirable grouping was to start the engine of a brand-new career in show business for Allan.

I was living in the Laurel Canyon area of Hollywood then, so I would spend a lot of time with the family that summer. Somehow over the years I had heard through the grapevine that Allan wrote hilarious parodies on familiar songs and then sang them for fun at dinner parties, much like what Carl Reiner and Mel Brooks did with their "2000 Year Old Man" routine. When I found out that Allan and Dad had introduced themselves to each other, I went to Allan's house and reintroduced myself to him. One day soon after, I asked Allan that if I played the piano for him, would he come over to Dad's house and sing a couple of his ditties. He agreed to the proposal, and when Dad heard some of the stuff, he instantly went crazy over it enough to arrange a party honoring Allan, who would at some point, entertain the guests with a few of his parodies. I had my trio, and there were Burns and Allen, Jack Benny, Mary Livingstone, Milton Berle, all five of the Marx Brothers, a bunch of behind-the-scenes "showbiz peep" and some hand-picked friends.

I remember playing for him "Glory, Glory, Harry Lewis," "How Are Things with Uncle Morris?," "There Is Nothing Like a Lox," as well as others from the score to his show, *South Passaic*. My friend Randy Wood, who was President of Vee-Jay Records, along with Dad and the blessings of others that were there that night, pushed Allan in the immediate direction of Warner Brothers Records, where he was to do his first hit album, *My Son, The Folk Singer*. Randy then got the bright idea for me to do an album of jazz parodies of all the tunes Allan parodied on his album, and we would call it, *My Son, The Folk Swinger.* With me were Victor Feldman, Vibes; Monty Budwig, Bass; and Norm Jeffries, Drums. Allan agreed to write my liner notes in his own unique way, and it was the beginning of a long friendship between us.

MY SON THE FOLK SWINGER. (ORIGINAL LINER NOTES FROM VEE JAY LP)

Bill Marx is my friend. If he weren't, he probably wouldn't have offered to let me write this album liner. (At last, I'm learning a trade.) I'm attracted by people who are honest. You'll agree that Bill Marx is honest by the way he plays. The feeling is so strong that I know he is living each mood. Take an ink blot. (I've got mine.) If you pass it among ten different people you wouldn't get two like impressions and you'd really be lucky if you got two like impressions out of fifty. Bill has arranged ten ink blots for this album so tastefully, that all four impressions are the same! One song...one mood...one personality...one feeling! Bill said that each song has its own personality and therefore wasn't difficult to arrange; don't you believe it... I'm a musical celebrity myself and I tried it. (The true title of this album should be 9 rawshocks and one wasserman.) The ten songs on this album are not usually heard in jazz circles as jazz, but being somewhat familiar with parodies, this tongue-in-cheek approach is sure to make an opening. The album speaks for itself. Listen. It has been said that no two people think alike, but this album proves that there are four minds, but with a single thought. Victor Feldman, vibes (who teases); Monty Budwig, bass (who plays dead inside); Norm Jeffries, drums (who enjoys driving); and Bill Marx, piano (who says many things with his tongue in cheek). You will also enjoy this album and Bill's unique "Baker's Dozen Beat"... you get more for your money. It's what I use myself. So, sit back and listen to my very dear friend Harpo's son, Bill Marx, the folkswinger.

—ALLAN SHERMAN

It was in late 1962 that Allan called from Las Vegas, where he was appearing at the Sands Hotel, and asked my dad if he'd be interested in doing four concerts with him—two on January 18 at the Santa Monica Civic Auditorium, and the other two on the 19th at the Pasadena Civic Auditorium. Dad loved the idea and Allan got permission from the head man at the Sands, Jack Entratter, to take two days off and do the shows with Dad.

Allan and my dad each did their own act and then did a few things together. It was a beautiful blend of Allan's songs with orchestra and chorus, and Dad's cutting of the skirt routine followed by his harp solo. In Allan's autobiography, *A Gift of Laughter*, published by Atheneum, he writes of how Harpo touched the harp like an act of love, almost too private for us to watch. He speaks of how you could feel his love for music and every other creature on earth in the way he played the music through his beloved harp.

Before the final performance on the 19th in Pasadena, Allan went to his dressing room and found a gift bottle of cognac and a note from Dad saying that he was retiring from show business and this would be his last performance. Allan went to him in disbelief, and Dad assured him it was true, but asked him to please wait until the end of the show to make the announcement.

That moment finally came, and with Allan blubbering to beat the band, he informed the audience that Harpo Marx, "the gentle, loving soul who had the good sense never to grow up," had decided to retire after fifty-six years in the business. Dad took the microphone and realizing that he had to do something for his last shining moment on the stage and owed the audience some kind of explanation or something, anything. He started with, "Now, as I was about to say in 1907 . . . ," then launched into his Bar Mitzvah speech, "For thirteen long years, I have toiled and labored for your happiness . . . ," and closed it out with, "I wish to commend all of you for your keenness and perspicacity in recognizing true genius and monumental megalomania, I thank you."

The constant barrage of laughs from the audience during his speech was followed by a six-minute standing ovation, each person, child and grown-up alike, all applauding because of their own personal thoughts about the very special moment they were sharing with Harpo Marx. Holding Mom's hand in the wings, I was thinking to myself that I was sharing this moment with my dad. That was *my* dad out there! The news spread quickly through the industry, and the responses from friends, fans and fellow entertainers were overwhelming.

"Good night, sweet props."

Years later, I accidentally uncovered one remarkable example of this outpouring of love, when I came across an extraordinary handwritten letter in pencil to Dad from another fellow professional clown, Red Skelton, who had written him with such affection and admiration upon hearing the news of his approximately forty-fifth, but final retirement.

Dad had recently appeared on Red's first TV show of the 1962 season, and it would prove to be one of his last television appearances. Red Skelton was at the top of the heap at the time, and as hot as the show was, the hardest by far of Red's shows to get into was his dress rehearsal. They were always lined up for over an hour, because everyone knew that they were bound to hear Red blow lines, screw up the choreography, the camera shots, and indulge in hilarious but frequently obscene language. The audience would then also be able to watch the final product at home on their TV and compare it with the dress rehearsal. Both shows were obviously quite different, but they still were always one hell of a "twofer."

In any case, the performance must have been poignant in retrospect for Red. I offer this complete document, exactly as Red wrote it, and I have purposely left it unedited to also reveal a profoundly eloquent side of this true comedic genius, the place inside of Skelton that few of us would ever get the chance to appreciate.

Dear Harpo,
When most actors announce their final performance, it's a meir crescendo to incidental music. But when greatness rings down the curtain, a lonely feeling shrouds our thoughts. We feel the stillness of an empty theater. There will never be another poetic figure, with your humanistic concern, who's philosophy is laughter, a kindly sort, with out belittling his fellow man. You dident have to speak, each gesture is shier elocution. Your very precence proved, "Silence is Golden."

The only time you made any one sad, was when you spoke to your audience, and bid them fairwell. We were privlaged indeed, that you dident decide to speek sooner.

We are proud to have been a small atom in your life, our appearance on television will be my most memorable hour how we displayed every trick in the clown's bag, romping our way through a harlequinade of farcical buffoonery.

A warm glow pervades, when I think of the nite you and your dear lady came to see me perform, and that extraordinary glow we get, when your name is mentioned.

The selfish will keep shouting for more, where happiness is concern aren't we all selfish. Man is always seeking laughter from their clown, you are theirs. But do they ever care if their clown gets tired. or wonder who diverts him with antics.

You've given to the world, enjoy the tributes long past due, your decision is your diploma from the school of adversity. Wisdom is now your teacher. Life has been good to you. Now you be good to your life.

Now you'll be able to enjoy your family, your play, and your painting your painting speek far more beauty than any poem written, and your music. Now you'll hear your greatness too. You'll learn why you are loved, depth will sing from the strings. You'll never have to say it could be better, or it has to be better. You will say, thank god I dident relize how great it is.

And your dear face, you won't have to wonder if they will laugh at its impish contortions. You'll see yourself and say there is a happy man with out half-formulated fears.

Give free rein to your enthusiasm, not to the whim of a box office. You'll have to curb your grumbles now. There is no performance to blame the quivering nerves on.

One thing certian you may not hear it but there is thunderous applause for you every day. You are beloved. We are all Gods children, if God puts his image in his children all I can say is, you sure look like our old man.
Love Always,
God Bless

Red Skelton (his signature)

"Hey, Dad, as long as you keep checking in on me, check this out. I'm sure you've always remembered Red's beautiful, heartfelt tribute and the fun you had working with him. Well then, I've often asked myself about how you might feel if somebody would bring you guys back with a Marx Brothers movie for today's audiences? Do you think it's possible to capture your magical spirit and humorous point of view somehow and actually make it work?"

"I have never been able to be very objective about stuff like that. My focus was strictly on performing."

"Yeah, well, I think it's possible. You guys as heroes sure had a unique way of dealing with the bad guys, and believe it or not, that technique can still work today. Also, think back of what heroes you were to so many audiences the world over at a time when we all needed heroes. We need them again now and forever. But to me you

always seemed to be the most heroic of all; you as Stuffy, the winning jockey in **A Day at the Races**, and you keeping the train going by chopping up the box cars for fuel in **Go West**, then you ruining the American operatic debut of the pompous Laspari in **A Night at the Opera**. I could go on and on and on. Why, if I were to make a Marx Brothers' movie today, I sure as hell would make you the most important hero."

"Billy, we were a team. Always. Different personalities, of course, but only as a *unit*. If we're talkin' about heroes here, the Marx Brothers was the hero."

"Okay, Dad, but we all tack labels onto people, and I am very much at peace with mine for you."

"Son, if I thank you for that, you in turn, must do me a favor. Though it was Woollcott's profession, I despise reviews. So please don't send me any when they come out. Promise?"

"Promise."

CHAPTER FOURTEEN

I was barely thirty by the time I started my steady gig at Dino's Lodge, and I had managed to rack up a lot of experience, professionally and otherwise. Of course it didn't hurt that my dad was a famous comedian—that offered me the opportunity to meet some of the most celebrated, talented and funniest people in the world. It also didn't hurt that my dad was a famous musician. Scoff if you will, but Harpo Marx is the most popular harpist whoever lived, and despite being self-taught, he was quite gifted. He almost single-handedly transformed the instrument from an occasional orchestral behemoth into a snappy, jazzy popular instrument. Because of my dad's musicality, I was able to experience first-hand some of the most gifted singers, songwriters, and professional musicians of the 20th century.

But my musical talent, such as it is, was not a gift from Harpo. I brought it with me when I arrived at 701 North Canon Drive, and I cultivated it in venues as varied as symphony orchestra concert halls and Las Vegas-like-after-hours lounges. I am eternally grateful to my dad for helping me develop my talent and our respective musical interests helped us form an unbreakable bond, but the seeds were there before we met.

The years before the Dino's gig came along were part of my long musical apprenticeship. In the very early 1960s, I was kicking around the music business, trying as hard as I could to make expenses from small jobs that came my way. I figured that I could supplement my income from composing and arranging by playing the piano in nightclubs if things got tight.

Things got tight.

So I got together with a bass player and a drummer and found a job for us in Palm Springs on weekends. The Whispering Waters Hotel was owned by Aaron Spelling, the prolific TV producer, and his then-wife, Carolyn Jones, best remembered as Morticia Addams on the popular television series based on the Charles Addams cartoons.

We were just barely good enough to have them put up with us for an eight-week run, but at least it was my first real chance to get some experience in a club situation. And out of town yet, just like New Haven.

Somehow I was able to track down a few gigs when we returned to Los Angeles, and I slowly built confidence in my playing. For the next year or so, in between writing assignments, I worked a lot of different clubs, some for dancing, some for jazz, and some for dining. You could say that we were becoming either a very popular trio, or we had trouble keeping a job.

I finally landed my first pretty steady not too "iffy" job playing solo piano at a steak house on La Brea Ave. called for some reason, The La Brea Inn. I can just see the owners sitting around the bar one day. "Hey, we got dis new jernt and gotta tink of a name fer it. Anybody got any ideers?"

Let me tell you that it was by far the best steak deal in town, and it enjoyed some well-deserved longevity because the food was good, reasonably priced and the restaurant had a nice, lowly lit, romantic atmosphere, complete with its burgundy leather booths.

One evening, in walked the tallest, biggest man that I had ever seen wearing a suit and tie. The only people that I had ever seen that big not wearing a suit and tie were basketball players. Much to my surprise, he was a basketball player, but I didn't recognize him at first, because he wasn't wearing his uniform. When he was introduced to me, I looked way up at him and there was number thirteen, Wilt "The Stilt" Chamberlain. I went to shake his hand, and, much to my amazement, my hand and arm up to my elbow disappeared into his palm. His hand was so big, I swear that it was possible for him to hold two basketballs at the same time. It was unnerving for me as a pianist to find that, for a brief moment, I had lost all sight of my fingers. The fact that I no longer had any feeling in them from his vice-like grip added to my anxiety. When he finally did let go, my fingers magically reappeared, along with the rest of my hand and half of my arm. I also breathed a sigh of relief when, in only a matter of three minutes or so, the blood returned to that part of my body. I then returned to the piano and dived enthusiastically right into the next couple of tunes. I wanted to show Wilt that I, too, was capable of rebounding.

There was a restaurant on Sixth Street in L.A. called The St. Francis Room. In the middle of the dining room was a big dance floor, and the tables and booths were all around the perimeter. On the ledges that connected the booths were aquariums with every wonderful variety of tropical fish you could think of. It made for a very peaceful, visually soothing atmosphere and something a little different for the customers. Our trio would play nice, soft music for both dining and the touch-dancing lovers.

One night, we were playing a ballad when we heard a verbal disturbance coming from two of the booths. From there it escalated into a shouting match between three and four couples. The next thing I knew, the altercation had provoked a fistfight between a couple of the guys, and within seconds, a full-scale donnybrook broke out with everyone jumping into the ring. Soon, a series of crashing blows sent a few of the hotheads careening into the awaiting aquariums, and before you knew it, the fish were boogieing up a storm on the dance floor, while people were slipping and sliding all over the ocean of water that accompanied the fish.

The band immediately launched into "Tea for Tuna," gracefully segueing to my bombastic vocal rendition of, "Fish gotta swim, birds gotta fly, I'm gonna love my fish till I die, *Can't help lovin' dat fish of mine.*" I got no applause, because everybody was just too busy to pay any attention.

The brawl lasted about five full exciting minutes, and I don't remember what the fight was all about or how it or why it ended. Someone must have thrown in their white table napkin, because it subsided rather quickly. I do know that the restaurant owners expressed immediate displeasure over the whole thing, and it kind of reminded me of those "B" Western movies I used to see when I was a kid, where the entire saloon was trashed. This melee replaced the cowboys breaking every stick of furniture over somebody's head. The place was a mess. It closed for renovation, and we were out of a gig. I must assume that when it did reopen for business, The St. Francis Room had no seafood on its menu. Sadly as well, I thought I would never again have the occasion, opportunity nor inclination to do my fish medley.

Some time later, the trio was working a barn of a club out near Los Angeles International Airport on Century Boulevard. We were up on a stage that looked out over this huge dance floor. It was our first night there, and apparently, some influential friends of the owners were invited to be a part of the evening. At one point, in walked two people out of Central Casting, whom the owners immediately fawned all over and escorted to a table near the bandstand. You would have had to believe this man in a white suit, white shoes, red tie, flashing pinky rings on at least five of his fingers other than his pinkies, and the tight-skirted blonde bombshell on his arm were descendants of Al Capone.

Moments later he jumped up and came over to the bandstand, and what was to occur became a classic case of misunderstood communication or understood miscommunication. He addressed me with, "Hey, you da bandleader? I wanna do 'skin.'" Something instinctively told me I was not about to deny him his unilateral request, but I didn't know what the hell he was talking about.

"Skin? I don't understand what you mean, sir."

With a touch of edginess, he responded with, "Waddaya mean ya don't know what I mean? Skin! Skin! Ya know, 'I've Gahchoo Under My Skin!'"

"I'm sorry that I didn't understand you. That's fine, we know the tune. What key do you do it in?" I queried, nervously. Very defensively he said, "I don't have a key."

"Well, sir, we have to know your key in order to play the tune for you properly."

"How da hell do I know what da f--- key I do it in? I'm nodda professional singer." And I reasoned kindly over the dilemma, "Well, we realize that you're not, sir, but we have to . . ."

He interrupted me with fire in his eyes. "You sonofabitch! Wadda *you* tellin' me that you know I ain't no professional singer?" You are some goddam sonofabitch." And as I was apologetically trying to assure him that he misinterpreted my meaning, Mr. Whitesuit jumped onto the stage and started to come after me, pinky rings and all. Fortunately, by the time he began wrestling with me and throwing a punch or two, the bouncer, who also doubled as the bartender, saw what was happening. He leaped over the bar counter, ran across the dance floor, climbed onto the stage, pulled the amateur singer off of me and forcibly escorted him and his moll out of the club.

It was hard for me to explain to the club owner about the misunderstanding, considering that the customer is always supposed to be right. It was a relief to hear him say that this was not the first time his buddy had gotten juiced up and caused a stir. I made very sure at the end of the evening that the bass player, the drummer and the bouncer/bartender safely escorted me to the parking lot, and waited until I turned on the ignition, to find out whether or not my car and I would blow up.

Even the pros have their problems singing, and as their accompanist, I've participated in some of their embarrassing moments, too many to chronicle. One singer I played for managed to forget the lyrics to "Try to Remember." One night at the Purple Onion nightclub, a wonderful black singer with an extensive operatic background launched into the Frank Loesser standard, "I've Never Been in Love Before." I played an opening arpeggio for him, and in warm baritone richness, with precise diction and without the need for a microphone, he began to sing in full operatic voice, "I've nehhhhh---vearrr---beeeeeeeeen---eennn---lllllloave---befoe."

I tried to control myself, but having real trouble doing so, I wound up playing the rest of the accompaniment from underneath the piano.

What the hell, it was a way to make a living.

Buddy Rich was one of those people who, if he liked you the first time he met you, by him, you could never do any wrong. If he didn't like you the first time you met, you ran like hell, because you could never do any right.

My jazz trio was up in Lake Tahoe, California at Harvey's Wagon Wheel in August of 1963. (This was just prior to my long-term gig at Dino's.) My friend and bassist, Lyle Ritz, and I had just gotten back to the hotel to hurriedly get ready for work after an outing in a rented speedboat we took on the lake. I knew it was time for us to end our afternoon of fun when Lyle, pushing the pedal at top speed, the spray hitting us in the face and both of us laughing uproariously, had his two hands firmly grasping a steering wheel. The wheel, by the way, was no longer attached to the boat.

In an act of great composure, Lyle smartly took his foot off the pedal before we crashed into something, and during the subsequent time we spent in the middle of the lake bobbing around aimlessly. I sat there waiting while Lyle, who has a Masters in Speed Boat Steering Wheel Assembly, figured out what went where, so we could get back to shore and get the hell to work on time. We made it, by the hairs of our chinny-chin-chins.

At this time I was with VeeJay Records, a small jazz and gospel label out of Chicago, and Randy Wood, the President of the company and close friend of mine, had arranged the gig to promote my latest album, *My Son, the Folk Swinger*. The schedule was a pretty grueling one, as we were also working with Shecky Greene, as funny and talented a comedian as there ever was, and one helluva good singer. I was also managing a trifecta by sitting in on piano with the legendary vibes man, Lionel Hampton and his big band.

What little time I had between breaks was spent across the street at Harrah's, where Harry James' big band, featuring Buddy Rich, was playing. Not much better than that. I was also lured there by the vocals of a young jazz singer named Ruth Price, who today is the proprietor of a top jazz club in Los Angeles, *The Jazz Bakery*. Her voice so effervescent, she was fun to watch and the perfect complement to that very swinging band.

A wonderful character named Red Kelly was the bass player, and, for reasons known only to Buddy Rich, was apparently Buddy's favorite to work within a big band situation. Red was a happy-as-you-can, go-lucky-as-you-can-be kinda guy, and I don't know how it happened, but we wound up hanging out with each other a lot. One night he came over to Harvey's to catch our little musical escapade, and then he invited me to come back to Harrah's when my gig was over, because he wanted to introduce me to Harry and Buddy.

We walked into Harry's dressing room and there he was—Harry James! Nobody's lead trumpet sound could fill a trumpet section any better than Harry's fully-rounded tone. It was between sets, but Harry was already so inebriated that he just sat in his chair and gave me an indifferent and gratuitous "Nice to meet you." And now, after years of admiring him from my childhood records back at Waring School or hearing him on the radio, I was finally having the opportunity to meet this great musical icon, and what happens? I get bummed, because he's too ripped to even care about my wanting to express to him what admiration and accolades I had for his music. He left me with less than I came in with.

Red then ushered me over to Buddy, who was standing over in the corner, and Buddy was at least gracious enough to shake my hand. But I could tell from Buddy that mine was just another hand to shake in a long line of hands he'd had to shake. Then Red said to Buddy, "Bill is playing across the street at the Wagon Wheel and, oh, incidentally, he happens to be Harpo Marx's kid."

Well, the lid came off of Buddy. He looked at me, smiled, grabbed my hand, and with Red trundling along behind, took me out the door and into his dressing room. He then said, without even knowing me, "If there is anything *ever* I can do for you, just let me know, and I'll be happy to do it, because of the story I am about to tell you."

His tale was about an incident during the time of World War II, at the Naval Base in San Diego, California, when my dad was there as the headliner to do a show for the troops. It was in the afternoon, and everyone had just finished rehearsal for the show, which was to be presented that very evening.

As Dad was picking up his props from the stage and reorganizing them into his coat, he looked down from the stage and saw a young man who was setting up the folding chairs to be used by the audience that night. But there was something about the young man that made Dad stop for a moment, a something that was familiar about him that my dad just couldn't pinpoint.

Out of curiosity, he motioned to the lad to come over to the stage and asked, "You a Jew boy?"

"Yes, sir, I am."

"Don't I know you from somewhere? I feel I've seen you before."

"Maybe, sir, maybe you have seen me performing in Los Angeles."

"Now I am beginning to remember. I did see you work some time ago, and you are that wunderkind drummer, right?

"That's right, sir.

"You are great, and it's a pleasure to meet you. I'm Harpo Marx."

"Honored to meet you, too, sir."

"You'll be coming to the show tonight?"

"No, sir. When I'm through here with the chairs, I go back into solitary."

"You're kidding! What the hell did you do?"

"I hit an officer."

"Why would you do a thing like that?"

"Because he called me a Jew, Kike Son of a Bitch. So I slugged him."

Dad went directly to the Base Commanding Officer and said that he would refuse to do the show unless he got a guarantee that Buddy was allowed to come to the show that night.

"Bill, your dad saw to it that I was there in the audience, that night, and in the same row as the Base Commanding Officer!"

Needless to say, my dad's wonderful impact on people's lives had given me entrée to a world I'm sure I would have otherwise never known. I was fortunate to have made Dad's acquaintance, just as Buddy had. Only my first contact with Harpo Marx was even far more improbable and unlikely than Buddy's.

Perhaps my most memorable moment in my years as a professional musician came one night in 1964, at a recording session for Impulse Records, and it was not at all a moment that was of my doing or instigation. The singer was one of the jazz world's all timers, Lorez Alexandria, and her album consisted of songs mostly from *My Fair Lady*. Once again, this was still the time in the industry where all the musicians and singers recorded at the same time, and so every take was a bona fide performance, good or bad. I had assembled a big band, whose list read like a "Who's Who" of nineteen of Hollywood's finest studio players, and we were in the middle of rehearsing "Get Me to the Church on Time," getting it into shape before recording it with Lorez.

That's me gettin' no respect.

It happened slowly, but at some point I felt that I was losing the band's attention. They started to giggle while whispering and murmuring to one another, and I could sense my authority as conductor was slipping away. I suggested that everyone please refrain from talking, and we'll take it yet once again from bar seventy-two, or whatever. Recording is all about "time is money." We were wasting both. But the developing scene was becoming more and more mutinous, as the band became more and more raucous. Now it seemed they were all laughing and poking fun at me at will, and in a moment of frustration, realizing I had lost all control and having had it with their intolerable insubordination, I issued an angry decree.

"I think it's time to "take five!"

I slammed my baton down onto the conductor's podium, stepped down from my so-called lofty position of power, and went to chew out the date's contractor for the unusual and highly unprofessional attitude the band was exhibiting.

But as I turned to walk away, I was completely floored to see what had caused the entire ruckus. There they were—what the band was *really* reacting to; Dad, Mom, Uncle George and Aunt Gracie! Without my knowing, they had sneaked into the studio, stood behind me during the rehearsal. Every now and then Dad would parade around with his chest puffed way out and his thumbs tucked under his imaginary suspenders, while occasionally pointing at me with an expression on his face of enormous pride as if to say, "That's *my* son!" Needless to say, when I returned to the podium, still overcome with tears of joy, the band accepted *my* apology for *my* outrageously unprofessional behavior.

So, there, indeed was Dad, the one who first validated me as a pro, returning to the scene once again, and for perhaps the last time before he would run out of "velvet," to confirm the suspicions he's had all along about his son.

CHAPTER FIFTEEN

In mid-1963, concern over my dad's health was temporarily shifted to Mom's. They received the sobering news that she had breast cancer. (Ironically, Bunny also had been the victim of the same thing, and in the same side breast, though she survived it.) I remember an incident that was an outgrowth of my fear and concern for Mom the day before her surgery. I was working a very popular club on La Cienega Blvd. called *The Losers*. It had two marquees, one on each side of the entrance. The right side displayed who was appearing at the club. The left side presented the "loser" of the week, always somebody newsworthy who had currently screwed up. It became so popular, that it was often a topic of conversation throughout the city regarding "who it is this week," or "who do you think will be crowned the next dummy."

As wonderful a singer as I have ever worked with, Ann Richards and I had recorded an album, *Live at the Losers*, during our previous engagement there. We had been treated beautifully by the owners, Pete and Sonny, probably only because they knew we had packed the place for them every night. This engagement was to be different. Pete and Sonny should have wound up on the left marquee trying to fix something that wasn't broken. For some inexplicable reason, they decided to hire a stripper to do her act between our shows. Although I have never turned away from the opportunity of watching a stripper work, both Annie and I were furious about this. She was upset because she was afraid that many of our following would come to the club expecting to see and hear us just like the last time we were there, only to be offended by something unnecessary they hadn't bargained for. I was hot because

I felt sad for the inconsiderate way they were treating Annie, and that it was a crass put-down.

After the first set, I expressed a rare display of temper and did something against my very nature, disregarding the consequences. I asked Pete and Sonny to step out in front of the club, and I told them how hurt and indignant Annie and I were about the addition of the stripper to our engagement. The more they tried to reason with me and justify their decision, the more frustrated I became with them and the whole scene. Finally, I couldn't take it anymore and sparks fired in all my cylinders. I went over to the marquee that informed everyone that "Ann Richards and the Bill Marx Trio" were appearing. I proceeded to take the letter "B" off of the marquee, flinging it like a Frisbee into the unsuspecting La Cienega traffic. I continued with this uncontrollable behavior until I had eliminated my name from view, all the while screaming at the cars going by that I didn't want anyone to know that I was playing in such a tacky joint.

Bass player/pal Lyle Ritz and Nick Ceroli, the drummer, both great musicians as well as quality people, were incensed as well, but we all agreed to play the night out and do the last three shows. The next night I apologized to Pete and Sonny. After having thought about my outburst, I had obviously over reacted from feelings that were brought about by my concern for my mother's tenuous condition and upcoming surgery. They accepted my apology, probably only because they knew we would once again pack the place for them every night. I guess Pete and/or Sonny, or both, had a one-night stand with the stripper, or vice versa. We never saw her again.

Luckily, they successfully got all of Mom's malignancy in the ensuing operation, but from then on, a new and uneasy sense of vulnerability about the future set in for her and Dad. Because he was twenty years older and not really very good at the practical and domestic aspects of day-to-day living, they had agreed in an unspoken contract that he was to go first. Dad knew that Mom, bolstered by her independent nature, would be able to carry on with her life securely. Both knew he would have a struggle on his hands if she went first. This reality was to settle into Dad's psyche, and I'm sure it had a major influence on the last year of his life.

He was the most positive man I ever have known, and he still maintained his belief in the good of his fellow man as an individual. However, he became more and more cynical about people en masse, citing how religious, political and ethnic organizations by their very nature tend to separate rather than unite people, spawning power grabs and greed, and quite often, hatred. If, God forbid, there were ever to be the ultimate downfall of civilization, he felt the masses would make a most considerable contribution. In thinking about Dad's thinking, it seemed to me that he felt just maybe the only possible way the human race might finally band together as one to eradicate bigotry, separatism and lemming thinking, would be if it was to be invaded by aliens from another planet. Then we'd be forced to unite in order to insure the survival of the human race, fully recognizing that we are really all brothers and sisters. Amen! And I second the notion.

I was with him at the hospital after his second heart attack, and we were watching the Rochester riots on television. He turned to me and said, "Isn't it sad when the only way you can get anyone to do anything anymore in this world is if you slam them up against an alley wall, and put a knife to their throat. Otherwise, negotiations tend to be nothing more than idle chitchat."

"Chitchat" was a phrase Dad also used often in describing mundane pleasantries, meaningless gossip or mere speculation. He was never much into any of that. He also got me into examining the word "tolerance," which I now find I can no longer tolerate. When I hear tolerance preached, I guess I'm supposed to put up with the intrusion of someone or something in my life that has not really been acceptable to me, so I should become tolerant simply to show that I'm civil. I much prefer the word "compassion." Compassion might eliminate perceptions for which tolerance is often espoused and possibly ultimately induce acceptance. For this reason, I would welcome as just an example, the idea of changing the name of The Museum of Tolerance in Los Angeles to The Museum of Compassion.

Dad felt that more than love, respect was what made the world go around. You can respect without love, but you can't love without respect. He gave me many things to reflect upon throughout the years, and they seem to rise to the surface now more often than ever before. Maybe it was by his design, believing all along that his influence would be greater after the inevitable were to happen to him.

He was right.

While Mom was recuperating from her surgery, Dad was pretty much a homebody filling his days in his studio, painting away. Golf became nine instead of eighteen holes. He continued to "live on velvet" and participate in a very active and varied daily schedule. But, accompanying that, was an underlying realization of mortality stemming from Mom's bout with cancer. The constant knowledge of his having an aneurysm that could erupt at any time started to prey on him more and more, just as, more and more, Mom was becoming her old self.

A real jolt occurred the day before his seventy-fifth birthday. Every American shared the same shock my dad experienced on that November 22, 1963, and most of us can recall exactly where we were when we heard or saw the incomprehensible news that President Kennedy was assassinated.

You might say Dad was *quite* a fan of JFK?

I know that Dad looked at this event as a metaphor that mirrored his own immediate existence. He saw that his health had caused more limitations on his ability to entertain and communicate the creativity and skills he so masterfully displayed throughout his life. He was also seeing Mom (perhaps once again she had called upon the Fates), mercifully saved in time to allow for the opportunity to participate in the prime of her life. Dad had crammed one hundred fifty years into his seventy-five. His beloved Susan still had plenty of time.

Gummo had been a card-carrying hypochondriac for many years, and always out of a loving concern, became my dad's advisor on all things medical. Unfortunately, Gummo's ongoing effort to keep everyone informed about everything was turning Dad from Harpo to Hypo. Dad had always identified with his mother, Minnie, who had succumbed to heart problems. Gummo only fueled Dad's belief that he would fall to the same condition. Mom always saw the light in Dad, sometimes a glow, sometimes a fire, and sometimes the sun's shine. Though he eagerly looked forward to every new day, she saw him become more obsessed with his health, and little by little, find less interest in his other quests. Oh, there still was the love of his harp, his clarinet and his painting. But quietly, he was committing himself to the implementation of his and Mom's unwritten contract.

And by the light Mom was seeing within him, she also knew.

It was September 27, 1964. Lyle Ritz and I had finished our gig at Dino's Lodge, and exhausted, we went to an all-night diner called **Theodore's** for something to eat. We wound up sitting with some other musicians who were also through with their gigs and just as hungry as we were. Many of us were into playing silly word games, and on this particular evening, we all chose to singularize song titles. My close friend, Cliff Norton, the wonderful character actor, (not the tailor or deli owner) and I would often amuse each other inventing and playing stupid games just to pass the time on long automobile rides. On one occasion, when we were overcome by singularization, we were inspired by our destination, which we proudly renamed La Vega, where we had reservation at the Dune Hotel. Hilarious? Hardly, but when you've been driving through the Mojave Desert for what seems like an eternity, you're usually going to

Cliff Norton

be rife for giddiness. We would go on and on about where our next trips might be, like Walla, Washington; [Phoenick, Arizona; Dalla, Texa, or maybe even Desert Hot Spring, California to stay at One Bunch Palm.]

Lyle and I were punchy from the long evening, so it was easy for us to lapse into some silly song titles. "I Only Have Eye for You," "Tea for One," "Day of Wine and Rose," "Thank for the Memory,"

"This Is the One of My Favorite Thing" got us going, and soon, everyone was contributing. We even got into lyrics like, "For it's one strike you're out at the old ball game."

The more dimwitted we became, the more raucous our table got that night.

That night I laughed as hard as I have ever laughed. The following day, September 28, 1964, would be forever memorable as "the yang of the ying." Gummo and several knowledgeable doctors convinced Dad that it was essential that he have an operation to correct his aneurysm. Mom was fiercely opposed to the whole idea, believing that it was too dangerous a procedure for a man Dad's age who suffered two previous heart attacks. Wouldn't it be better to let everything just take its course and maybe allow him to pass away on the fifteenth hole of his beloved Tamarisk Country Club golf course that he created along with his Hillcrest pals? But Mom was out voted, so she did the best she could by acting as if it was nothing to worry about. Dad chose to have the operation, and so, on the 27th, the eve of their twenty-eighth wedding anniversary, Mom drove him up from Palm Springs to be admitted into Mount Sinai Hospital in West Hollywood. It had been a quiet trip, and Dad seemed to be peaceful enough, though in some kind of spacey funk. Mom described to me an eerie moment in the admitting office when he was asked his full name.

"He didn't seem to hear, and I had a feeling he was looking back in time. The administrator gently asked him again, and Dad answered vaguely, "Duer, Arthur Duer." Oh, God! I wanted to grab him and run. Alice Duer Miller, one of his closest friends, had been dead for many years.

That afternoon, Alex, who was into his finals at college, came to the hospital to see Dad, bringing him words of good cheer and positive thoughts about the success of tomorrow's operation. Jim wished he could be there, but Dad knew Jim was serving his time in the Armed Forces, and he was just unable to get away. Instead, Jim sent his spirit as a proxy.

That evening, I showed up to wish him well just before I went to my job at Dino's and told him I'd see him tomorrow. Later, Minnie and her fiancé, Jerry, came to his room with a chocolate cake to represent them at an anniversary party, which was now going to be celebrated differently. They had wanted to have their wedding date the same as Mom and Dad's, apparently something to do with establishing a tradition. Minnie and Jerry had accepted Dad's feeling of urgency about his operation, so they would wait until November 28, at least staying with the same number while giving him a couple of months for a full recuperation. They had to get back to college, so they kissed him and left.

Felix Unger and Oscar Madison.

Mom told me, "I didn't want to leave, but there was no excuse to stay. Trying to hang onto him, I reminded him firmly, tomorrow is our twenty-eighth anniversary. I'll be here with the other kids as soon as they let us in. So you be in good shape, or it'll spoil the party."

He looked up and said, "Okay, Mom. You go now. I'm going to take a nap."

Mom had been staying with Gloria Stuart, her closest friend, in Brentwood. Gloria's career in motion pictures has spanned over

Mom self portrait.

seventy years, culminating in an Academy nomination as Best Supporting Actress for her work in the remake of **Titanic**. Gloria and Mom were perhaps the female version of **The Odd Couple**, as was evidenced in the varied artistic endeavors they shared over their years together. First of all, Gloria's personality was outgoing, Mom's was more introverted. Gloria loved acting, Mom hated it. Gloria painted beautifully, mostly in the "primitive" style. Mom was a wonderful draftsman, being very "representational" in her work. Gloria loved having gallery exhibitions of her art; Mom put her art in the closet. Gloria became a world-acclaimed printer of rare art books; Mom chose to hand-carve exquisite frames. Gloria loved her white wine; Mom stuck to vodka. One thing they agreed on artistically was that silk-screening was too damned backbreaking a medium. The one thing their personalities unquestionably had in common was that at the drop of a fedora, they both would let you know exactly how they felt about any subject in the world, pulling no punches when offering their opinions.

On the morning of September 28, we all received the news in the morning that the operation to eliminate the aneurysm was a success, and Dad was resting comfortably. Whew! It was truly a day to celebrate. We went to the hospital later that afternoon, only to have found otherwise. Dad didn't make it.

Because the operation took four hours to perform, it was too much for his heart to take, and about six hours later, it went into shock, which led to a massive coronary. Mom had been right. At his age and with his history of heart problems, the operation never should have been sanctioned. But there was another factor involved. It became evident that he had already decided to honor his end of that unspoken contract. Mom told me later that she had seen it coming, and he had willed himself that it was time. For him, he saw Mom's mastectomy as triggering a new vision of their future, recognizing that sometimes we have no control over our own lives, and that unforeseen things can happen at any time. He was aware of how fortunate he was to have been able to play his own hand for so long. Mom had overcome some bad cards she had been dealt, and now it was her turn to take over his place at the table.

She was twenty-eight when they got married. Now it was the 28th and the day of their 28th wedding anniversary. It was the one day Dad didn't make it. He no longer needed to.

That night, Mom and I went back to Gloria's house with a different reason in mind from the one we had planned. Gloria had champagne on ice to celebrate what was to be a day of both a successful operation and, of course, their anniversary. When we all decided to pop the cork, we toasted Dad's life, his achievements and contributions. Then we went on to get drunk, at least numb enough to accept the fact that Dad had now completed his engagement on earth, breaking all records for living life to the fullest.

The critics even loved him as much as his old friend Alexander Woollcott did. Adolph Arthur Harpo Marx had attained the rare distinction of having died without an enemy.

"You know, Dad, I have worked so damn hard over the years to forgive you for abandoning me and all the rest of the world when you did."

"It was time for me to go."

"Come on! You weren't ready at all. Your health was under control, Mom won her bout with cancer, the kids were off on their own, professionally you were as busy as you ever were, and we still had more tunes to learn and some golf to play. What the hell are you talking about?"

"I had lived all of what life had offered me. I was tired. You guys still had your youth and energy. It was now your turn."

"Sounds instead like you were being pretty damn selfish. You denied us. Christ! You took away *my* role as your father. My job was over. I was lost. I even wound up in therapy. Thanks a lot."

"That's not my problem. When you're confronted with your own moment of truth, you will only find peace when you do what truth tells you to. I did what I had to do, Son. And you'll do what you have to do."

"What's that?"

"How should I know? See ya later."

Neither Mom nor Dad wanted any kind of memorial service, but against their wishes, Gummo insisted on having a get-together at his house in Beverly Hills. That way, every one of Dad's friends could have an opportunity to pay their last respects before we left town for Palm Springs, where Mom and I needed to start dealing with some of the problems that now confronted her as a widow. Just as we expected that afternoon, everyone was somber and there was a dreary pall that permeated everything, including the tray of cold cuts from **Nate 'n Al's Deli.** Mom kept looking at her watch wondering when we could get the hell out of there and beat the traffic going home. The whole "tribute" was teetering on the imperceptible line between the maudlin and the morose.

All of a sudden, as if on-cue, in walked George Burns. George had lost his beloved Gracie a month earlier, so he knew what Mom was going through. He found his way across the living room to the couch where Mom and I were sitting. Then he knelt down in front of Mom, took her hand in his, looked up at her and said, "Susan, I know Harpo and Gracie won't mind. Will you marry me?"

In a split second, George had transformed the place from a mausoleum into an Irish Wake, and Dad wasn't even Irish. Neither was Mom nor George. He had just demonstrated a perfect example of what he had once told me—Never walk into a room without an opening line. Everyone loosened up and for the rest of the afternoon; Gummo's home became the site for a joyous celebration of my dad's extraordinary life. George had also made our drive to Mom's home in the Springs much easier.

The hardest thing for us to deal with was losing the roles we played in Dad's life. Over his last ten or fifteen years, Mom had become his mother, and since I had been sixteen, (by that time he was already sixty-four) I had always felt a fatherly protection toward him and the responsibility to look after his practical as well as musical needs whenever possible. Now Mom and I would have new roles to play. Mom and I were confronted with something that we didn't know, but would ultimately learn. It was something that Dad didn't ever have to learn, because it was what he already instinctively knew. Be yourself.

We still had each other.

I returned to immerse myself in the world of score paper and piano keys. It gave me a purpose in what I now came to view as a purposeless life. No more harp arrangements for Dad. No more golf with Dad. No more anything with Dad. I was afraid to think about that, because I felt I was not quite ready enough mentally and emotionally to allow myself to become vulnerable to my feelings. So I lost myself in my work to shut out my memories. That would be all right for then. The memories were to surface later.

Among a myriad of things that Mom had to address was the question of what to do with Dad's two harps. One was with Mom in the Palm Springs home, and the other was at my place in L.A., where he would stay when he had to do a television show or whatever. Mom continued to be in touch with Teddy Kollek, whom she and Dad had met during their trip to Israel. He was still the mayor of Jerusalem, and Mom had the bright idea of contacting him, because she had remembered that the harp has always been Israel's national instrument. In her correspondence with Teddy, he put her in touch with A. Z. Propes of the Israel Ministry of Tourism. The timing was perfect to do this, as every third year, Israel hosts the International Harp Contest, and this was the year. Mom agreed to sponsor the second prize money, and she and I were honored to be asked to serve as judges for the competition.

As presentor of the harp contest awards, Isaac Stern, the great violin virtuoso and humanitarian, accepts our check for sponsorship of the second place winner.

Further correspondence with Mr. Propes revealed that in the land of history's most famous harpist, King David, there were only two harps in the whole country. One belonged to the harpist for the Philharmonic Orchestra in Tel-Aviv and the other with the harpist who played for the Philharmonic in Jerusalem. Both of them taught as well, but their many students would have to practice on the harps of their teachers, depending on the availability. So Mom arranged to donate Dad's harps to Israel, helping to solve the problem of the scarcity of harps, while extending their life by having them played.

Simple enough? Not quite. We were notified by The Bureau of "Fly in the Ointment" that all musical instruments entering Israel had to be charged a one-hundred-percent import tax of each harp's original price of twelve-thousand dollars. Unless this sum was waved in some way, Mom would give them for the same purpose to the school, Cal Arts, right in Los Angeles. She wasn't offering a work of art to be viewed, but an instrument to be used. Unlike the violin or piano, the harp does not improve with age. The extreme tension created by the strings on the sounding board shortens the life of the instrument, and causes the beauty of its sound to deteriorate unless it is played and lovingly cared for. But Mom insisted we make the trip, with or without the harps, so Mom and I were off to Israel for eight weeks for the competition, the presentation of prize money and a lot of sightseeing to get a feel for the "cradle of civilization."

As it turned out, Mom had appealed to Max Targ, president of the Chicago Board of Americans for a Music Library in Israel, who persuaded the Israeli Ministry of Education to accept the harps through Targ's agency. This was a marvelous group, sensitive to the need of music for emotional survival in the immigrating Jewish nation. It created an all-important means to supply musical manuscripts and instruments along with the money to pay the exorbitant Customs fees. So thanks to Max, the harps arrived in Israel; one was sent to the Rubin Academy in Jerusalem and the other to the Rubin Academy in Tel-Aviv. Hopefully, in future competitions, there would be one or more Israeli contestants that would qualify, now that they had something to practice on. I find it ironic that, though a famous harpist, Harpo Marx, never was involved in the world of musical academia, at least his two harps were now a part of it.

It was a good thing Mom and I got out of Los Angeles for the two months. It was August 1965, bloody hot, and heat can often make people very angry. The mood of the city was perfect then for the Dodgers/Giants baseball rivalry, which is always hostile anyway. The Giants pitcher, Juan Marichal, was the hitter at the plate, and suddenly he turned, and with his bat, tried to brain the Dodgers catcher, John Roseboro. The reason? Marichal claimed the last pitch was thrown much too close to him. And his nearly hammering of Roseboro into unconsciousness was in retaliation for what the Giants team had been claiming; that Roseboro had been calling for too many "brush back" pitches in order to keep the Giants hitters from "digging in" against the Dodgers pitcher. The benches cleared, and all hell broke loose as the bad blood flowed. Marichal was ultimately suspended a year for the indiscrete assault that got the city of Los Angeles up in the bullpen, to warm up for their upcoming riots.

We, however, were in another part of the world that also had a heated but much more serious rivalry going on, adding to the personal experience of sightseeing in Israel. We got to see it all that which was right in front of us, while imagining what it might have been like throughout its turbulent history; King Solomon's Mines, The Dead Sea Scrolls, Masada, Nazareth, The Sea of Galilee, Mount Scopus, the highest point of the Judean Hills. One doesn't need to be deeply or even superficially religious to sense the profound purpose ingrained into every inch of the country. And every inch of the country and its profound purpose is forever ingrained in my heart.

Israel has impacted my thinking about existence for all people. After all, none of us asked to be here on earth in the first place. We just showed up one day, and so we all should have a right to participate equally in a crap shoot called life. Throughout the human hardship, sacrifice and bloodshed this hub of civilization has endured throughout the ages, how ironic that it should be the home of the "Prince of Peace." I often wonder if it's possibly too much to ask that finally, one day that entire region will mercifully embrace His message of "love thy neighbor." Believing myself to be much more an idealist than a realist, maybe that's why I've always rooted for any underdog and against the New York Yankees.

Taking in some serious history in the cradle of civilization.

I'm at the Truman Forest in Israel, in the same place where Dad had visited four years prior. His spirit is with me.

"And now, ladies and gentlemen, for your listening pleasure, the International Harp Contest!"

You would think so. Twelve days of competition engaging the finest harpists in the world, with beautiful music wafting from their heavenly harps. Guess again. The compulsory Hindemith piece is wonderful for a few hearings, but when you have to sit through it fifteen times, it becomes something akin to Chinese water torture. As a composer and not a harpist, I had to rely as a judge more on the contestant's interpretation rather than their technique to make my assessment of a performance. Mom's knowledge of harp literature amounted to whatever she heard Dad play. The rest of the judges, all of whom were harpists, were able to blend technique and performance in their decision-making process. Apparently we all came to the same conclusion anyway, when we voted a little French girl to be the exquisite winner in a grueling duel with three Russian girls of almost equal skill that took second, third and fourth prizes.

Because of Israel's sophisticated appreciation of the arts, you almost come to expect twelve days of harp competition to fill auditoriums every day with music-wise audiences. Their serious attention to the quality of each gifted contestant made us doubly focused on our job as judges. Their attention would also help keep us from the occasional embarrassment of being caught nodding off. Especially during the Hindemith. It takes a hell of a lot of courage to expose oneself to the probability of losing your dream of winning. Somehow, Mom and I wanted everyone to win, mainly because losing goes deeper than any success. It's also very hard to handle when you have to be unnaturally sporting as the door to the future is shut in your face. These brave and talented contestants gave me a far greater understanding and appreciation for the dedication and discipline it takes in pursuing whatever goal you choose.

I suppose the thing that stands out in my mind more than anything else about the event was either a misprint or a bit of humor we found in the official program: "Once again our land echoes to the sweet gentile notes of this most ancient of musical instruments."

And in Israel yet.

(Incidentally, for you trivia buffs, the harp is not the most ancient of all musical instruments. It was something called the "Kinnor," a form of Lyre mistranslated as "harp," with which King David exorcized the evil spirits from King Saul.)

(Thanks, Bill)

Neither Mom nor I remember very much about the final evening and the presentation of the awards. I guess there was a reception afterwards with the traditional buffet, and of course, a lot of broken hearts. But they all passed the true test, that of putting all their preparation on the line to show everyone the very best that they could do. *That* they can carry with pride for the rest of their lives. And just like in baseball for many teams, there will always be the perennial battle cry, "Wait'll next year!"

Back home! Back to work! Back to something I never had to deal with, the "M" word. I had been dating a very nice Jewish girl whose mother was turning a deep shade of blue from holding her breath until her daughter got 'M'arried. Stara had lost her father, Al, when he was only thirty-seven, to a weak heart caused by rheumatic fever as a child. He was taken at the top of his career as an arranger/conductor, which he started as musical director for Olson and Johnson's ***Hellzapoppin'*** stage show. He later became the protégé of Paul Whiteman, working for the West Coast part of radio's Blue Network. During the Golden Age of Radio he arranged and conducted for such programs as ***Take It or Leave It, The Tony Martin Show***, and even had his own hour-long show. Because he was a dead ringer for the fine actor, Leslie Howard, he doubled for him in all the long shots in the movie, ***Intermezzo***, and it was his hands in those close-ups playing all those difficult violin solos.

Stara and me

So, of course, Stara and I would have in common a love for music. Humor and animals were high on the list as well. If you can imagine hearing a female Mel Brooks or Myron Cohen, you would be listening to Stara. She can do dialects like Cohen and remembers every line of Brooks' "Two Thousand-year-old Man" albums and from all of his movies. Also, she was much cuter than both of them. She was particularly influenced by her maternal grandmother, Yetta, who came with her sister from Poland to the United States at the age of fifteen.

Yetta Kornitsky, Stara's grandma.

In all her eighty-plus years on the planet, she never lost her Polish accent, and never got a good grasp of the English language. If she was angry about something, she could throw a "transom." If she was tired, she would lie down to "relapse" for a little while. Her favorite flower was a "hybiscuit," and she loved any building that had "ivory" growing up the walls. Yetta had a canary that used to sing all the time, so she named it Frankie Sinatra.

Often, after throwing one of her "transoms," she would go down to the Wilshire Boulevard bus stop and announce to anyone who was standing there that she was going to commit "sooscide" by throwing herself in front of the next bus that came along. Then, instead of following through with the threat, she would go back home, call us up on the phone and always give the same reason why she didn't let a bus run over her. She said that she was afraid it would hurt. Ask her what her favorite movie was? "Oy, vhat's da use talkin'. *DA VIND VENT."*

Almost everyone's favorite.

Stara and I were awakened one night at 2:00 A.M. with a call from the rest home where Yetta was living. They requested that we come down the first thing in the morning and remove her from the place for violating one of their rules. It seems that they found Yetta, then eighty-seven, in bed for the third time that week cuddling with the ninety-two-year-old man that lived down the hall. The rules prohibited this kind of behavior. It was a tough decision to make, because the rules are the rules. But we also felt that it was tragic that they would think that Yetta and the old guy were doing anything other than just cuddling to get a little human warmth. I mean, what harm in that? To think about it, the greater tragedy was in that it was probably the only thing they were doing.

Stara has always adored animals. From her very first dog, Tuffy, to our dog throughout our marriage, Esther Marx, and her present-day companion, Noodles, she has always had a very large place in her heart for them. Even the vast arrays of cats I have had were special to her. To name just a few over the years, there were the ever-present cat hair and fur balls of Blanche, Irving, Harvey, Mister Morrismarx and Gregory, who I never saw much of. However, one day I was more than surprised to find under my house Benny, Jake and Lou, all kittens from a litter produced by

Gregory! Now I knew why I never saw much of Gregory, whose name incidentally was immediately changed to Lady Gregory.

If there was a flaw to Stara that was to haunt her for much of her life, she was a compulsive consumer. But Stara did it with a different spin. Before I would trundle off to work at Dino's Lodge at night, she would make dinner for us. The table was always set thoughtfully with a colorful tablecloth and matching linen napkins. We both were very neat eaters, rarely if ever spilling anything or soiling her table setting. One day I suddenly came to realize that I never saw any of these settings more than once. The following day, Stara would fold up last night's tablecloth and napkins, put them in their original box and return them to the store where she bought them. After explaining to customer service that they clashed too much with the décor of her dining room, Stara then made an exchange for another equally pretty tablecloth and napkins that were to grace our dinner table that night, once again, for the last time. This constant behavior of hers was buttressed by a genetic overdose of chutzpah, something I always admired about her, even when it was misdirected.

Martha Stewart has had nothing on Stara.

Oh yes. Dino's Lodge!

CHAPTER SEVENTEEN

Now you didn't really think I would forget, did you? And also that glass of wine. Well, I am at Dino's playing the first set. Sitting at a coveted two-table is Jim Morin, dressed in his three-piece Brooks Brothers suit having dinner by himself. Jim is a management consultant for Hughes Aircraft. For the last six months or so he has come in once a week, and whenever I play his favorite song, "*The Look of Love*," he sends over a glass of wine and an invitation to sit with him on my break. As a result of this downright neighborly habit, we have come to know a little bit about each other in these very casual moments together. This particular evening is not particularly different, the song, the wine and the invitation. But as I sit down at his table, Jim raises his glass of wine and immediately proposes a toast. I ask him what the occasion is. He and his wife, Donna, have just adopted a baby boy, named him Paul, and he wanted to share the news with me because he had read **Harpo Speaks!** and knew that I was also adopted. We both take a congratulatory sip of our wine, and then I ask Jim, "Where did you get him from?"

Before I finish posing the question, I sense what his answer is going to be. "The Children's Home Society."

"I know."

"But how would you know?"

"Thirty years ago I was adopted from the Children's Home Society."

We both sit there a little stunned and take another sip.

"Bill, I know enough about you to be convinced that you would be a perfect choice for what I'm going to ask you. I know that you had a Godfather, Alexander Woollcott. I thought it might be a nice idea for our son to have one also. Might you please consider being the Godfather of our new child? One day he may need someone other than his dad to confide in, or maybe show him how to throw a curve ball or whatever he might need."

This time I take a gulp. I think the request is rather odd at first, and I tell him that there might be a problem in that I know he was Catholic and I'm not. He says he doesn't think that will stand in the way at all. So after a minute of thoughtful consideration, and I really don't think the wine had anything to do with my response, I tell him that I am most honored by his offer, and that I will be happy to accept.

Jim and his wife Donna live about an hour's car ride east from Los Angeles in the town of Loma Linda. Jim stays in an apartment in L.A. Monday through Wednesday for easier access to his job, and then he returns to Loma Linda Thursday night and stays through Sunday. He asks me if I am available to come to Loma Linda that Sunday for the baptism ceremony and meet Donna and their two other children, Peter and Stephanie. I tell Jim I think I can forego a pro football telecast for a change and make the trip. He is thrilled, but I am a little apprehensive, as he describes the parish as being somewhere in the boonies, situated right in the heart of an orange grove.

Somehow that Sunday, Stara and I find the way to this somewhat attractive and obscure oasis in a desert of orange and green. As we arrive, there is already plenty of anointing of the child going on. Jim introduces us briefly to all the players, Peter, Stephanie, Donna, my Godson, Paul and the presiding priest. The place is teeming with doting relatives, each one playing tweaky-cheeky with baby Paul. Not long after, the Priest asks that Jim and I come to his office to clean up all the legalities. We follow him there, where he pulls out a pen and some official looking papers. The priest's first question is the exact name of the adopting father. Jim says, "James Morin."

"Could you please spell out the last name?"

"James Morin, M-O-R-I-N."

"And the name of the Godfather?"

I respond with, "William Woollcott Marx, M-A-R-X."

"May I please have the name of the adopting mother?"

Jim's turn, again. "Donna Morin, M-O-R-I-N."

"No, I mean her maiden name."

"Donna Klapperich, but I'm not sure if there is one or two 'p's' in Klapperich."

I immediately chime in with, "There are two 'p's' in Klapperich. K-L-A-P-P-E-R-I-C-H."

Jim and the Priest look at me quizzically, and see that my face had turned ashen. Jim asks me how I know the spelling.

"Because thirty years ago when I was adopted from the Children's Home Society, my name was James Klapperich."

"Wait a moment," Jim blurts. "You must be kidding. If you're not, was your mother's first name by any chance Verna?"

"No, I have my birth certificate and my adoption papers, and on them they say the name Veronica."

"Would you know if she taught piano? Donna had an aunt who taught piano."

"On my birth certificate it says under mother's occupation, 'pianist.'"

We all realize that right then an amazing coincidence has occurred in that I had the same unusual last name as Donna, my birth mother and her aunt both played the piano, both their names began with a "V," and yet we aren't related. When we are through with the rest of the information that the Priest needs, we are still intrigued enough about this weirdness to tell Donna of the coincidence. It is a good thing that she is holding baby Paul very, very firmly in her arms when we inform her of our update. She tells us that her heart has just skipped a beat, and her legs are wobbling.

Regaining her composure, she also agrees for sure that there is no possibility of our being related, if for no other reason than she knows her Aunt Verna never had a child. The rest of the day proceeds without any more *Twilight Zone*-type occurrences. I think about the whole day on the drive home with Stara and later at dinner over yet another fancy table setting.

A couple of days later I receive a phone call from Donna thanking me once again for becoming Paul's Godfather and for my making the trek out to Loma Linda for the "Big Day." She then tells me that she has called her mother and talked about the coincidence at the Sunday baptism ceremony. When Donna mentioned the fact that, along with us having the same last name, my piano-playing birth mother's name was Veronica and she also had a first name beginning with "V," her mother informed Donna that though her piano-playing aunt was always known by everybody as Verna, her real name was, in fact, Veronica. That made what happened that Sunday even more bizarre, but her mother confirmed the fact that Donna's Aunt Verna never had a child. It is great that Donna has followed up with the phone call to get the extra information, and I thank her for her interest and concern about the whole thing.

At Dino's with legendary studio bassist, Steve La Fever.

Dino's starts out spacey for me that night, but it's amazing how music always has been able to refocus my mind, blocking out whatever is on it, and so before long, the trio is swinging, business as usual. I guess Jim is still in shock, because I don't see him for a while, but I am already into being back at the old haunt doing my music thing. There is Harrison Carroll in his booth with tonight's "maybymightbe" actress. And of course, Richie, the bartender is there pouring for a lot of the regulars, Max, a waiter, at a table about to secretly add two more extra pats of butter to his most popular scrumptious, cholesterol-riddled Alfredo sauce simmering before his pouring of it over the waiting pasta, and at the door, Luigi, the maitre di, doing his typical Luigi thing of making you feel so special by his "going *way* out of his way" in case you hadn't made reservations for finding that one *extra* available table just for you. (And if you tipped him real good for it, from that day on, he'd remember your name forever.)

Another night at the office.

The next day I receive a call from Donna who tells me that her mother has called her back, admitting to a long-standing family secret, that Verna once had a child.

Recent photo in front of one of Dad's paintings with cousin Donna, also a very gifted artist.

CHAPTER EIGHTEEN

McAllen, Texas. Maybe some of you are not familiar with the city or its location. Well, it's right next to Pharr. Now you know. These cities are situated near the Mexican border and the climate is just perfect for raising citrus fruit. That is basically the reason that Raymond Klapperich relocated his family to this region from what was once the town of Conde, South Dakota. I say what "once was," because I can't find the place on any map I've ever looked at. Conde, I mean. South Dakota is still there.

Conde, S.D. circa 1910. Verna (in front) and the farm-family Klapperich.

Like every other city in the United States, except apparently Conde, McAllen has grown considerably since the Klapperiches moved there in around the early 1930s. During that time, Ray became perhaps the most formidable of all growers of Texas grapefruit. He and his wife, Anna, had five children; among them were Tex, Florian, Wilfred, Mayoma and Veronica. Ray Klapperich's wife and five children certainly bought into the picture Ray painted of himself.

Ray and Anna Klapperich

Though he was not an imposing-looking man, being tall with a wiry build, he was the archetypal patriarch, ruling with an iron hand. You would find him at the end of the day, right in his big living room, sitting in his big, black leather chair, which he placed right in the middle of his big living room, with his big brass spittoon fortuitously right next to his big, black leather chair. Ray played the fiddle and Florian played the viola, and both instruments could be found on the floor of the big living room, placed there to avoid the sun's damaging rays.

Ray's big living room also housed a piano and organ. Everyone in the family sang to the best or worst of their abilities during the almost daily musicals they had, which were only interrupted by their other pastime, that of playing all kinds of card games. Ray was a devout Catholic and extremely rigid in his beliefs, with a view of life and people that made him a very intolerant man. Anna was far more commanding looking than Ray. Standing barely at four-foot-eleven with the figure of a middle linebacker, she was born, I swear, with a permanent scowl etched in her face of granite. Well, let's just say I never saw a picture of her with any other expression. But through the cold exterior image was a rather easygoing woman, designated

Veronica Klapperich

Veronica Klapperich

by Ray to be a second-class citizen while dutifully carrying out all the requisite activities of a mother and farmer's wife. Eventually, she would betray the role of a trusted wife to her domineering husband.

Veronica was the eldest of the brood, and at the age of ten, she was stricken with spinal meningitis. It rendered her more than just partially crippled on the right side of her body, and it caused her to drag her foot when she walked. Her right hand was deformed as well, and the disease also affected her speech. Having her posture visibly affected, she would compensate for this misfortune by making her own clothes to hide her deformity. Deemed and ridiculed by her family as homely, she was self-conscious about her looks and very cautious about dating.

But Veronica had something no one else in the family possessed—an innate talent for music. And throughout her life, music was her sublimation. It was manifested in her love for the piano, and in spite of her deformed right hand, she became a professional pianist, making a decent living by teaching, playing for the silent movies, various functions, performing on the organ for her church and often working as an accompanist for singers. Veronica was a take-charge person, and was the one child that Ray could always count on to properly carry out his orders. Her strict Catholic upbringing was responsible for a much disciplined and hermetically-sealed existence. Of course, there are always exceptions to the rule, and one of them was to cause quite a stir.

Irving Weisfeld

Irving Weisfeld, his brothers and sister all found their way out of Poland during the late 1920s for obvious Jewish reasons. One brother wound up in Brazil by some mysterious decision, while Irving and his brother, Morris, came to visit their sister in McAllen, Texas. She had settled there a few years prior, having married a man in the textile business. Irving decided to stay for a while and went to work for his sister's husband. His real dream was to become a cantor, so his life in McAllen was spent between earning a living and developing his singing technique.

A Capella is a musical term meaning without accompaniment. Because of its difficulty in staying on key, any singer worth their life savings doesn't usually sing without some kind of instrument accompanying them. The piano is the most popular because of its flexibility, and it can closely resemble the fullness of an orchestra. Irving definitely needed an accompanist. One night he decided to go to the movies and there he found Veronica musically following the silent action projected onto the screen. They met, and soon came to recognize each other's dedication to and passion for music. They also fell in love.

For Veronica, Irving represented something she thought would never happen. To have someone in love with her meant that, for the first time in her life, someone saw beyond her looks and deformity. They both thought of it; a future cantor and a working pianist were to be an ideal coupling and a prayer answered by both. So one day, about four or five years into their secret relationship that publicly seemed nothing more than a fulfilling musical collaboration, Irving and Veronica decided that it was time that they did something that they had desperately wanted to do for so long, but had been afraid to take the chance.

Irving went to Ray Klapperich and asked for his daughter's hand in marriage. He was met with the strongest possible objection to the idea, which confirmed why they were always afraid to take the chance, as it was certainly influenced by the social attitudes of that time and place. Ray, in so many uncarefully chosen words, and there were so many words, told Irving how dare he even come to him with such a absurd, outlandish request, that he would never allow his Catholic daughter to marry a Jew and forbade them to ever see each other again. To Ray, Irving and Veronica was not exactly an ideal coupling. To Irving, this kind of bigotry was why he fled from Poland. To Veronica, it was the start of a heartbreaking battle between saving her relationship with Irving and continuing to please her father. But Ray could never take that big step to compassion. He could only be in control of himself and everyone else by what he knew, and not by what he could learn. This was to be his family's cross to bear.

Plan B was set into action. Knowing that Irving was the only love of Veronica's life, Anna and Mayoma secretly decided to help by arranging a long series of clandestine meetings for the lovers without Ray ever knowing. This Plan B was a pretty courageous mission for Anna and Mayoma to engage in, for their very behavior signified a betrayal of Ray's prejudicial edict, and risked irreparable damage within such a strict Catholic family. The excuse that Ray was given was that Veronica was either working at the silent movies or playing organ for church services. Ray would never know.

Dallas, Texas. I'm sure you all know where that is. I've never seen a map of Texas that didn't have Dallas on it. It was summer at the State Fair, and Veronica was working a job demonstrating pianos, when she suddenly felt ill, fainted and fell onto the floor. She was overcome by heat and nausea. This upstanding thirty-six-year-old Catholic woman had sinfully become pregnant out of wedlock; hardly the way the nuns had taught her to conduct an appropriate church acceptable life. Accompanying the accompanist's physical pain was the frightening thought that when she returned home, she would have a lot of explaining to do to a lot of people. Saddled with this huge dilemma, Veronica and Irving would have to make one of those tough life decisions.

Meanwhile, back at the citrus ranch, Plan C would now go into effect. Anna, Mayoma and Veronica decided on a story that would be in the best interests of everyone, especially Ray. Veronica and Irving agreed that this would definitely work for them and solve one of those tough life decisions. Continuing to hide any signs of pregnancy by the clothes she made for herself, Veronica went to Ray and asked him to allow her the opportunity to go to Los Angeles, because she has always wondered if she was really good enough to make it as a pianist in the big city. She was already at an age where it might be her last chance to find out. Ray reacted reluctantly but finally sanctioned the idea, probably because once when she was twenty, he had enough confidence and trust in Veronica to allow her a vacation to Venice, Italy.

Veronica in Venice.

As you might have guessed, permission from Ray was much to the relief of Veronica, Anna and Mayoma. Part two of Plan C was that Irving was to meet Veronica in Los Angeles, get married and settle down there as a family.

Los Angeles, California. I am absolutely positive all of you know that Los Angeles and California have the Pacific Ocean to the left of them on any map. They are to the right of the Pacific Ocean. You have to look quite a ways on a map to find the states on the right or on the top that border California, because it is almost as big as Texas. Veronica arrived in L.A. by train at Union Station and immediately found an apartment downtown on Beacon Street. She got everything together in preparation for Irving's timely arrival. That day came, and Veronica went back to Union Station to greet him when he stepped off the train. It was right on time, came to its crunching halt and the passengers started to slowly disembark. Her heart was racing with the thrill of seeing him, and the suspense grew as she waited eagerly for Irving to be the next passenger to get off the train. She then sat down on a bench and continued to wait until the very last passenger was accounted for.

It was not Irving.

The rest of Plan C was now apparently left up to Veronica alone. Not an iota of communication was forthcoming from Irving. Why not even one lousy word? She would deliver soon. He knew that. How could he do this to her? Veronica was devastated, hurting all over from his cruel and prolonged silence. She was now faced with the rejection she had so carefully protected herself from all these years. One can only imagine the courage she must have had in having to fight a lonely battle of survival through her despair. But she was a responsible and resourceful mother-to-be, and soon her inward depressive state turned into an outward anger that would be the fuel for her survival instincts.

The day finally came. That meant it was time for Saint Vincent's Hospital, and at 9:52 A.M., on January 8, 1937, James Wayne Weisfeld was born. It was a bittersweet occasion for Veronica and the first occasion of any kind for James. The love Veronica had for Irving would now have a new recipient; a dependent little boy recently arrived on earth who had no idea about anything that was going on.

The first two or three months for Veronica were spent simply taking very good care of the two of them. No doubt a natural bond between mother and son had already formed. They were forged together in the big city, and Veronica could no longer afford to look back, but forward to what the future would have in-store for them. That future was to depend first on her ability to make a living, as her finances were running low. Her new mission was to check out some nightclubs in the area that hired pianists. Certainly there would be a job for a woman in one of the clubs. So she began her quest, always having some sitter for baby James while she was gone.

It turned out to be much more difficult than she expected. She was met with more rejections and for more reasons; we already have someone, we don't hire women, we are discontinuing entertainment, we're a union house and until you join, we can't use you, and on and on. She got all kinds of excuses having nothing to do with her piano playing. After auditioning for one particular nightclub owner, he told her that she played all right, but he couldn't use her unless she showed some cleavage. That gig became a dead end because her deformity made it impossible for her to wear anything décolleté. Peripheral interferences were denying her the chance to measure her talent on the big city's musical barometer.

Time marched on, and one day Veronica noticed that time was marching on much too fast. It was November of 1937, and the reality that Christmas was right around the corner was weighing heavier and heavier on her mind. As a good Catholic, she knew how important for the family this religious holiday was. She couldn't use the same excuse she had last year for not being home, when she had just gotten to L.A. and needed the time for getting situated in her new apartment and the hang of the big city life. Frankly, she had no job, had no money and had no believable reason for missing this year's Yuletide season. If she chose to stay in L.A., her father would likely have a heifer and start to imagine some pretty rotten thoughts about Veronica's feeling for family and church. If she went home, she couldn't take baby James with her, showing up with, at that time, the popular tainted term "bastard child." If she was to leave the baby in L.A., who would she leave him with until she returned? The pressure of the predicament mounted with each passing day. Through a combination of careful exploration and practical reality, Veronica made another one of those tough life decisions.

Plan D was to be the hardest of all to successfully execute. It began with a trip one morning to a Five-and-Ten-Cent Store, where Veronica purchased a cheap gold-plated wedding ring. She then proceeded onto her next stop, a place that she had been investigating for some time as an alternate choice in her tough life decision-making process. She found the right building, walked in and asked to see one of their social workers. The lady that was assigned to interview Veronica was both a highly sympathetic woman and a skillfully trained professional. It wasn't long before the questions started coming toward Veronica. She had come with the possibility of placing her baby in their care, while she continued to look for work. The social worker then asked for the baby boy's birth certificate.

"I notice here that it states that the father's name is Irving Weisfeld."

"That is correct."

"He is your husband?"

"Yes, he is"

Noticing Veronica's wedding ring, the social worker asked, "Are you really married?"

"Of course I am."

"I'm afraid I don't believe you. What I do believe is that you are, in fact, not married, and that you're wearing a phony wedding ring you probably bought yourself." It became immediately obvious to Veronica that others could now see through her, for she had become as transparent as a cheap motel towel. She then admitted to being an unwed mother and was left to answer truthfully more red tape questions from the social worker.

The interview concluded with Veronica signing papers that would put her own baby James in their care. The stipulations during a required probation period were that she could have visitation every other day for one month only, or until she had proof within that same time frame that she was financially solvent enough to take back her baby. He was then admitted to the agency and became known as James Wayne Klapperich. Veronica had so much to do and think about in such a short period of time. She continued looking for work, this time as a salesperson as well, but she was having no luck in the one area of expertise she had.

Time was marching on faster than ever before, exacerbating her frustration.

With love and hope in her heart, every other day she came to see her baby boy. And with love and hope in his heart, he must have been ecstatic whenever he saw her and filled with such painful feelings of abandonment every time she went away. Especially the last time she came to see him. Veronica Klapperich's decision to give up her baby boy for adoption surely was the most pivotal moment in her life. It certainly was in the life of James Wayne Klapperich. Did she make her choice from having baby James' best interests at heart, or was it for her own self-preservation? A bit of both?

Veronica and baby James never could have returned to McAllen together. It would have been hell for them. By going home alone, no one would have to know anything about anything, and by leaving her own child in L.A., there was that chance that a family might come along one day soon and provide for him a much better life than she was capable of ever giving him. Veronica returned home to McAllen, Texas, to share with family and friends that most joyous and festive time of the year, I'm sure all the time wondering what her excuse will be for not going back to Los Angeles when the Christmas holidays have passed.

CHAPTER NINETEEN

McAllen, Texas. You know where that is. Mission is also right next to it. When Veronica returned to her family and friends in time for the Christmas holidays, everyone was filled with great anticipation to hear all about her adventures in "glamorous" Los Angeles.

"Who did you meet that was famous?" "Did you get to see Jean Harlow or Clark Gable or any other Hollywood movie stars?"

Everything they wanted to know was everything she was not interested in talking about. There was only one thing on her mind. There was only one thing occupying the space in her heart. It's not easy to kindly respond to peoples' questions, while you're painfully thinking about something else. That would just about sum up the holidays for Veronica, and I was told, much of the rest of her life.

Ray was thrilled to have his eldest little girl back home and was helpful in getting her back into the flow of things, especially when she announced that she had said adieu to L.A. once and for all. I was never able to find out for sure what explanation she gave for this decision. Though in fact, I believe that there must have been at least two that she offered; the one she gave to Anna and Mayoma, and the one she gave to Ray and everyone else. However, the one reason most probably used was that she couldn't find any permanent work as a pianist. What was left for her was an occasional gig here and there. She also had no emotional support from anyone in L.A., and so in time became just plain discouraged and frustrated knowing that she wasn't making a living playing piano, which was really the only thing she knew how to do.

Anyway, whatever reason she gave certainly worked. Ray was so happy to have her back that he bought her a trailer to hitch onto the back of her car. He customized the inside all by himself, building a table, chairs and cupboards for lots of her sheet music, and topping it all off with the additional installation of a brand-new white spinet piano. This way Veronica could provide curb service to all of her students in a very attractive and most practical setting. She could now go from home to home teaching little children how to play the piano. As many of them as she taught for the rest of her life, fate was to keep me from ever being one of her students, and she was never to be one of my teachers. Anna and Mayoma remained silent, and would have swallowed their cyanide capsules rather than give up Veronica's agonizing secret.

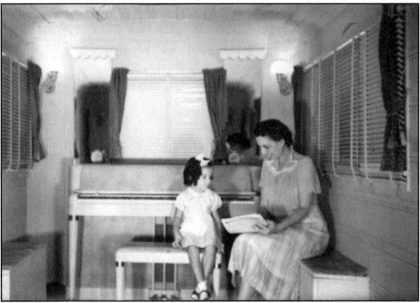

Curb service as Veronica teaches inside her trailer.

And what about Irving? It turned out that he couldn't handle the pressure of a non-sanctioned mixed-religion marriage along with the responsibility of being the family breadwinner in a new city. So instead, he went to Brazil to visit his brother, and stayed there until he found out that Veronica had returned to McAllen for good without their child. After he came back, they would meet now and then on the street, awkward as those times must have been. But they both remained civil to one another, thus avoiding any possibility of instigating gossip in their small town. Not long after, Irving fell in love, married his first cousin and had a daughter. Because of this rather strange circumstance, I have a natural second cousin, who is my step-mother, and also a natural third cousin that is also my half sister! (One more family indiscretion like that, and I could've been my own grandfather!!) A few years later in 1943, while still working for his brother-in-law, Irving was transporting some textiles on the highway to Houston in a truck, when the driver fell asleep. As the truck swerved, Irving's elbow hit his door handle on the passenger side, causing the door to unlock and open. Irving was thrown from the truck and crushed to death by the oncoming traffic.

Veronica never married and continued to teach little children until 1963, when she was visiting Mayoma and her husband in Pontiac, Michigan. Mayoma told me that during that short visit, Veronica confided with great concern, "If I only knew that he was all right, then I could have some peace."

Two days later she passed away in bed at her sister's home at the age of sixty-three from a heart attack.

Much of what I know about Veronica was told to me when Jim Morin and I went to visit Mayoma after the shocking revelation that Donna and I were first cousins. Mayoma was most gracious with information, but she also gave me a few of Veronica's personal effects, including photos, sheet music and a recording of her emceeing Ray's eightieth birthday celebration. I even had the opportunity to catch a quick nap on the very bed Veronica had died in.

But, wait, there's more!

When I was about twenty-five years old, I was dating a girl whose closest friend was married to a guy by the name of Hal, who was about seven years older than I. The four of us went out on a number of occasions to a movie or dinner, and we got to know each other pretty well. But apparently not well enough, for when I uncovered the true story of my birth background, I came to find that Hal was also my natural first cousin! On Irving's side.

Yes, I guess the Fates, that Susan so strongly believed have controlled everything that ever happened on earth, were at it once again. And what if the Fates had written my life vice versa? Suppose

Harpo and Susan were too busy with their movie careers and other outside interests to deal with raising a kid? They had heard through the grapevine that there was a couple in McAllen, Texas that desperately wanted a little boy to adopt. Today, I might be a nice, well-respected Catholic in the McAllen community, holding down an executive position for my uncle in textiles. And think, under the astute tutelage of Grandpa Ray, I could also be a genuine card-carrying, narrow-minded bigot.

I confess that I never even thought about my being adopted, nor did I have any interest or concern about who my birth parents were. One day when I was around four years old, my dad went to his safe, opened it and pulled out my adoption papers. He explained to me what adoption is, and why he and Mom adopted me. Dad then showed me my real name on the document, "Klapperich." I responded to the name as any four-year-old would, and Dad and I had a good laugh together when I asked him if that is something you have to go to the hospital for. That was the extent of my concern about my having been adopted. Only the chance meeting with the Morins would change my mind about seeking out any information as to who my birth parents were and how I came to be adopted by Susan and Harpo. Then the whole situation became just too weird to not pursue. My sister, Minnie, was once asked how it feels to be adopted. I thought she put it best when she replied, "I don't know. How does it feel to not be adopted?"

Minus some physical or genetic restriction, anyone can be a mother or father. That's the easy part. But it takes a special couple to understand what parenting is all about. Not everyone has those skills. I was just plain damn lucky as hell to wind up with two people that really had what it took to guide me, my brothers and sister with true parental care and understanding. We were chosen, and all of us were ready.

There are some things that I will never come to know the why of. I shall leave that to the Fates, if I have any smarts left at all.

CHAPTER TWENTY

"Dad, does it bother you that I found out who my parents were?"

"That depends on what you mean."

"I had mixed feelings about all of it. Two people who had plenty of problems even without me. I feel sadness and pity for the lives they had to live.

"I feel sadness and pity that they didn't get the chance that we did, watching you grow into the person you are."

"But they gave me music, or at least the ability to appreciate it."

"That's a nice gift."

"At one" with my score paper.

"What strange thing it is to learn about your parents in your thirties."

"You've always known who your mom and dad are."

My years at Dino's Lodge had come to an end and I started scoring scary movies for American-International Pictures, because they gave me more of an opportunity to utilize some of the musical influences of Bartok, Stravinsky, Shoenberg etc. that I had been exposed to back in my Juilliard days. I was able to write more "farther out" than the conventional movie would demand.

My first, **Count Yorga, Vampire**, turned into quite a cult classic. I also scored its sequel, which was thoughtfully titled **The Return of Count Yorga**. (Sometimes you just can't keep a good vampire down.) Garlic was becoming my favorite food. I even had some hanging outside my front door. Then I went on to do **Scream, Blacula, Scream**, which I am proud to say won a Golden Turkey Award for the year 1973. But the more pictures I did, the less I was enjoying my life. The pressure I felt from directors, who were both indecisive yet demanding ("I don't know what I want, but whatever it is, I gotta have it yesterday"), was making me so stressful, that I was starting to get my asthma attacks once again. Therefore, I decided to temporarily bow out of film scoring in hopes of incorporating a less intense way of making a living in music. Besides, after having underscored so many "kills" in so many movies, I feared that I had finally used up all my musical ideas. Horrified at the thought of being asked once again to compose one more cue for even one more "kill" was enough to make me believe that it would surely kill me instead. So I bade "Sayonara for a while" to film scoring.

My marriage to Stara also came to an end. In spite of our love for music, humor and animals, we wound up taking a stroll down boredom lane, and one day three years into our marriage, ended up getting a divorce. I found out during the process that it was another form of abandonment with which to deal. It probably would have been easier for us just to stay together, but at some point in life you have to have the courage to say no. It's simply survival—are you going to take the lessons you've learned from life and apply them or are you going to bury your head in the sand? As much as it hurt, we did it. Crummy as it was, years later we realized how right we were and we've been dear friends ever since.

After that I moved to Topanga Beach, a "nude-optional" little cove off the Pacific Coast Highway. Though I never participated in the buff life, I sure as hell learned that eroticism exists in your brain, not your eyes. Dad would have loved the place, being an amateur nudist himself. He was so comfortable with who he was that it was no problem for him to doff whatever exterior disguise he was wearing in order to be more fully, freely himself. I, on the other hand, have never felt that comfortable with my stuff to go gallivanting across the horizon like a jay-bird. One more way that Dad was ahead of me in the self-actualization process.

I remember driving home one day listening to the all-news radio station, and they had just received word that nine people were arrested on a beach up the coast in Malibu for alleged nudity. I had to pull over to the side of the road to ponder this late breaking news story. How could you be allegedly nude? You either are or you're not. I know when I am not. It's a pretty easy thing to describe. (I'm pretty sure my dad was never allegedly nude. He only was or he wasn't.) And in a court of law, aren't you considered dressed until proven naked? Imagine how confused those people who were, wondering if they were really nude or going around just thinking that they were. As I recall, the judge changed the charge of one count of alleged nudity to one count of nudity.

At about this time I went in pursuit of my new dream. I got commissioned to compose a work for the Hollywood Chamber Orchestra by its fine musical director/conductor, Jerome Kessler. I hadn't written anything for the concert world for so long, that just being able to finish the damn thing was enough to give me a great sense of accomplishment. The fact that it turned out to be a rather sophomoric and self-conscious effort didn't deter Jerome from asking me to write another piece for the orchestra. Either he wasn't paying much attention during the performance of my first piece, or maybe he just wanted me to keep doing it until I got it right. I

had an awakening during the time I struggled to write my "Celebration Suite for Strings," which I chose to make as my present to Mom on her seventieth birthday.

Shortly after having gotten started, I got writers' block and stopped working. I had been preoccupied with the fear of whether Jerome, the orchestra or especially Mom was going to like what I was writing. It took me three days away from the piece to understand that I shouldn't be concerned with other people's assessment of my work; I must write what *I* want to hear and hope to hell someone else wants to hear it, too. Being true to my *own* musical taste is what must come out, for better or for worse, and I found the rhythm and flow for the rest of the piece. Happy Seventieth, Mom!

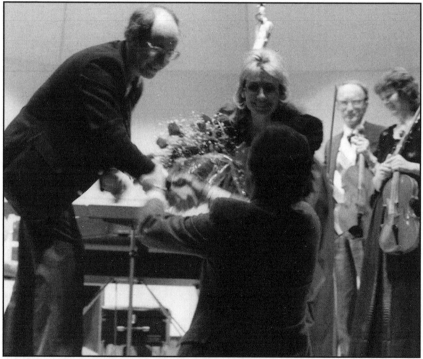

Jerome the conductor gets congrats from Bill the composer.

It was also during this time that, after several very-nice-for-a-while, then failed relationships with two lovely Marilyns, the first an actress/singer and the second a piano teacher, out of the blue, I became happily reunited with the concept of family. My pal, Cliffie Norton introduced me to one Sherrie Dong and her three children, Kim, Trish and Aaron. For nine wonderfully enlightening years we all watched each other grow, blossom and flourish. I was in there composing more concert stuff, interspersed with a piano gig here and there. Like the fadeout at the end of a tune came the time when we were to simply and unfortunately drift apart. But by then, her kids were solid citizens, Sherrie would now know the *best* delis in Los Angeles, and I would be hip to the *real* Chinese, both restaurant and her Mom's home-style cooking.

I still can't believe this was the time when I also spent three years or so as an actor trying to make it doing TV commercials.

My eight-by-ten glossies for all those un-erring commercial casting directors.

I did manage to be a pitchman for one or two piano stores in Southern California, but that was as me and not as an actor. The rest was a silly waste of time, except for the chance to hang with some of the actors I met at what is known as "cattle calls." I don't know about now, but at that time, these were auditions whereby every agent in Hollywood sent every actor in Hollywood that appeared to be the perfect type for a particular commercial, and we all sat around sometimes for hours on our ends to wait for the chance to be rejected by the Producer, Director, Writer, Cinematographer, Account Executive of the Advertising Agency, and yes, especially the Casting Director. All the times I was sent by my agent to answer a call as a pianist or conductor, I never once got the job, and I'm a pianist and conductor!

An actor friend told me he was once up for a commercial where they were looking for a specific elegant British butler type, someone that fit the description and demeanor of an Arthur Treacher. As he was waiting for his audition, he noticed, sitting right across from him was . . . Arthur Treacher. My friend knew right there and then that he had absolutely no chance to get the role. As it turned out, apparently Arthur Treacher wasn't right for it either.

Eventually, I finally quit my pursuit when I came to the emotional realization that any more rejection in my life may be hazardous to my health.

Most probably the very last picture of Dad and my four uncles together.

Oddly, while involved in my failed acting thing, I was getting to know the surviving Marx Brothers better than I'd ever known them when Dad was alive. The two younger brothers, Gummo and Zeppo, lived down in Palm Springs near Mom.

Gummo appeared to me to be the least Marxian of all my uncles. Exhibiting an inner calm and passivity, you had to listen carefully to hear his soft low voice, as he spoke very slowly, taking all the time in the world to finish a sentence, even if it had only three words in it. Of all the uncles, he was the most comfortable for me to be with, and like Groucho, he loved his cigars.

Zeppo was another story. He was easily the most aggressive personality of the Brothers. He had a very short fuse, and because of it, would often wind up duking it out with someone twice his size, and still make the fight quite interesting. Zeppo had been a remarkable physical specimen. Pound for pound, he was put together as well as anyone. The chest expansion of the great heavyweight champion of the world, Joe Louis, was two and a half inches. Zeppo's was an astonishing six inches. You can't begin to imagine the sight of him puffing himself out like a peacock.

After Zeppo and his wife, the soon-to-become Barbara Sinatra, had divorced, he sold his house and moved to a place in Rancho Mirage called Desert Island, which was completely surrounded by a body of water that was always stocked with fish. Zeppo's no-nonsense approach toward people made him the perfect selection to be the Fish Commish of Desert Island. It was his job to see to it that the fishing limit was two fish per person per day. One day he saw a guy pulling out many more fish than the limit.

Bristling with anger, Zeppo ran out to confront and admonish the man for breaking the rules.

"You SOB! Don't you know that there is a limit of only two fish per day?"

"Yes, I do, but I'm only down here on weekends, so this is two for Monday, two for Tuesday, two for Wednesday . . . "

Zeppo was about to haul off and deck him, when suddenly controlling his temper, he responded, "Hey, fella, you're good. Real good!," and walked away.

Zeppo's later years brought on serious ear problems. He had lost all hearing in one ear and was preparing for an operation to save his hearing in his other ear. He was dating a nice blonde girl named June who was blind as a bat without her "coke bottle" glasses, which she could never find to begin with, and for obvious reasons. I was at Zeppo's house one night having cocktails, and this was the conversation I heard between the two of them:

"Oh, June, darling, would you come here for a minute?"

"Where are you?"

"What?"

End of conversation.

It was in 1970 when I really got to know Groucho. These were his later, failing years, and creeping senility was his enemy during a time rife with surrealism. Erin Fleming, a feisty young gal, answered a "girl Friday" ad and became the puppeteer that would resurrect

Groucho from the embers of diminishing capacity and create reasons for his still being interested enough in living. From his start in show business at the age of nine, Groucho was always a "performing seal" and was never really comfortable unless he was working to an audience. Knowing this, Erin would continuously concoct various events that would honor Groucho, such as his receiving an Academy Award, or those wild parties she would throw for him at home and away. The parties at his house were the weirdest that I've ever been to, every single one like something out of a Fellini movie. Sooner or later, almost every major movie personality would make the trek up Foothill Drive in the Trousdale Estates to pay homage to Jeffrey T. Spaulding, Dr. Hackenbush, Wolf J. Flywheel, and Rufus T. Firefly et al. In a way it was tragic to me to know that those hysterically funny characters were no longer there for the people to appreciate once again. And they had left no forwarding address.

What you saw instead was a meek, tired, frail old man who would sing, "Peasie Weasie was a bold bad man, Peasie Weasie will catch you if he can," and then go to his bed around nine o'clock, where he would always be flanked by two gorgeous girls for a photo-op. Groucho would then fall fast asleep, but the party would continue on, stretching itself into the wee small hours. Elliot Gould was always there, sitting quietly, rarely interacting, and just taking it all in. Liza Minnelli was her usual flamboyant self. Bud Cort, "Harold" of the unusual and brilliant movie with Ruth Gordon, **Harold and Maude**, actually lived there for a while during this most bizarre of times. Sooner or later, Edie Adams, Carroll O'Connor, Sally Struthers, Berle, Hope and others were there to nosh and josh with "the one, the only . . . Groucho!" Thank you, Fenneman.

I will always hold dear, the evening when I spent most of the time (get this) playing piano along with Jack Lemmon. Jack was a much, much better than average pianist, with a special affection for the music of George Gershwin. So at about 11:30 P.M., he sat down at the treble part of the piano, and I sat at the bass part, and we played and played and played every Gershwin tune you could think of. We even played portions of his "Rhapsody in Blue" and "Concerto in F." Long about one in the morning, Jack's wife, Felicia, decided she wanted to go home and notified Jack it was time to call it an evening. He told her okay, in just a few minutes.

I'm with Uncle Groucho, about three weeks before he passed away.

He was not only having fun with the piano, but also he was having a fun time with ol' man Scotch.

At one fifteen, Felicia returned to remind him of the hour, and that it was time to go. He agreed with her, and said he'd be right there. At one thirty, Felicia was now really pissed, and issued her final request to Jack, who was by then, really in his cups. He told her to go get their car and he'd be right out as soon as we finished this last tune. At one forty-five, Felicia appeared once again, this time beaming with pleasure from ear to ear. She had taken another approach. She told him that, with great delight, she had purposely backed their Rolls-Royce into the outside wall adjacent to the driveway. You think the wall looked bad, you should have seen the Rolls. Jack then decided it was indeed time to go home, thus ending one of my most memorable and favorite of all my evenings. I am sure it continued to be that for him as well; for many years, whenever we would occasionally see each other walking the streets of Beverly Hills, he waved, pointed to me and himself, then proceeded to wiggle his fingers in mid-air, playing Gershwin on an imaginary piano, followed by a wink and a smile.

Jack Lemmon at a political fundraiser for Mom, who never did learn to play the piano.

I was always invited to these soirées, and I would accompany Groucho and any of the guests that wanted to sing a song or two. Erin would also arrange small dinner parties with various writers and show people. One such evening was with Mae West and her entourage of five guys, as unique a sextet as I have ever been around. There was a guy that looked exactly like Bela Lugosi, somebody else as I recall being the first centerfold for the then new **Playgirl** magazine, and the other three bodyguards reminded me of saloon bouncers I have known. At eighty-three, her body really wasn't worth guarding that much. This little gathering occurred just before the making of Mae's last movie, the much-maligned **Sextet.** (For me, both of her "sextets" will be memorable for all the wrong reasons.)

Groucho's stipulation to all of his celebrity guests who accepted his invitation to dinner was that they perform, or sing for their supper, but of course, only after Groucho sang "Peasie Weasie." All during dinner, I tried to convince Mae that Groucho meant what he said about performing, but she kept on saying no. Finally, at the end of desert, I cajoled her into doing her signature number, "Frankie and Johnny." The five guys lifted her off of her chair and slowly maneuvered her into the living room, frequently catching her from falling over and then propping her up again all the way until they reached the piano. "Bill, while I do the soliloquy, you just noodle around in the background until I give you the nod for a D7 arpeggio. Then we'll do the tune in tempo in G. Got it?"

"Got it."

So we started and she did a most remarkable, riveting performance of the three-and-a-half-minute soliloquy and then gave me the nod for the arpeggio. I went into tempo, and she launched into what everyone was waiting for, "Frankie and Johnny were sweethearts . . ." That was all. Suddenly she went blank on a song she must have sung four or five hundred times in her life. And after having remembered the entire soliloquy! That night, the audience got the appetizer but no main course.

Another evening at one of Groucho's intimate dinner parties, it was just Groucho, George Jessel, me and a Groucho biographer, Charlotte Chandler. Everything was pretty much about vaudeville and show business. Jessel asked what I thought was the most memorable thing about Groucho when I was growing up. It was at a rare dinner party at our house with all the brothers. Zeppo was regaling us with stories of their vaudeville years. This one was about the time when the two guys who were to be the front and back end of a horse that was an integral part of some silly sketch, got sick at the last minute, so Zeppo and Groucho, who weren't in the sketch, agreed to fill in and be the horse for that performance. Unfortunately, neither one of them had ever been inside a horse to practice the coordination between the two that was required.

As Zeppo was describing their ineptitude, Groucho started to laugh out loud, and when Zeppo got to the point where they couldn't see where they were going and wound up falling off the stage and onto the musicians in the pit, Groucho was himself falling off the couch with uncontrollable laughter. I turned to my mom and said, "I've seen Groucho crack a smile at a good joke. I've seen him even sort of laugh at a good story. But I've never seen him with tears in his eyes with laughter like I am seeing tonight."

Mom told me that Zeppo was the only one she knew who could make Groucho laugh like that. Zeppo was a very funny, gifted raconteur and accomplished dialectician, who somehow was able to tweak Groucho's funny bone like no other person.

Another favorite of mine was one of Groucho's recollections he also told me when I was young. What I remember most about the whole thing was that even *he* was amused while telling it. Appearing to enjoy anything was so unlike Groucho. The story I refer to occurred when the Marx Brothers were at the height of their Broadway success. As you probably know, the overwhelming desire to unsuspectingly pull the rug out from under any deserving pompous individual was always one of their primary goals on stage or in the movies. But their unified ego, when ruffled, would surprisingly surface on occasion in real-life situations. Well, as a kid, I always secretly wished that I could have the chutzpah that Marx Brothers had. I still wish.

It goes like this. The Brothers were asked by a very upper-crust society couple to briefly entertain one evening at their black tie party on Park Avenue. The couple had heard how popular these "Groucho, Harpo, Chico and Zeppo people" had become. The money was good, so the Brothers agreed to take the gig, as long as they could then get back to the theater in time for their regular nightly performance. In full costume, the Brothers arrived promptly at this most lavish apartment's front door and were greeted by a most stuffy, Arthur Treacher-like butler. After explaining to him that they were the evening's entertainers, the most Treacher-like butler informed them that anyone here who is hired as an employee is only allowed to come in through the back service door. As you probably already know by now, that's just not something you should ever say to the Marx Brothers.

Without putting up any kind of argument, and remaining cheerful, they fully cooperated with the edict and proceeded to the back door. Upon entering, they found themselves having to go through the kitchen in order to get to the living room where the guests were congregating. On their way there, all four of them thinking as one, surreptitiously, filled their pockets with the hors d'oeuvres and veggies that were waiting to be transported out of the kitchen.

When the Brothers finally reached the living room, they were greeted with great enthusiastic restraint by the host and hostess, who announced to all that the entertainment was about to begin. As the guests assembled, Groucho, like a circus barker, harkened to all, "Step right up, ladies and gentlemen! You're in for a real treat tonight! And so now . . . the show . . . must go on!"

The Brothers were still their cheerful selves as their unscripted act commenced. With impeccable timing and well-coordinated disdain, they launched every bit of food they had in their pockets in a torrential outpour at the stunned guests. Before anyone could stop or apprehend them, their performance concluded when the Brothers escaped hurriedly through the ugly mess and total chaos, out the not-to-be-used front door. They never got paid for that night's very personal appearance, but at least they did get to the theater on time.

I continued to compose for the concert world, getting more requests from various other orchestras, including at this time my previously eluded to "Violin Concerto," commissioned and performed superbly by the world renowned virtuoso, Israel Baker. However, another, more powerful awakening was developing within. It was a dream I had that started about two years after Dad had passed away, and continued resurfacing every couple of years with the same basic theme occurring in different venues. I would meet Dad and always be angry with him. I sounded like a Jewish mother admonishing her child. "How come you never call or write me anymore? You express absolutely no concern about me or my career and how it's going."

It was about this time that I finally figured out what this was all about. I was angry, hurt and disappointed in him for having abandoned me by dying. Would I now be left to my own devices to find my way through life? Maybe he was suggesting that perhaps I didn't need him any longer for his guidance. Or was I the one suggesting that to myself? My recurring dream of abandonment continued, and I was to remain angry at him every time he and I got together.

Until one day, many years later.

In 1984, the world, contrary to Orwell's prediction, had not come to an end, so I decided to go back to playing the piano. I was really missing the pleasure of playing for people in live performance. A few hotels had a piano in the lobby, so I took a job or two, until I wound up at the Century Plaza Tower Hotel. There was a small, romantic, intimate, wood-paneled holding room/bar adjacent to the Chaumiere Restaurant, which was there for your complete upscale, expensive, fine-dining experience. I opened the room in early 1985 and remained there till the end of 1992. During that time, I would take off the first three months of each year from 1988 through 1992 to pursue another aspect of my varied musical career.

In 1986, I got a foreshadowing call from one Carrol McLaughlin, who told me she was a harpist writing for some harp magazine. She wanted to get my permission to do an article on Harpo Marx and include an interview with me as well. We got together, and in the course of the visit, I found out that she was probably the leading touring harpist in the world, having done so for Columbia Artists Management for a number of years. When I told her that I had all of Dad's harp arrangements, she and I thought what a wonderful idea it would be if we did a concert where she played all of his arrangements exactly as he performed them on recordings, in motion pictures and TV. I would accompany her by playing the orchestral parts on the piano and also tell stories about my relationship with Dad. We tried it out a couple of times, before Carrol arranged an audition in New York for Columbia Artists in Steinway Hall.

Only three times in my life did I ever get a muscle spasm in my lower back, and this just had to be one of them. It was me with an unwilling demonstration of the "Groucho Croucho." I showed up the day of our twenty-minute performance after somehow having ladled myself into my tuxedo and doing my best to keep from tipping over from the pain. When it became our turn to show them what we had to offer, I torturously went from my forty-five-degree posture into a thoroughly vertical human being. Apparently, we were successful enough, because they decided to book us on tour for the following season. When I went back from the audition later that day, I found out, much to my horror, I had done the entire audition with my fly open. Carrol always wondered if that was the real reason we wowed them that day in Steinway Hall.

Carrol, who also did a great Harpo in the show, shown here with me being just me.

For the next five years, usually from January through March, we were on tour with our comedy/concert show, doing one-niters all over the country and parts of Canada. To give you an idea of what travel is like for anyone on the Columbia Artist's circuit, I believe it was 1991 that we drove 12,750 miles during the three months we were out. The van we drove housed Carrol's harp, all of our props, tapes, records, CDs and our wardrobes, yet it still had a tiny space where one of us could take a nap. But it was obvious there was just no room for my piano.

Now, musicians are very sensitive to the idiosyncrasies of their own instruments. This intimate knowledge establishes the expectations and limitations they must use in affording a comfort and confidence during performance. A true bonding, just like Carrol with her choice of harp. When you are on tour as a pianist, you don't have the luxury of that bonding. You never know what kind of instrument you'll get, or the condition it's in. Some good, some well . . .

You can go from the majesty of a Steinway down to a piano that sounds like it gets tuned at least every six years. Thank God for the attention. Some keys produce no sound because of broken hammers, so you have to learn quickly which ones they are to avoid them. Sometimes you'll be cursed by keys that stick, thereby having to pull them back up while continuing to play. Referring to the old but true anecdote about the club owner who, when questioned about the condition of his piano, remarked, "Oh, you'll love it. We just had it painted yesterday."

Well, I can recall one such key-sticking incident that occurred at a fancy country club.

I was checking out their very nice piano prior to my performance, when I noticed that one of its keys kept rubbing against and thus sticking to a slightly warped place on the wooden strip found in front of the piano. I thought, hey, by prying open the area between the key and the strip, I could create enough space to allow the key to move freely. So I quickly summoned a passing waiter and asked him if he find me a screwdriver as soon as possible. Sensing my urgency, in no time at all he hurried right back with a glass of orange juice and vodka.

Our daily tour routine was chiseled in granite. Up and out of the motel early morning and on road to next town. Check into motel rooms in afternoon. If time, take nap. Shower, get dressed and go to theater. Unpack stuff from van for show and go through sound and lighting tech rehearsal. Sit around in dressing room until show time. Do show, and then sell tapes and CDs in lobby. Pack up van, go to reception or try to find restaurant that's still open at 11:30 P.M. Go back to motel and sleep, until up and out of motel early morning and on road to next town.

One-niters can disorient you. Because of location, time and space become distorted and your reality is nothing more than seeing that you get to the next town on time. I remember us playing a number of consecutive dates in the Texas "Panhandle." We had always enjoyed working Texas, so this was no different to us, as we were acing each show. This particular night we got a standing ovation and then proceeded to the lobby to sign autographs and sell our tapes and CDs per usual. An old guy came up to me and told me how appreciative he was of us having come to perform our show for him and the good folks of his city. I thanked him and told him that of all the forty-plus states we had performed in while on our tours, we had always felt that Texas audiences maybe were to be our favorites of all, because they always appeared to be the most demonstratively appreciative. The old man put his hand on my shoulder, looked me square in the eye, and in an informative tone of voice, he informed me, "Son, you're in Oklahoma."

I knew that the intense rivalry between Texas and Oklahoma extended way beyond the hundred yards of a football field, and I was so embarrassed that I tried to recover with things like, "Oh, we love the Oklahoma audiences also! They're just like the Texas audiences, sometimes even more so!" He wasn't buying. I explained to him about our being on the road, hardly ever having the faintest idea of where we really are, and how the only thing we know for sure today is that we play Ponca City tomorrow night. He nodded, smiled and then with a big wink wished me good luck in Ponca City, that is, if we were to ever get there (heh-heh). We got there, and I guess with some of his luck. We must have been good that night, because the audience made us feel like Hereford, Texas had come all the way to Ponca City, Oklahoma, just for lil' old us.

One night I was brought to my senses in a way that my senses had never been brought to me before. Carrol and I were in the middle of our comedy/concert. In front of an audience of a thousand people, I delivered one of my punch lines. As I heard the audience break into laughter, in a split second I thought to myself, "My God! For a brief moment I just made all of these people forget about the six o'clock news. I have taken them away from themselves and made all of them someone else. I'm actually listening to a thousand people all at once laughing at the same time. What a remarkable contribution I have made to them, but what's more, how lucky I am for having had the opportunity to do so."

That was the magic moment when I came to believe that, of all the professions, as a comedian, they make the greatest positive impact on society. They are my real caped-heroes, having dedicated themselves to a most noble and rewarding life of making us feel good.

All this touring had me aware of just how close it must have been to those days in vaudeville with its one-nighters and "two-a-days." At one point, I wound up in Allentown, Pennsylvania. *"Symphony Hall,"* as it was now called since its complete refurbishing, was the beautiful venue we played in. It had once been used for vaudeville circuit shows and out-of-town tryouts. After our show, I was met by and cordially introduced to a man in his thirties that had been there to review us. Good God, a critic! And Good God, young! But his real purpose for our meeting was to inform me of the fact that in 1928, his grandfather was a trumpet player in the orchestra pit of this very theater, and one of the shows he worked was the out-of-town-try-out of the Marx Brothers' *Animal Crackers*. He wanted me to know that I had just performed on the very same wood floor of that very same stage that Harpo had performed on, and that I had dressed in the very same dressing room that Harpo had dressed in sixty-three years prior.

For me, thinking about being on the road reminds me of a letter Dad wrote to us when he was on tour with his own show in 1950. Mom saved it throughout the years, and one day gave it to me to keep. It was written in a hotel just a few days before Dad was to celebrate his sixty-second birthday, on the road, alone.

Dear Ma and Gang,

"It is now 11:30 P.M. after the show. The theatre was 2 miles out of town, business bad. I am sitting in the lobby, it is dark. I can't go in my room until I am ready to go to bed as it is cold. A Victrola is playing a hillbilly song. I drove in, and every town and people looked like Lil' Abner characters. I made a mistake after I spoke to you of taking a fisick. I spent the entire day and night on the can. At four in the morning last night on one of my trips I took a swig of Kayopecktate. My hynee was sore. I put some Zink ointment on. When I got back in bed, I smelt toothpaste. I realized my mistake but even that felt good. I played in Nashville last night in the dirtiest theatre I have ever been in my life. But I am hold up fine. I miss you all terribly. Just eight days more. I love you."

That was the last tour Harpo Marx ever did.

In 1985, in between my gig at Le Chaumiere, I agreed to another, shorter tour to promote the Limelight Editions reprint of Dad's autobiography, **Harpo Speaks!**. I guess it was about a ten-day trip, and long about the seventh day, I had clearly come to understand why God was ready to rest. And the wall of loneliness had come to hit me, big time. I was more than ready to go home, yet I still had three or four more dates to do before winding up in New York, beat as hell, to do the *The David Letterman Show* and the *Today* show with Gene Shalit.

It's the night of the Letterman show and I'm in the Green Room, which is where they hold all their guests prisoner before and during the show. I am so tired and about to drift off into dreamsville, when the Assistant Director bursts into the room to inform me I'm next on the show. He tells me to follow him, and I am yawning all the way as I stumble through a door, leading to the very dark backstage. The sound of the band is deafening, and it rouses me from my stupor. I notice right in front of me is a full-length mirror framed with exotically flashing strobe lights, flickering at high speed, and right in the middle of this, I see my whole being staring back at me and screaming, "I'm here to help you get your act together!" I looked into that mirror, straightened my tie, checked the puff in my hanky, saw that the hair was nice, and with the band blasting away at mach volume, I became so energized that upon hearing my introduction as the next guest, I flew onto the stage. I did all the right "It's in the book, *Harpo Speaks!*" stuff I was taught to do, (making sure I said *Harpo Speaks!* at least three times in the five minute segment when hawking your product on TV), and then I had enough time left over to relate a rather unusual story about Dad and me.

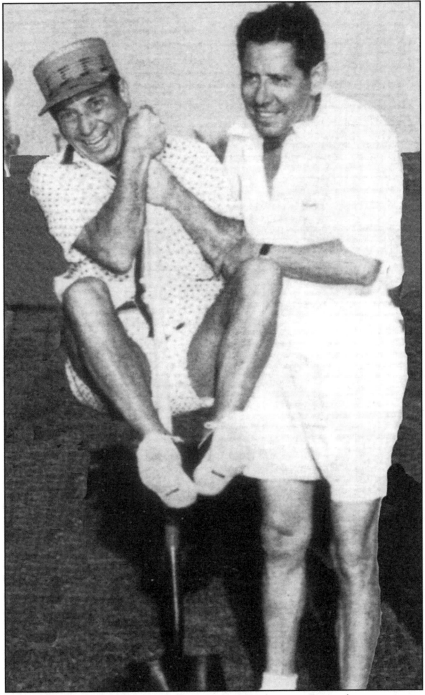

Tamarisk ground breaking with his producer pal, Harry Tugend.

Dad, who helped create and was one of the founders of Tamarisk Country Club in Rancho Mirage, with its golf course conveniently right across the street from the house, thought that it might be a nice idea just to play a little golf. It was off-season, no dress code to adhere to, and there would be very few people if any on the course. He said to me, "Bill, I'll go get the golf cart and meet you around at the front door."

It was as hot-as-hell, one-hundred-and-ten degrees, so I had on just my swimming trunks and golf shoes. He picked me up, and when I got in the cart, I noticed that he didn't have *any* clothes on. At first, I wasn't at all sure how to deal with what I saw or didn't see before me. And because he was seventy-three at the time, I surely didn't want to make him think that I might think he was starting to "lose it" mentally. So I decided rather than bring any attention to the fact, I would simply treat his nudity as commonplace and not make any mention of it.

He drives us to the first tee, gets out of the cart, selects his driver, tees up the ball and hits it his normal one-hundred-eighty-five yards straight down the middle of the fairway, then gets back in the cart. After I hit my drive, Dad shuttles us to our next shot, and the same modus operandi is underway for the rest of the round of eighteen holes. Because most of the people couldn't take the heat like Dad could, they would leave their homes for the summer. And so occasionally, he would hit his shot and then, to cool himself off, jump into any available neighboring pool that was adjacent to the fairway, climb back into the cart, and off we'd go again to our next shot until we had finished our complete tour of the Tamarisk Country Club golf course. That my dad was a true sun-worshiper and loved the desert heat was perhaps the reason I was probably chosen to have the distinct honor of being the first person ever to play an entire round of golf with someone who was totally nude. At which point, Letterman concluded the interview by saying, "I suppose I shouldn't ask where he kept his tees."

Somehow I managed to get through my following morning interview with that charming man, Gene Shalit, and then onto the plane that, and most gratefully for me, was soon to refute Thomas Wolfe's claim that, "You can't go home again."

"I'm getting kind of used to you popping in on me like this. I am even beginning to expect it. Afraid I might write about something you may not want me to divulge to the world?"

"I'm not afraid. I never had anything to hide. I have no regrets. Not even for my mistakes."

"Mistakes? Funny you should mention that, because during the twenty-plus years that we had together, Dad, I don't remember you ever making *any* mistakes, except for a wrong note now and then on the harp."

"First of all, Son, you couldn't possibly know what I considered to be a mistake. Hell, sometimes we're not even aware of our goof and/or its magnitude till after the damage is done. Other times we know of it right during our doing of the damage. You know that we all live with our own out-takes. So what? Mistakes are always a major part of living. Fortunately, I managed to recognize mine and chose to learn from them."

"Well, I've made more than my share. Looking back, I can't believe how dumb some of my life decisions were. What the hell was I thinking? But apparently they were correctable in the passing of time. All except for one. It was a real humdinger. Knocked me clear out of the batter's box for almost a whole season."

I made the decision to bow out of our tour after the 1992 season, and I finished out the year back in the Chaumiere holding room/bar. I was now truly beginning to feel that, at last, I was quite ready enough mentally to make another one of my life's decisions. Yeah, sure I was. 1993 was to be a pivotal year for me, starting with the decision to sell my house of twenty-six years in Pacific Palisades and move to the Palm Springs area to be closer to Mom, who was now already eighty-five years young.

As the eldest child, I felt it was my responsibility to look after her on behalf of our family, not that she needed my help or anyone else's. What I couldn't have possibly known then was the role reversal that was to happen between us.

I had been married to my second wife since 1988 for five very rocky years, rockier than the rockbound coast of Maine, which is why I haven't mentioned it until now. In spite of these most stressful of times, I did manage to do a couple more film scores, including the second Marx Brothers' documentary, ***The Unknown***

Marx Brothers, the first having been *The Marx Brothers in a Nutshell*, produced and written by already then two very talented up-and-coming young men, Bob Weide and Joe Adamson. For the concert world, I was also able to crank out my *Concerto for Two Harps and Orchestra,* and used it as a good excuse for me to return once more to Santa Fe for its World Premiere. (Apparently I am first to have ever tackled such a challenging musical task, as there appears to be no other work of its kind in harp literature.)

So in October of 1992, I thought that the change from L.A. to the desert would be good for all concerned. My "wife of then" agreed. I had enough money to live carefully but comfortably. I could go into semi-retirement while still gigging around to keep up my piano chops. I found a two- or three-nighter at the Westin Hotel that was the salvation for my fingers. Never had I ever looked so forward to those nights I could melt into some music. It was practically the only positive emotional experience I would have for the next year and a half.

CHAPTER TWENTY-ONE

Oy vey!!!!

CHAPTER TWENTY-TWO

Twice the amount of "oy vey," or for you mathematicians out there, "oy vey2." June of 1993. Carrol McLaughlin and I had been endorsed by Victor Borge to play some kind of international harp conference thing taking place in Copenhagen, Denmark. Whenever we had been away from the show for a while, Carrol always and wisely insisted on a run-through in front of a small group just to jostle our memory of it. So we had one of these at Mom's house the day before we departed for Victor B.'s homeland. I called around town to muster up enough bodies for our afternoon refresher course, and a pianist friend, Bob Ross, brought with him as his guest, his friend, one Barbara Herzog. Bob and Barbara also kindly offered to look after our animals while my then second wife, her son and I were out of the country for two weeks, including taking a side trip tour through Burgundy, France. When we were to return home, not surprisingly, the animals were still alive! That called for a celebration, so one evening, we all went out to dinner, and during the salad, my then "wife to the second power," who did nothing but chat with Barbara and no one else the entire evening, learned that Barbara loved to play golf. My then "wife after my first one" suggested that her thirteen-year-old son and I go with Barbara from time to time to a driving range and hit some balls.

Now you'll just have to believe me when I tell you the following; that because I have yet to lie to you this far into the book, there is no reason for you to think that I'm going to start now. This was nothing more than a nice, simple, uncluttered, innocent, fun-for-the-whole-family kind of plan that was put into effect. It became a regularly scheduled activity for some months, and I found that she was also comfortable to be around and a woman I could talk to, which was something I desperately needed that I wasn't getting in my marriage. The driving range was a metaphor for communication between us, as it became something I always looked forward to. But as time went on, as our marriage was crumbling from crummy to really lousy, my second wife suggested we separate for a while. She asked me to move out.

Mom had given me a room at her house to begin recuperation from, thank God, my one and only nervous breakdown. I was left shaking and unable to drink soup for a year.

I really knew I was in serious mental trouble the evening I was watching a rerun of the marvelously absurd Monty Python gang. You see, I have a comical dependency. Always having been a huge fan of theirs, *that* particular night was most extraordinarily different. As the show unfolded with its non-sequitor sketches, I found myself mumbling to the various "Montys" and "Pythons" as they scampered across my screen. I found myself telling them, "You're not funny, and that also goes for the crappy skit you're doing. Your whole show is one giant suck!"

Grabbing the remote, I hit the off button and shut them all up. I had inconveniently misplaced my sense of humor. And then in an instant of darkness, it became . . . . "the dreaded bedtime!"

Every night until I somehow drifted off to sleep, I would have a panic attack thinking about how my life would never be the same again, having lost almost everything I had worked for. I had managed to make some bad stock investments. After falling in love with a magnificent piece of property in Rancho Mirage, I spent a fortune remodeling the house that was on it, which should have been torn down or become a centerfold for **Lesser Homes and Gardens**. And there was the little money matter of how much of what I had left I would have to fork over in case it turned out we couldn't reconcile. Then I would wake up the next morning, once again starting my day with another panic attack thinking about the very same things.

One morning I got out of bed, went into the living room and sat in a chair, just staring out at what appeared to be nothing at all. I must have been there for at least twenty minutes before Mom came into the room, saw me in my self-induced funk and then dropped a piano on my head.

"Now this is silly, and you must stop this nonsense immediately. If you want to change what you think is your pathetic melodramatic situation, then do something. Anything. It doesn't matter what, just do something. Eventually you will start to do other somethings that will lead to other somethings. But you mustn't just sit there feeling sorry for yourself and expect a miracle to get you back among the living."

My morning routine was to change immediately, and it did. After first being greeted by a cup of coffee followed by a lovely song from the "Bluebird of Prozac," prescribed to help me out of my overwhelming depression, I would take a walk for a couple of miles. On one of these occasional traipses, a Jeep Wagoneer pulled over next to me, and a familiar solo voice came out of it. It was that of music publishing legend, Howie Richmond, who, along with his wife, Anita, was a very close friend of Mom's. Howie's varied career included being publicist for the Larry Clinton, Glenn Miller and Woody Herman bands, press agent for the Andrews Sisters and Gene Krupa, and managing Sarah Vaughn. Howie developed his own music publishing company, TRO, into one of the biggest, most successful in the industry, owning the catalogues of such artists as Kurt Weill, Anthony Newley, and Bill Evans to name a few. Our chance meeting on a residential, rarely traveled back road was to be pivotal in my putting Humpty-Dumpty back together again.

For the next fifty minutes, we sat in his SUV and chatted about poor Willy's "woe is me" condition. No matter how hard I tried to convince him of my justifiable desperation, Howie always had a positive answer for every negative notion I would bring forth. He was wise and slick, street slick, and by the time we said adieu, he had put me in a far better mental location than I had ever dreamed possible at the time. And doesn't everything important in life always come down to "location, location, location"? Even my gate became sprightlier as I sauntered down the barren back street, now with the new desire to get home to "do something." Thank you, Howie.

My personal restoration was a gradual process aided by those much needed nights I spent churning out my music at the Westin Hotel. It was also being exacerbated by that someone I had met only six months earlier, and through a strange circumstance was becoming more and more an important part of my life.

A great group called "Howie and the Richmonds."

So help me, I still will not lie to you. The day came when Barbara received a startling phone call from my then "wife of five years" asking Barbara to meet her for dinner. It seemed to be very peculiar indeed, in that they had not developed any kind of relationship nor had Barbara ever shown any interest in doing so. They had virtually nothing in common, yet my then "wife of sudden mood swings" was talking to Barbara as if the both of them were lifelong friends. What possibly was behind all this, and what might it lead to? Would Barbara's instinctive and very female curiosity eventually get the best of her? You bet your life! (Thank you, Groucho). So she warily accepted the invitation.

Barbara could tell there was definitely a strong message to be conveyed that was the main, if not the only reason for their getting together to share such a unique dining experience. It came quickly, even before the salad, and in the form of a most unusual request. My then "still my wife" began explaining how the twenty-four-year age difference between her and me was a troublesome problem. We no longer had the same interests to share and were drifting apart. Soooo, she thought it would be a good idea for Barbara and me to start dating!

Barbara as house model in Milwaukee at Gimbel's, (ironic?).

Superb singer, Jack Jones (son of Allan Jones, singer and leading man in *A Night at the Opera* and *A Day at the Races*), with Barbara in mid-1960s, also at Gimbel's.

Well, there was Barbara Herzog, a beautiful blonde from Milwaukee, Wisconsin, brought up to live with very Midwestern social attitudes of propriety, suddenly blindsided by the unexpected proposal set forth by this young lady sitting across from her. It was a wife recommending and sanctioning a relationship between her husband and another woman! All happening at the same time, Barbara rolled her eyes, breathed a huge sigh and responded incredulously, "Only in California!" The dinner ended with Barbara in absolute shock and also stuck with the check.

The next time Barbara and I spoke, she told me about this bizarre encounter. Quite frankly, throughout our entire marriage, my then "wife for not much longer" always pulled my strings. Now she was also pulling Barbara's. I have never been a fan of speculation. Just show me the existing facts, so I don't have to engage in supposition and the same old kind of "chitchat" that Dad found to be such an unnecessary, time-consuming exercise. And we, too, then found it to be unnecessary as well, because one irrefutable fact was coming into play that was to affect our decision-making process; we were falling in love. March 1994. My then "wife numero segundo" filed for divorce.

I suppose in retrospect, my now "second ex-wife" helped me get out of the mess she helped put me into. Her role as a matchmaker both aided and expedited my quest to be able to once again drink soup normally. The acceleration of my recovery was equal to the acceleration of my relationship with Barbara. And there was Dad, right in the middle of my metamorphosis. He had told me on a number of occasions that usually something fortunate will come out of an unfortunate situation, if you are willing to look for it and learn from the experience. I know that Dad would have approved of Barbara, and Mom sure did. Three weeks after my divorce became final, Barbara and I got married in front of the fireplace in Mom's living room. Being the archetypical traditionalist she is, Barbara "borrowed" a beautiful and delicate antique handkerchief of Mom's to satisfy the one of the "somethings" in that time-honored ritual.

I have always had trouble crying over sad things, but no trouble in shedding tears over things of joy. By another standard edict, Barbara would not allow me to see her the day of the wedding. So when she descended the stairs to finally appear that night, being escorted and given away by her maid of honor's husband, I started sobbing uncontrollably from the vision of her beauty.

As the ceremony proceeded, I recognized I was in serious need, so without thinking, I grabbed Mom's handkerchief from Barbara, and produced one hell of a honk into it while the justice of the peace rambled on. Traditionalist as she always is, Barbara was horrified that such a special heirloom could ever be selected for such crass usage.

Paraphrasing what Dad used to say, "When ya gotta blow, ya gotta blow."

Later that evening during the reception at Morningside Country Club, I took Barbara away to a quiet corner, where I felt like repeating to her the words that Dad honored my mom with fifty-nine years prior, "You are now Mrs. Marx forever."

Perhaps another, more important reason Mom was so happy with my getting married to Barbara, was that she was tired of finding different ways to explain away the fact that her fifty-seven-year-old son was still living with her, and even worse, his being only *half* Jewish. Our marriage became a merger of Barbara's house, her furniture, her dog and every other damn thing that were hers, and my family memorabilia, though I must say she had some of hers as well. Howard Herzog, Barbara's father, better known in the Midwest and elsewhere as "Buck" by the adoring readers of his column, was for many years the entertainment editor for the ***Milwaukee Sentinel*** newspaper in the days when they actually used typewriters.

For Buck, it couldn't get any better than hanging out with Frank and Der Bingle.

When Buck passed away, the city had a motorcade through the streets of Milwaukee, and thousands turned out to say their fondest of goodbyes to him. But Buck, none of those people would ever come to know that your greatest single contribution, your daughter, would one day find her shining way into my life. Thank you, Buck.

WE INTERRUPT THIS BOOK TO BRING YOU A MOVIE!!

Yes, folks! I, too, like everyone else in America, have written a treatment for a screenplay to be produced by a major studio that surely will make me a lot of money. When writing is not a person's chosen profession, one will then usually write about something that has happened in their life. Familiarity breeds content.

So, my inspirational content for such a lofty endeavor has come from the time when my mother chose me as Successor Trustee of the Harpo Marx Trust in 1998, and I was immediately confronted with a very surprising, most sudden and serious legal problem, imperative for our family to address and overcome. The gist of the matter, much to our satisfaction, was ultimately resolved in court and became grist for a new Marx Brothers' movie that I have since written, produced, distributed and screened many times, but of course, only in my own mind's eye.

However, I am now compelled to introduce the Marx Brothers to the twenty-first century by sharing with you their latest, long-overdue return to the silver screen. So, I implore you to just sit back in your favorite easy chair and transport yourselves to the world of the Surreal. (Popcorn not included.)

DUCK THE SOUP

THE MOTION PICTURE
THE TREATMENT

[CRAWL ON BLACK BACKGROUND]

Attention, all Marx Brothers' fans! Alas, there has been a *"trentino"* in our midst, using surreptitious manipulation to empowerment that is most undeserving. His arrogance represents a display of unconscionable disrespect for our beloved country, *Freedonia*, and all of its loyal subjects.

It has been his effort as head of the dreaded country of *Sylvania* to annex us by usurping our rights, thus ousting our fair and just ruler, Mrs. Teasdale, and uniting fairest *Freedonia* with his country through a series of well-calculated deceptions. But at last, our crack (adjective) undercover operation's team has harvested some irrefutable evidence that will surely expose his antics to the entire world, thereby causing all to rejoice in knowing that no one need fall prey to his misadventures ever again!

And who then has been summoned to lead our forces to a most convincing final victory, you must ask? The answer is as simple as duck soup.

[DUCKS SPLASHING AROUND IN A SOUP TUREEN UNDER MAIN TITLES]

EXTERIOR MONTAGE OF GORGEOUS COUNTRY LANDSCAPES, EROTIC FOAMY SEA SHORES, BUSTLING, PRODUCTIVE RETAIL AND WHOLESALE CITY LIFE AND A WEATHER MAN PREDICTING YET ANOTHER BEAUTIFUL DAY IN *FREEDONIA*

SIR LAWRENCE OLIVIER SOUNDALIKE NARRATOR:

When we last left the fair country of *Freedonia* only one movie ago, they had enlisted a crack (same adjective) undercover operations team to help unravel a plot to sign away an array of the country's economic rights without their knowledge or consent. As you might have guessed by now, their revered leader, Mrs. Teasdale chose a team that would use the most unorthodox and outrageous methods to expose this sly and insidious **Sylvanian** power play. Who then would heed her call?

THE MARX BROTHERS TO THE RESCUE! For all the faithful fans of the Brothers and fair *Freedonia*, a bit of background history is in order.

(THE FOLLOWING IS THE ACTUAL MOVIE OUTLINE IN ITS RAGGED ENTIRETY)

One apparently fine and harmless day, "*trentino*," the unctuous leader of the country of *Sylvania*, came to Mrs. Teasdale with a business proposal for his country and her country to enter into, in tandem, leasing out various property rights they owned, in order to help the neighboring country of *Balgesia*, a tiny monarchy one can barely find, situated due west of the *Cape of Little Hope*. *Balgesia's* use of these licenses would help to revitalize its sagging economy, while the spirit of trade between the three countries would continue with unquestioned trust.

After careful scrutiny by *Freedonia*'s top legal experts of the ensuing contract presented by "*trentino*," Mrs. Teasdale signed the document, securing the deal, and then she and everyone else in *Freedonia* all went out and had a drink.

Everything seemed to be running smoothly for all three countries and their economies, until, by a remarkable and purely accidental happenstance, the Marx Brothers stumbled upon a very troubling discovery, one that would ultimately have a negative impact on *Freedonia*'s ability to negotiate trade with other countries, thus stifling their once robust economy for years to come.

Why had they suddenly become neglected by the rest of the world's business community? What indeed did the Marx Brothers find out in their own unique fashion that would be of great consternation to every decent, law abiding *Freedonian*? Why also would this be of concern to any and all loyal and adoring fans of fair Fredonia and the Marx Brothers, as well?

"*trentino*," who needs additional assistance to carry out his master plan, hires Harpo and Chico as his left and right hand men. He would have enlisted Groucho as well, but he ran out of hands. Little does he know that they are <u>Freedonian spies</u> assigned to monitor "*trentino*'s" every move!

The fruits of their counter spying were to come into evidence, when, during a gin game with Unfortunato, ("*trentino*'s" minor Domo), Chico, after going down with twenty-seven and easily winning the hand, found out in a weak moment from the dejected Domo, that a licensing deal had been made by "*trentino*" with *Balgesia*, including in it Fredonia's participation for a tidy <u>eight</u> figures, (not referring to the figures the Brothers usually chased after). Chico dutifully reported this information, as was his job as a counterspy, and upon being told of this news, Mrs. Teasdale immediately went into shock and fainted in a very lady like fashion.

When she returned to consciousness three days later, she explained to everyone that the deal with *Balgesia* that was presented to her by "*trentino*" was for only <u>six</u> figures. This created many a furrowed brow in all of *Freedonia*. It was now time for Mrs. Teasdale to appoint Groucho the "Official Ambassador to *Sylvania* as

Liaison in Charge of Getting-to-the-bottom-of-it-all."

Meanwhile, having been told of this huge financial discrepancy, Harpo, elected by everyone who didn't want to take on the risk doing it themselves, is asked to somehow get into *"trentino's"* safe, where all of *Sylvania's* legal documents are kept. Not knowing of the possible danger that could lie ahead, with naive stupidity, he destroys the tape and accepts the mission.

As luck, and a blow torch would have it, along with rather wretched *Sylvanian* security, Harpo, after a considerable time taken in sawing open the front door, entered *"trentino's"* mansion unnoticed by all, blew open the safe, creating a noise heard way back in *Freedonia*, and then despite the enemy's lukewarm, strategically pathetic pursuit, still narrowly but successfully escaped into the night, hailing down a waiting ostrich on loan from *Walt Disney Studios,* and trundled merrily back to fair *Freedonia*, having absconded with a bulging raincoat full of papers.

Upon Harpo's triumphant return, Mrs. Teasdale, in traditional manner with her tribunal looking on, proceeded to ceremoniously empty the raincoat's contents, which included take out dinner menus, invoices from *"trentino's"* personal tailor, and unpaid parking tickets. Suddenly, at last!

What to everyone's wondering eyes did appear? Emerging from the heap was the very document providing the very answers that fair *Freedonia* was looking for!

This discovery made fair *Freedonia* really upset. They had uncovered a contract that *"trentino"* had *secretly* entered into with the Prime Minister of *Balgesia*! By not having known of the agreement's existence, until of course Harpo's heroic effort, this information was to represent a monumental affront to the trust that Mrs. Teasdale had so graciously placed in the coexistence of the three countries.

What was particularly rankling was that the document divulged an enormous personal *economic windfall* for *"trentino."*

Mrs. Teasdale was also filled with enormous rancor at the *Balgesian* Prime Minister, until, during the urgent phone call she placed to him generated by her harboring un-Mrs. Teasdale-like thoughts consisting here of unprintable nouns, adjectives and adverbs, he became equally shocked and disclosed to her that he had no idea "*trentino*" was *clandestinely* and *illegally* representing *Freedonia*'s interests without her knowledge or consent. Mrs. Teasdale was so relieved to find that there was not a conspiracy involved, and immediately sent the Prime Minister, on behalf of all *Freedonians* anywhere, a heartfelt letter of apology and a basket of *Freedonian* fruit.

She then spent no time in unfilling herself of the rancor she had filled herself with, misplacing it on the unsuspecting *Balgesian* Prime Minister, and immediately redirected it at the unscrupulous "*trentino.*" When he heard at a hastily called summit meeting that *Freedonia* counterintelligence (a job Chico was well qualified for, if you catch my drift) obtained the contract that "*trentino*" had entered into, specifically *assigning all of Freedonia's trade licensing rights to Sylvania and to himself personally as president of some Sylvanian production company,* the ever slick "*trentino*" calmly responded to this most grievous accusation, "THERE MUST BE SOME MISTAKE."

Groucho, a very discerning and understanding Ambassador, upon hearing this reassurance by "*trentino*" that there was some mistake, agreed with him that in fact, there was indeed some mistake. Concluding that "Boy, that *was* SOME mistake!"

Groucho took from his pocket, a glove he uses while playing right field in the *Freedonian* Softball League, and without even having any rehearsal, simultaneously was able to strike "*trentino*" across his cheek while declaring, "THIS MEANS WAR!"

Meanwhile, on the field of battle, the hostilities commenced, but the litigation lingered on. And on. And on. And, like most litigations, on. There were a number of Counts to be addressed, but most of them were home sick or on vacation. So instead they smartly dealt with the ones in the lawsuit.

Soon, news of a possible settlement spread through the gallant *Freedonian* troops like a bad bowl of grits, helping them to turn the tide of battle their way to an ultimate and lasting triumph.

Back in the courtroom, after endless verbal infighting, a breakthrough finally occurred, and so it became time for the presiding judge to read the terms of the settlement agreement that had been reached! This turned out to be more than just a lopsided judgment in *Freedonia*'s favor, and more than just.

Not only did the court and three different judges agree that "*trentino*" was *guilty of fraudulent behavior* in his negotiations with *Balgesia*, but most importantly, *Freedonia got all its licensing rights back in perpetuity, along with a sum of 90,000 Krellmans,* which were sure to help defray some of the legal costs stemming from those undecipherable legalese phrases that forever lurk in mystifying billing practices.

Oh, to be fair, one decision went in favor of *Sylvania* on a stupefying technicality (something you can always bet is bound to happen), because *Freedonia* had not filed in time to comply with law 3344.1 that had something to do with registering your country with an international organization that allows people the world over to find out where *Freedonia* actually is, just in case they want to license their name, character or likeness. But by comparison, it was quite a hollow victory for "*trentino,*" who was obviously shaken by the results of his "SOME MISTAKE."

It is interesting to note that in researching the case for Mrs. Teasdale, her designated law firm of Hungadunger, Hungadunger, Hungadunger, Hungadunger and McCormick (recruited from a previous movie and unanimously recommended by the Marx Brothers), had cleverly turned to decisions of recent court cases involving the very same issues, only to come across amazing coincidences regarding the arguments presented to and the ultimate findings of the courts of law that are now a matter of public record in the neighboring Kingdoms of *Klopstockia* and *Kallephornya.*

In spite of the court's rulings and overwhelming condemnation of "*trentino's*" nonethical behavior, he has never nor most probably ever will admit to any guilt or offer an apology for his wrongdoings to Mrs. Teasdale and all the subjects of fairest *Freedonia.* But Mrs. Teasdale also believes he won't, because she feels that he's just plain incapable of doing so.

As "*trentino*" jumped to his feet in his moment of public humiliation in protest over the decisions just handed down by the judge, who had already left the courtroom to get some hot chocolate, he found out very quickly that while engaged in *their* moment of jubilation, the good citizens of *Freedonia,* exhibiting such rarely exhibited euphoric jubilancy, had become so jubilant that they started hurling invective at him, any and all the invective they could find to pelt him with, along with carefully selected 'rotten only' *Freedonian* fruits and vegetables, until the moment they heard Mrs. Teasdale with abounding pride, suddenly burst into song, with a most overly enthusiastic and remarkably high-pitched rendition of a tune uniquely having a lyric of only one line: "VICTORY IS OURS. VICTORY IS OURS. VICTORY IS OURS! VICTORY IS OURS!" The *Freedonia Symphony Orchestra* was seated off to the left throughout the entire court proceedings just in case Mrs. Teasdale would suddenly submit to this kind of urge as she so often has in the past, and sure enough, they heard her exactly the same as they always have heard her all those times before. This made them also want to participate in the now rampant fun and festivities, and the Marx Brothers were to feel the orchestra's desire to contribute in their own way as well.

So with Chico hitting on the lady Concertmaster, and Groucho suddenly from across the courtroom proposing marriage to Mrs. Teasdale, gay divorcee, Harpo grabbed the baton from the conductor and then gave the full orchestra a completely unclear, indecisive downbeat, and with all the musicians understanding its obvious and appropriate implication, turned (almost as one) and heaved their instruments directly at *Freedonia's* own aspiring diva, still in full song, Mrs. Margaret Teasdale . . .

[AS WE FADE TO BLACK AND THE END CREDIT CRAWL]

CHAPTER TWENTY-THREE

Meanwhile, when we returned to our book, you may have by now come to find that it has not been laced with stories about sexual exploits that proudly point to my prowess for prowling through the streets of life as a natural male animal to terrorize the female villagers. This is not to say that over the years I haven't had my share of day to day or night to night dalliances. I am just rather shy about divulging such personal data about myself and any of my roamin' conquests. And I don't think of myself as anything special with regards to your "a good time was had by all."

To paraphrase the great line Texas Senator Lloyd Bentsen once said when comparing Dan Quayle to JFK, "Bill, you are no Wilt Chamberlain."

But I don't mind occasionally referring to the raucous behavior of the Marx Brothers in this line of work. It's much easier to tell you about what a ladies' man Chico was, and how the boys would have great glee from time to time even sharing their women. Of course then, they had extraordinary opportunities to make merry, or whomever, what with being constantly surrounded by the beautiful showgirls that were always present in any Marx Brothers' stage or screen offering.

If it would come to my never-ending "stream of consciousness" mind that there was anyone with any concerns about performance other than on the stage, it would be Groucho. I was told a story about a time Groucho had a problem with becoming vertically aroused. He mentioned this most unfortunate situation to one of his pals at Hillcrest Country Club, and the guy gave Groucho the name of a doctor who should be able to straighten him out, so to speak. The next day Groucho wanders into the Roxbury Medical Building and gets in the waiting elevator, which already has four or five passengers. Now in those days, there were elevator operators that would spirit the Otis to your rightful destination. So, when Groucho was asked by the operator, who instantly recognized him, "Where to, Mr. Marx?"

"I don't know. On what floor do you go to get a hard-on?"

Another time he had the opposite problem. There was a period when he was having no trouble rising to the occasion, but was now fighting a recurring bout with premature ejaculation. To add to his concern, Groucho was to have a date the following night with a lady he knew he could get in the hay. So he went to his Hillcrest buddy again, who highly recommended a specialist in that field to hopefully solve the nasty little problem.

Back to the Roxbury Medical Building Groucho went. The operator knew which floor. After explaining about the upcoming evening's possibilities and the trouble he was having, the good doctor gave Groucho a prescription for a topical cream that when applied to his member, about five minutes later it would create a condition that would allow him some much needed control during the unfolding antics of the evening.

The next day Groucho returned yet again to the Roxbury Medical Building with "the reviews." The doctor asked how it went the night before, and did the topical cream work?

"Perfectly! I came while I was putting it on."

Now, my reason for consulting a doctor about something sexual had a totally different spin than Groucho's consultations. I decided in my fifties, during the time I was married to my "second wife before she became, as previously noted, an ex," that I would like to find out whether it would be possible for me to have a child. So on referral from my doctor/bass player/friend of then thirty-seven years, Ralph Gold, I went to see the eminent, world-renowned specialist who is a pioneer on the cutting edge of those male fertility kinds of things, Dr. Cappy Rothman. On my first visit, he explained to me what my duties and responsibilities would be in order for him to make a definitive analysis. It appeared that judging from what he said, I thought it might be something "fun" to do.

When I next returned to his office to begin carrying out this good doctor's master plan, I walked in being normally apprehensive and self-conscious, even in spite of having lived for years on a nude beach as I reported earlier. I had on the comfortable, loose-fitting jogging suit like they told me to wear and carrying a Time magazine, my reading material while I waited for my orders. A male nurse (thank God) handed me a clipboard with a bunch of papers attached to fill out before step number two. I sat down and proceeded to write. I felt so relieved that I was the only one there in the waiting room, until a guy walked in and sat down next to me. We now were both to know that we were where we were because of something of a very personal nature found within the area of our groin.

As you know me by now to be an affable sort, I asked him what he was in for. Believe it or not, I still haven't lied to you in this book, and I have no reason to start now, so here goes his response. He told me that his girlfriend was giving him oral sex, when suddenly the under skin of his penis somehow got stuck between her teeth, and they had to call someone in to cut them apart.

"Arghh!"

When he said he was there for a check up to make sure everything was, thanks to this good doctor, back to normal, I figured that what I was about to go through was now *really* going to be "fun" by comparison. Just then the male nurse, (thank God), called my name and escorted me through the door where I was met by, yee gods, a *female* nurse, who in turn escorted me to a room that was affectionately named "The Masturbatorium!" She explained to me that in the room there was more written information to fill out and to please bring it to us when you are through along with the plastic jar that is provided. Also, if you experience any trouble at all, there are some magazines there that may help speed you to victory. At no time during the entire spiel did I make eye contact with her. Before entering, I looked up and around, only to see that there were three or four other female nurses looking at me and thinking, "We know where you're going, and we know what you're going to do!" Completely embarrassed now by everything, I opened the door to "The Masturbatorium!," and everyone watched me disappear into its confines. Once I shut and locked the door, I felt some relief being alone.

I looked around and found the room to be nothing more than a restroom with a fancy name. The sink was on the left, the toilet was to the right, and, but wait! Directly in front of me was this huge aquarium filled with all kinds of tropical fish, all staring at me! They were probably thinking, "We know why you're here, and we know what you're going to do!"

For a brief moment I was amused, but I quickly caught myself before giving myself one more chance to reprise my "St. Francis Room" fish medley. Then I was confronted with the decision as to what I should do next, fill out the information first or take care of business first. I figured that I might be too tired to fill out the information after taking care of business, so I chose the info before it would be too late. Upon completion of that task and feeling some sense of accomplishment, like I had passed the DMV's written driver's test, it was now time to take care of business.

In my other hand I had the jar, and though I do not wish to go Freudian on you, it was very soon after that I started to have questions about my sexuality. I found that I could not evade the looks I was getting from the fish, as they certainly were acting like anything but cheerleaders. But they remained fascinated, like if they were slowing down to see a traffic accident. Their whole attitude about my mission was so counterproductive to my mental state, that I felt I had no other choice. Suddenly, the old joke about the thirty-year-old gal and the eighty-five-year-old guy, who wanted to marry, popped into my head. But though she truly loved him, she vowed to marry only if she could have a child with him. Like me, he went to where you find out about things like that. They gave him a jar and put him in a room to exact a specimen. About an hour later, someone noticed that he had not come out of the room. So they opened the door only to find the poor old guy tired and exasperated as hell.

"Are you having problems, sir?"

Forlorn and dejected, he said, "I spent the first twenty-five minutes trying with my right hand until it got tired. Then I tried for the next twenty-five minutes with my left hand, and frankly I just can't get the goddamn lid off of the jar!"

My recalling that joke certainly did nothing to help me out with my situation one bit.

Oh, well, the lady nurse told me that's what the magazines were there for.

Indiscriminately, I picked up one of them and turned to page whatever. Slowly, as I kept turning and viewing, turning and viewing, and turning and viewing, I was starting to, yes, giggle. For some reason, all of those airbrushed twenty year olds with their pointy, perky boobs, everyone in the same kneeling pose, with their tushes in the air, all having their index fingers planted ever so delicately orchestrated in their pouty little mouths eventually sent me into gales of laughter. This prompted the fish to swim around furiously, as under normal conditions, they had never seen this kind of patient behavior before. Suddenly, I realized then that even though barely audible, I was able to hear noises from outside my room, which meant that *they* could probably hear what was going on with me in . . . "The Masturbatorium!" My laughter subsided immediately, and there I was, a ship without a sail, a man without a country. I had to be left to my own devices, so I launched into a half time, Knute Rockne-like–"Win one for the 'Capper'" pep talk.

"Men! Excuse me, I mean man! You've always considered yourself to be a professional, and now is certainly not a time for quitters. Get in there with your head held high! And do what you've got to do, do, do."

I have either forgotten completely, or I blacked out for a short while, but somehow I found that I had managed to have done what I did, did, did. I swear there was some slight applause from the fish. I made myself presentable once again, gathered up my papers, the plastic jar, waved goodbye to the fish, and took a deep breath before opening the door to present someone with my recently acquired bounty. When I walked out trying not to be chalant, sure enough, the nurses welcoming committee was there to greet me with approving smiles, mentally applauding me for what I had just done, done, done.

I was told to take it down the hall to the lab technician and after that, I was free to go. I found it as embarrassing and surprising a moment in my life as I've ever had, when I handed my plastic jar to the *lady* lab technician! Explaining to her that this was not my usual way of presenting this to a lady, she said she understood, and that I would be hearing from her with the results she got, including whether I appear to be normal or abnormal regarding such goodies as sperm count and semen volume. And there is nothing like looking forward to having a nice conversation with a perfect stranger about my sperm count and semen volume.

More so, would I ever get to see Dr. Rothman again? I got the call the following day for what I thought was to be my final consultation with him. When he called me and my "then curious, as well as present wife" into his office, he had us look into the microscope to see why he has determined what he has determined. I didn't know what I was supposed to be seeing, but suddenly something appeared that looked like an aerial view of the Aleutian Islands. I have nothing against the Aleutians, but as I kept on looking, Dr. Cappy was describing to me how malformed my spermatozoa was, and that not only could I probably never be able to have children, but even if there was a remote chance of doing so, it was a very good thing that it never happened.

He then ordered an ultrasonic on my most private of areas, because of something else abnormal that he noticed as a result of my test findings. Whatever dignity you might have thought you had, disappears into thin air as if by the wave of a magician's wand when one goes through the process they use to discover a very common occurrence in forty-percent of all American men called a "varicocele." I do not wish to discuss here the matter of this problem of "male blockage," other than to tell you that as they were wheeling me down a hall on a Gurney for the operation itself and the anesthesiologist asked me if I was allergic to anything. Funny, but it only brought to my mind the time the same question was asked of Buddy Rich as he was going in for heart surgery.

"Yeah, only one thing; Country and Western Music."

The upshot of all this, pardon my painting the disturbing visual, is that I cannot have children.

"Dad, are you disappointed that I never had any kids? I mean, just maybe I might've. . ."

"Why should I be disappointed? It just turned out that way."

"Well, like coming from a family with kids, you know, that kind of atmosphere, you woulda thought maybe I'd . . . ."

"No. *You* thought maybe."

"Yeah but, knowing what it meant to me to be a part of a family, it is one of my life's great regrets that I did not somehow find a way to have a kid I could share that experience with also."

"Son, you already did. You had me. I was your kid."

CHAPTER TWENTY-FOUR

A mom is a mom is a mom forever. To a mom, a son is forever. It's a nonnegotiable contract with no bail out or option clauses, no free agency, and Susan Fleming and I entered into it way back in March of 1938. It was time for me to assume her dependency as she had done for me. Being the eldest of the children and geographically available, I decided to modestly repay her for her dedicated guidance through the years of my most grateful indentured servitude, by being accessible to her for emotional comfort or carrying out normal mundane daily activities.

Recently, we were watching some politician making a speech on television, and he was spewing the same old bromides we'd heard as far back as Herbert Hoover. To bring confidence in him to the voters, he bravely and unabashedly announced that, "We must move forward to the future . . ."

Mom finished his provocative pronouncement with, ". . . so we can be there to catch it if and when it falls."

Mom's 90th Birthday

I suppose it was just Mom's belief that the Fates were in control anyhow, and it was eventually always going to be their call to get us on the right track or derail us. The secret potion of Mom's perpetual "fountain of youth" was the joy she got from anything that smacked of the absurd. The punch line and its variations to the following creakingly old but charming jokes is what we used over and over to justify any unjustifiable stupidity or silliness we would usually find in the daily news or those normal mundane activities:

So, there are these three guys in this mental institution who are up for their semiannual assessment of their faculties by the "in house" psychiatrist. The shrink tells them that he will ask the three of them the same question, and if anyone gets the answer right, he will gladly sign papers releasing them from the institution.

He asks the first one what's three times three. After pondering for a moment, he answered, "Two hundred seventy-four!"

"I'm sorry, that's not the right answer. You are not ready to leave. Next person; what is three times three?"

"Tuesday!"

"No, you're not ready to go yet either. Next; it's your turn. What is three times three?"

After careful deliberation, he said quite calmly, "Nine!"

The shrink was astonished, surprised and delighted.

"You are absolutely correct, and as soon as I sign your papers and turn them into administration you will be free to leave. Just for the record, how did you come to your conclusion?"

"Oh, it was simple, Doc. I just took two hundred seventy-four and divided it by Tuesday."

This punch line would continue to release Mom's endorphins, adding years to her life, and almost every day it appeared as an explanation for something that definitely needed a better explanation than the one that was being offered.

"What do you think is the solution to the Middle East problem, Willy?"

"Tuesday."

"You're sure about that?"

"Of course, Mom."

"How do you know it's Tuesday?"

"I took nine and divided it into two hundred seventy-four."

"Sounds good to me."

Once at a lunch after my passing through a salad bar I concluded, "Mom, don't go near the coleslaw, it's bad."

"How could you tell?"

"I took Tuesday and multiplied it by nine."

Sometimes a simple salutation in a harmless phone call would set her off.

"Hi, Mom. How are you feeling today?"

"Two hundred seventy-four!" And then she would lapse into hysterics.

I think supposition takes up around twenty-three hours of "what if" speculation about what might, could, maybe, perhaps, or possibly happens in the news every day. Or is it two-hundred-seventy-four hours? Mom's conclusion would probably be Tuesday.

Mom remained as sharp and rapier-like throughout her furniture-walking years, but if there was one source of befuddlement for her, I think it probably was the advancements of technology. It seemed to bring out a little bit of her friend, Gracie Allen, in her. Once I explained that a FAX machine transmits almost instantly, paper communications and documents through a telephone line, thus eliminating the two or three-day wait when sending them by postal mail. This concept fascinated her.

"Well, tell me how do they get all those papers to go through those telephone wires?"

Thank you, and say goodnight, Gracie.

Whenever she had trouble with her TV, she would call me frantically. "Willy, I can't find my thing that changes the channels for me."

"The remote control?"

"Yes, and I've looked everywhere for it and I can't find it anywhere. I have looked absolutely everywhere. Why, I even looked under the piano, and I don't even have a piano!"

Once she had a *real serious* dilemma! She couldn't get her ball game on ESPN! So she called me for help. I said that it's very simple, so follow me along. ESPN is on channel thirty-two, so just press three first, and then two, and the game should come right on. She verbally reiterated simultaneously as she pressed them. "First I hit three, and now two," as I heard two very carefully selected beeps on my phone, "Damn, nothing happened! I've still got the same channel."

"Mom, it might work if you try instead doing it on the remote control."

Embarrassed over her lack of technical prowess, she would start to giggle, which would turn into great waves of laughter.

Some people say things that are intended to be funny, and they are. Mom would say things that were not intended to be funny but they were.

Her honesty would often bring about the truth of the moment.

We were coming out of a restaurant when someone tapped Mom on the shoulder. When she whirled around to see who it was, the lady said, "Oh, I'm so sorry, but I thought you were somebody else."

"Well, I am."

Mom and I were tooling down a golf cart path at Tamarisk Country Club, when all of a sudden she announced, "Ah, what a beautiful smell that was!"

I responded with, "What do you mean? I didn't smell anything."

"I know you didn't."

"Really? How do you know?"

"Because, if you had, you would have said, 'Ah, what a beautiful smell that was!'"

At the age of ninety-three, she told Cliffie Norton that she has finally given up on the idea of "kicking the bucket." After having had cancer, jaundice, double pneumonia three times and a heart attack, she continued, "I just can't understand why it's taking me so long to die."

Yes, once a mom, always a mom. However, this "moment of truth" was never brought home to her once a son, always a son philosophy any better than the time I had to conduct a world premiere of one of my symphonic works. It was a very difficult piece to get a handle on because of its constant changes of meter, and we had very limited rehearsal time. Of even greater concern was that it was my first time ever conducting a huge symphony orchestra (all symphony orchestras being huge by nature).

Well, Mom was there for good old moral support.

The performance's ensuing nine minutes was accompanied by sheer terror and a bucket of flop sweat. Still in all, the orchestra and I somehow managed to survive the major pitfalls, overcome the minor potholes, and much to our relief found us all ending at the same time.

World Premieres and unknown works are generally programmed to end the first half of a concert. So it was intermission, and I came off the stand dripping wet from anxiety. I spotted Mom, walked over to her and with some trepidation asked her, "Well, whadya think?"

Without batting an eye, she offered, "You need a hair cut."

Mom always had a thirst for seeing the world's topography and studying its various cultures. Even at the age of eighty eight she was one of only six non-crew passengers on a cargo ship that sailed from Long Beach, California to New Zealand and back, a trip lasting almost a month. When a friend and Mom were discussing the sensitive subject of "passing on," Mom calmly revealed, "When I die, I want my ashes cast out to sea." Her friend then queried why Mom had settled on that particular choice. And as only my mom could with her pure honesty, she reacted with, "Oh, come now. You've always known how much I love to travel!"

It was Thanksgiving, 2002. Barbara and I had a small dinner party which included Mom. Thanksgiving has always been our family's favorite of all the holidays. We were all sitting at the dinner table eating and chatting. Every now and then, I looked over and saw Mom smiling at a portrait hanging on the wall behind Barbara. It was a John Decker painting of Dad with a seductively impish look on his face as Thomas Gainesboro's "Blueboy."

The Decker "Blueboy."

Back I went to eating and more chatting. The dinner continued, and everyone was still enjoying themselves, in spite of the fact that volume and discomfort were becoming bedfellows. I kept glancing Mom's way, only to see her looking up often at the painting, and I began to believe it was as if she was saying to him, "Hold on, Poppy, it won't be too much longer now."

It was a little more than a month later that Barbara and I, after some luncheon charity event we had attended, decided to stop off at the rest home where Mom was living to see her and just say hello. Her sliding glass door was locked and we could see she was sitting in her chair watching television. We motioned to her to open the door for us, and she saw us but couldn't seem to get up out of her chair, so we went around to the front desk and got a key to let us in her other door. When we got into her room, we tried to get her up from the chair, but to no avail. It was clear that she wasn't right, so I called the home's nursing department. They came quickly and felt it was going to be necessary to make an immediate and most urgent call to the paramedics. In almost no time they arrived, and it even took *them* some doing to get Mom on the stretcher. As they were wheeling her out of her living room on their way to the ambulance, Mom looked up at me and half whispered, "Now Willy, you take good care of yourself."

I knew.

The next eight days at Eisenhower Hospital were spent with the kids coming in from out of town to see Mom, knowing that it wouldn't be long before, as the Fates would so ordain it, she and Dad would be chasing each other through the clouds, reunited once again, this time for eternity. I had long ago agreed to do a fund-raising speaking engagement at Temple Sinai on December 22, 2002. Minnie, who came in town driving some eighty-plus miles every day from her home in Orange, CA, stayed with mom at the hospital that evening until Barbara and I would get over there the minute my engagement was through. When we returned to Eisenhower, there was Minnie holding Mom's hand.

I looked down at Mom, who was not in any pain from the heart attack they finally had narrowed their diagnosis down to, and I assured her that I was a much bigger hit at the temple than David and his harp could have ever hoped to be. She made an attempt to

smile. As Dad had pointed out,

"The only weapon you are born with is a sense of humor."

Thank God she hung onto that precious weapon to comfort her right to the end. I took Mom's other hand, and Barbara held onto Mom's feet. Within a half an hour, we were to see the line on her monitor flatten out.

And I knew that Mom had been waiting for me until I got there, so she could hear the reviews.

Like Dad, Mom died without an enemy. (In her case, having always been her outspoken self, she managed to outlive all of hers.)

Mom's Memorial service on her 96th Birthday, February 19, 2003.

One night less than a year later, I was having another one of those now-and-then dreams about Dad I'd been having over the years. But this one was decidedly different from all the others. I was immediately surprised that it was the very first time I found myself not being angry with Dad for having left me in this life with the feeling of abandonment. As the perfect poster child for Surrealism, he was just standing there in front of me, with this big stupid grin ear to ear, dressed in red "Doctor Denton's" (with the feet and rear flap like long johns), wearing swim fins, goggles, a snorkel and carrying one of those big "Neptune" pitchforks.

Stunned, but not completely speechless, I asked him, "Why in God's name are you dressed that way?"

"Because *this* is the way I *chose* to look, and the only way I could look like this was by wearing exactly what I have on."

"But why, what's the purpose?"

"Because this is what I *wanted* to look like."

Before I could ask a deeper rational question, I suddenly bolted out of my dream and into a very puzzling waking state of mind. I asked myself what the hell *that* was all about! Was he trying to tell me something? Or maybe it was *me* trying to tell myself something? Slowly, the fog was lifting, until I came to realize what the message of that dream might just have been beckoning to me.

Reflections.

Dad always became the overall vision of any goal he wanted to achieve. There would be a process to go through to reach his goal. It mattered not to him whether other people might think of his goal as silly or frivolous. What they thought was not important enough to allow their view to impede his pursuit. It was his goal and no one else's, his choice of what he wanted to order from life's vast menu, and he never lost sight of what was necessary to make it come true. There would always be some brass ring available to him to reach out for, a ring for comedy, a ring for music, a ring for family. Sometimes the brass ring was nothing more important than, or could *not be* anything more important than the desire to just lie on his back on some soft green grass, look skyward and be royally entertained by the graceful and unpredictable ebb and flow of a colorful kite in its dance with the wind, all the while feeling comforted by the knowledge that the other end of the string was ever so securely tied to his big toe.

Dad was a clown with a silver lining. He was in a class all by himself, and not because he was the only one who didn't graduate from the second grade. No, indeed. For me, Dad made wisdom from intelligence. When I was young, he told me that it wasn't what you do in life that's important; it's how you feel about yourself while you are doing whatever it is you are doing. As long as you aren't hurting someone else in the quest of your dreams, always look for things to do that can bring you pleasure and personal fulfillment. Dad had a clear channel to himself for living life the way Adolph Arthur Harpo Marx wished it to be lived. He most assuredly *was* elemental. The guy just knew how to live. How strange I still feel perhaps, it was the Fates that had me dream that surrealistic dream on that very special day, November 23, his birthday. I have had no dreams fearing abandonment since.

"Dad?"

"Yes, Bill."

"This has been weird for me. Talking to you like this, obviously, considering the circumstances. And looking back over my life. Weird, and sad. And great."

"Are things more or less the way you want them to be?"

"I think so. I've gotta admit that life is pretty good. Good wife, good home, still jazzed by music the same way it was when we were together. Hey, what else is there?"

"What else, indeed."

"I guess I'm happy with who I am. Who you made me into."

"I played a part in helping you become who you are, a lot of us did, but nobody made you into anything. That was you all the way, Son."

"Composer. Pianist. Entertainer. Friend. Husband. Whatever. I'm just glad to be Bill Marx."

"Nobody does it better. You're the best at it there ever was."

"Thanks, but it's just giving it my best."

"I'm gonna run."

"What for? Where are you going?"

"I'm finished. Time to go. Gotta see Mom. I'm proud of you, and I love you very much. Goodbye, Son."

"I love you too, Dad."

There I go again. Yesterday I wept. A lot. Unmercifully. In public. No, I didn't get married again. I am still very happily attached, thank you. Barbara and I went to see **The Producers**, as many have and many more will. But just like when we were taking our wedding vows, I was in dire need of a hanky, as I cry at happy things. Perhaps the producers, along with Mel Brooks, Susan Stroman, the cast and everyone connected with the show shed tears of joy finding out that the critics hailed it as a smash hit.

However, I may be the only person in the audience of multitudes who has enjoyed this comedic romp that ever cried throughout the entire performance. There was the song about one's hopes and dreams. There was another song about believing in yourself. Corny? You bet. And there is always the time when the show is over. I have never met a curtain call I didn't cry through. Yesterday was no different.

I suppose I am wont to over romanticize the feeling I get when an actor gets to "steal that extra bow," or when the entire cast joins hands and bows in unison as if they have, as one, completed their mission to entertain. But I think of the lifetime of hard work, competition and dedication to their craft they endured for you to get to see the maturation of the product—that performance. And whether you were a star or an understudy during the show's run, you all shared coming together as a family, the same experience of having realized your hopes and dreams. You made it, baby!

But yesterday was different for me. I was out there on stage as a youth, in my angel's outfit, placing Dad's harp in the right position for his solo and then anxiously waiting for my very own "Eat at

Olivelli's" laugh. I was backstage in the dressing room loading up Dad's sleeve with the four-hundred knives and making sure that the carrot was in the upper right inside pocket. And I was there in the wings, watching Dad hearing the applause, receiving the reward he so richly deserved. Oh, how I wish that I could do it just once, more, just one more show with my dad.

The only time on stage that I ever completely lost control of myself was a few years ago at a curtain call taking a bow with Kitty Carlisle. I was her accompanist this one evening for an autobiographical piece about her life both in show business and in general.

The show ended and I went over to this ninety-one-year-old treasure of the theatre, took her hand and together, as if we had rehearsed it, took our bow. As I was staring out at the audience's standing ovation, I realized, "Hey, I'm standing here holding the hand of a woman who worked with my dad in their biggest movie hit ever, *A Night at The Opera*, sixty-six years ago!" Another time, and now, another Marx. I burst into a flood even Jamestown would have been envious of. Later, at the reception, I asked her, "Don't you know when to quit already with us Marxes?"

All my life I have cried at curtain calls, and at least once I can say, just like at my circumcision, I cried at my own.

Kitty Carlisle Hart and me.

CHAPTER TWENTY-SIX

This book, much to my surprise, has turned into an exercise in self-discovery. As I have progressed through the recapitulation of my own experiences, I have found that as subconscious recollections and feelings rise to my conscious mind, I have not really magnified them in their importance to me, but simply clarified them in an objectivity that only the passing of time could bring.

I'm the only person I know whose second wife fixed him up with his third wife even before the second marriage ended. (I like farsighted women.) I'm the only person I know who received an anonymous gift from parents I never really got to know. I credit them for giving me my innate musical talent. I know of no one else who could have nurtured nor appreciated more those talents than my adopted father and mother. In a much truer sense, I belonged with them more than I belonged with my star-crossed birth parents. Stumbling upon the identity of my "other" family was as enlightening as it was miraculous. But again, music was the conduit that led me back to them. I think sometimes that we're connected to the people we belong to not by genetic or family ties, or even by proximity. We're connected at some cosmic level that transcends time and space and life and death, and perhaps we're drawn closer to them in our grand journey. Certainly that and perhaps fate might very well account for us four adopted children coming from totally diverse backgrounds with distinctly different personalities, having had the good fortune in being given the opportunity to pursue our own unique brass rings of life.

We four children were surely raised in a time of great simplicity and innocence. Now the immediacy of my every day is also a time for new self-discovery. Maestro, a little soap box music if you please.

In today's world of rapid technological sophistication, computers provide our fingertips with correct answers without our knowing the process that gets us to the solution. It appears unnecessary to know the "why" of it. No longer is there the curiosity or the need to care about *how* the work was actually done. But I guess with the faster paced life we now live, the end product must come quickly at the expense of the journey. (I know without my computer, it would have probably taken me at least ten years to crank out this book.)

In my view of today's increasingly faster-than-a-speeding-bullet pace world, half-second subliminal editing cuts on TV commercials bombard my senses with fleeting, often improbable images. I am left wondering what the hell any of it has to do with the purpose, substance or quality of the what they're trying to sell me. These snippets appear to be more for entertainment purposes than giving me valuable information about the product. (All this invariably leads me to rarely if ever remember the product's name.)

Today, we appear to have an insatiable appetite for negative news stemming from our morbid fascination about bad people doing awful things to good people. In this society of escalating aggressiveness comes the enormously rising appeal of football's innate manifesto of physical force for territorial imperative, which makes me believe that *it* is perhaps becoming our new national pastime, replacing the inherent skill requirements and intellectual maneuverings of my beloved baseball. Basketball also appears to display a more antagonistic attitude toward the opponent than ever before. It seems our present society demands that sport be that way.

In this world of two-bar musical phrases, all too often do I feel its player or some band just loves to hammer them out repetitively, with the presumption that its profound musical significance was not appreciated the first time it was offered. I grew up in a generation that didn't need predictability to satisfy their lives. From my perspective, predictability does not represent one's artistic evolution, and I shun the presence of it in other artists' work as well as my own. Also in today's whirling world, I sure as hell find a most disturbing absence of a thing called grace. I have always felt it something to be necessarily appreciated. Arts and entertainment apparently do imitate life.

The complex world of what I see and hear today redefines, by very obvious comparison, that simplicity and innocence of the past, because for me, I believe those qualities don't exist anymore. Nobody knows what I loved. Nobody remembers what made me laugh. Nobody cares how I spent my days, and with what distractions. They're all gone, and other generations have come along to take my place. But then again, I suppose way back around 60 A.D., Pliny the Elder was expressing the same feelings. It's the way of the world, I guess.

Still in all, I welcome the challenge of blending my memories with the seductively new ideas that are being offered me by our evolving planet. These purely personal observations about this changing society of ours will never keep me from continuing each day to contribute my time and energy to others. It is now my purpose. More than ever, it is my time to do so.

Though the past makes me miss things I may never participate in again, it does remind me that "once upon a time" was the prelude to the wonderful life I've had so far. I occasionally look into my curio cabinet that houses many memories, and I take particular note of my Astarte fertility goddess, an Amlash bull and various oil lamps, all of which are authenticated Persian relics over five-thousand years old. I got them during my sojourn to Israel with Mom, and little would they know when they were first crafted that their destiny would be finding me and becoming part of my family. Just like all the rest of my brood, they, too, are placed strategically so their antiquity can both see and be a part of my contemporary world.

Though I am now without Susan and Harpo, I am no longer emotionally the same as I was without them before they adopted me. I suppose those feelings of abandonment I have found so frighteningly fearful in the past were nurtured by the fact I had lived fourteen months of a life fortunately lost. But in the life I found, I am now at peace, with Mom and Dad, who still comfort me with their presence as if they were in the next room, available to me any time I may need them.

Music is still my staff of life, and so I will continue to take piano gigs whenever possible. Also I'm sure there is at least one more symphonic piece in me to discover and perhaps one more film to score.

Jack Jones, years after Barbara first met him, and your friendly piano player lost in a musical moment.

Barbara and I share Bill Asher's special day for receiving his Star on the *Palm Springs Walk of Fame*.

From my early days to the present, I've come life's full circle with two all-time singer/actors, the late Howard Keel and my dear musical and spiritual colleague, Herb Jeffries.

I, too, believe the notion that everyone in the world has a book in them. Surely though some books will be better than others, we still must not be afraid to write our own unique story. So, with prodding by some sadistic friends, I have come to find out just recently that I, too, have had one in me. However, one thing continues to trouble me greatly. If, in fact, as Mom believed, that the ever-present Fates; Clotho, Lachesis and Atropos have already

written everything that has ever happened, then why did I have to write my autobiography in the first place? Thank you, my sadistic friends.

Now, in my world here in Rancho Mirage, with my wife, Barbara, I *still* might not be quite ready enough mentally for what lies ahead, but I *do* have an ace up my sleeve—my greatest resource has always been and will continue to be from the people I've met along the way that have helped to shape my journey through life and blessed me with their unique presence. They are my perennial mentors and shall forever serve as an illuminating beacon guiding me through what is left of my ongoing voyage into the next dimension.

Thank you all.

EPILOGUE

I now know there are certain things I will never come to know, though I must forever press forward in my Quixotic pursuit for their answers. There are some things life has taught me, and I must continue to use that knowledge as a solid foundation to be converted into wisdom. There have been some things I just instinctively knew without having to learn. Still, no matter how curious and extraordinary it was for me to have already known the answers to those things, I have now found it unnecessary to know how I knew.

All because I have had the luck of the draw.

Thank you, Clotho, Lachesis and Atropos.

CODA

Adoption tells me that I am chosen. I have no rational answer, nor do I wish to pursue one, as to why I have been chosen. I, along with Alex, Jimmy and Minnie, am a pawn of the Fates, having experienced such a strange series of events that led me down a pre-ordained path into the lives of Harpo and Susan Marx. I can never be thought of as an "accident." When I was chosen, that made me special; not better, not worse, not different; just very special. Those who choose are also very special. They make a voluntary commitment to provide as good a life for me as they are capable; so in return, it must be my responsibility to honor their commitment to me.

Aside from the fact that my heart goes out to my birth mother, especially because of how she must have felt during the time of her excruciating decision and then having to live with it forever on, one important thing rings a bell for me personally. May I once more step onto my soapbox for a moment, please? Thank you.

Because we are no longer living in the dark ages, I feel that there should be a federal law, even international, that allows all adopted children access to their birthparents' medical history. You can put together all the arguments opposing a law, and they still will not add up to the most important thing any human being must have the right to; all the knowledge one can obtain that applies to one's own health. When I learned that my birth mother died of a heart- related condition, perhaps exacerbated or caused by what we now call cholesterol, I was luckily able to control what I have inherited with proper medication and nutrition. (I happen to be a major manufacturer and distributor of LDL, Low Density or so called "Bad" Cholesterol.) Let all us adopted kids know what we have lurking inside us. That necessary knowledge will help toward seeing to it that we all experience healthier and more productive lives. And it won't hurt anybody, especially us!

I wish to heap praise all over Matt Hickey, master documenteur, whose literary insights guided me through the fog shrouding my memory and into the mist clouding my reality. Without his tireless attention to both detail and economy, this book would have been twelve-hundred and forty-five pages long. Surely we all owe him a debt of gratitude. While there is just no end to his talent, he is still looking for the beginning of it. I am proud to say from the bottom of my heart, and vice versa, of all the people I have met along the way, Matt certainly is one of them.

Thank you, Matt.

I am also most grateful to Lt. U.S.N., Daniel Kinske, for taking time out from his normal duties like, well, protecting our country from impending peril. Staunch, stellar and even stout are apt adjectives in describing his supportive participation and vital contribution to the collating, scanning and, with great deft, helping with the appropriate placement of these rare, previously unpublished-never-before-been-seen-by-the-public-photographs that pepper the pages of this book. I salute you.

Thank you, "Dan, The Scan."

ACKNOWLEDGMENTS

To my attorney of so many years, Eddie Ezor, who, for those so many years through his indefatigable pursuit of justice, has accidentally stumbled upon all the possible legal loopholes necessary to have kept me, but barely, out of harm's way.

To Sandy Krinski, a longtime friend and Emmy Award-winning writer of comedy and drama, who also crafted the book of my touring comedy/concert show with Carrol McLaughlin for **Columbia Artists**. Thank you, Sandy, for my blatant use of your talent, your sense of humor and for your life-long love of the Marx Brothers.

To my friend Jimmy Bryant, singing voice in cinema for Richard Beymer in **West Side Story**, and James Fox in **Thoroughly Modern Millie**; and master orchestrator, for all his help in our various collaborations, and who always feared at the end of a job that he'd never work again, is *still* working again.

To Rob Bader, huge fan of the New York Mets, oh, and incidentally, curator extraordinaire of Marx Brothers rare film and video footage, and master producer of many wonderful DVD anthologies including that of Uncle Groucho's classic radio and TV show, **You Bet Your Life.**

To Paul Wesolowski for keeping the Brothers "out there" with a passion that can only define him as one uncontrollable memorabiliac of mind-boggling proportions.

To Ray White, our man in the United Kingdom, who continues to champion the Marx Brothers throughout Europe on blind faith alone.

To just some of the additional diversions that filled my early years and stayed deep within me all these years; Gleason; Cronkite; Ed Wynn; Captain Midnight's space decoder; Tom Mix's whistling ring; "Holy Moly;" *The Green Hornet; Time for Beany;* the song, "Ticonderoga pencils, are on their way to fame, a fine American pencil, with a fine American name;" Saturday afternoon serials at the "Hitching Post" theater; "You betchum, Red Ryder;" Roy and Dale; Bob Nolan and the Sons of the Pioneers; Gene and Champion; The Lone Ranger and Silver; Tonto and Scout; "The William Tell Overture;" *The Huntley/Brinkley Report;* Eric Severeid; Edwin Newman; Jack Paar; "Uncle Miltie;" *Burns and Allen; I Love a Mystery;* Jack Doc and Reggie; Bergen and McCarthy; *Inner Sanctum* and its "Won't you come in for a kindly thought, hmm?;" Sheldon Leonard and his "Your Money or Your Life," Jack Benny and his "I'm thinking It Over!;" Dennis Day, Alice Faye and Phil Harris; Fred Allen and his "Alley;" *The Gillette Friday Night Fights*, with Don Dunphy; Red Barber; Mel Allen; Russ Hodges and his proclamation, "The Giants win the pennant!!!, The Giants win the pennant!!!;" L.A. Rams; The Los Angeles Dons; *Your Hit Parade* conductors Axel Stordahl and Lud Gluskin; Music by De Vol; *The Tonight Show* with Steve Allen; Louie "Hi-ho, Steverino" Nye; Tom Poston; Don Knotts; Sergeant Bilko; Skitch Henderson; Lamont Cranston and Margo Lane; Bulldog Drummond; *The Fat Man* with J. Scott Smart; Jack "Just the facts, ma'am" Webb; Nick Carter, 'Master Detective'; Sam Spade, 'Private Eye'; Dick Tracy; *Alfred Hitchcock Presents; Lux Radio Theater*, hosted by Cecil B. DeMille; *The Longine Symphonette*; *Information, Please; Can You Top This* and its Senator Claghorn; *Queen for a Day; This Is Your Life* with Ralph Edwards; *You Are There* with Edward R. Murrow; *Crusader Rabbit; Ozzie and Harriet; Vic and Sade; The Bickersons; The Great Gildersleeve; Our Miss Brooks* with Eve Arden and Richard Crenna; "Faster than a speeding bullet!;" *Terreeeee and the Pirates; Jack Armstrong, the All-American Boy;* Joe Palooka; The Katzenjammer Kids; The Little King; Blondie,

Dagwood, J. C. Dithers; Lowell Thomas; Gabriel Heater; Walter Winchell; Jimmy Fiddler; Hedda; Louella; and Manny, Moe and Jack. These are but a few.

To Jim and Jackie Lee Houston, who, through their kindness and generosity, reunited Mom, Dad and me with our adjacent stars on the Palm Springs Walk of Stars, providing a most memorable day for me, and, fortunately, for Mom, who was there for her honor to enjoy as well.

To "Aunt" Barbara Sinatra, for loving my mom and dad, and having the foresight to realize that The Mrs. Zeppo Marx Center just didn't sound right, so no way could it have ever achieved the success that The Barbara Sinatra Center has had over the years in helping to make a better life for abused children.

To Miriam and Maxine and Bob, my special Marx cousins, for making me feel so special being their Marx cousin.

To my dear cousin, Donna Klapperich Morin, in appreciation for her vital contribution to this book regarding the Klapperich family history, and mine as well.

To all you loyal Marx Brothers' fans the world over . . . .

To life, it definitely has been.

ABOUT THE AUTHOR

Bill Marx is a musician of some note. Many believe it to be E flat, as those familiar with his body of work find it woven into the very fabric of his angular and probing melodies. He uses it a lot. As a jazz pianist, Mr. Marx has recorded numerous recorded recordings that are really hard to find or are no longer available. As a composer, he has indeed distinguished himself in Hollywood, California by his scoring for the Silver Screen. Many of the movies Mr. Marx has penned for include film, picture and sound. He has drawn kudos for his sensitive yet perspicacious musical contributions to defunct and probably never to be seen again television shows. And for very good reason. Mr. Marx has written countless, count them countless works for the concert world that have been performed in their entirety from beginning to end.

It has been said, by whom we are not exactly sure, that the measure of one's true artistic musical genious is found in the tenser tympanums of his or her adoring fans. If, in fact, this is the ultimate accolade bestowed by an audience's recognition of a truly creative soul's unique aesthetic brilliance, it is then the axiom by which Mr. Marx is so dubiously forced to live out the rest of his life. Upon closer examination, this postulate, as others might prefer to call it, includes the notion that the "bigger picture" comes in to play when the artist receives a well deserved "retrospective" for lifetime achievement. This unfortunately usually occurs after said artist's passing. And for some reason beyond reason, it apparently heightens public awareness, hence building into enough of a frenzy to exact even more appreciation of said artist's relentless contributions to the free world, and, of course, the justification for subsequently having one helluva going away party.

Thus Mr. Marx currently is living in fear of this reality.

<u>CREDITS</u>

CONCERT WORKS

OPENING REMARKS (STRING ORCH.)

CELEBRATION SUITE FOR STRINGS (& FULL ORCH.)

IMAGES FOR HARP AND STRING ORCH.
(ANN MASON STOCTON, SOLOIST. CARROL MCLAUGHLIN, SOLOIST. ANN PILOT, SOLOIST)

RHAPSODY FOR ALTO SAXOPHONE (STRING & FULL ORCHESTRAS)
(VICTOR MOROSCO, SOLOIST)

CONCERTO FOR VIOLIN (STRING ORCH.)
(ISRAEL BAKER, SOLOIST)

CONCERTINO FOR FLUTE, "THE PROMISED LAND"
(FULL ORCH.)

"FRIENDS" (CELLO & HARP)
(STEVEN ISSERLIS, CELLO, SOLOIST)

MUSIC FOR STRING QUARTET (& FULL ORCH.)

FANTASY FOR PIANO AND ORCHESTRA
(JOANNE GRAUER, SOLOIST)

CHORALE FOR FOUR CELLOS

TEXTURES FOR SOLO HARP (CARROL MCLAUGHLIN, SOLOIST)

"MUSINGS" (SEXTET)

CONCERTO FOR TWO HARPS AND ORCHESTRA
CARROL MCLAUGHLIN, ROSALYN SIMPSON, SOLOISTS, WILLIAM KIRSCHKE, CONDUCTOR)

DIALOGUE FOR TWO HARPS
(CARROL MCLAUGHLIN, JOSEF MOLNAR, SOLOISTS)

"SHAPES" (FULL ORCH.)

FANFARE FOR ORCHESTRA

RECORDINGS

PRODUCED, ARRANGED, CONDUCTED AND PERFORMED:

JAZZ KALAIDESCOPE (VEE JAY)

MY SON THE FOK SWINGER (VEE JAY)

LIVE AT THE LOSERS (VEE JAY)

NIGHT TIME IS THE RIGHT TIME (VEE JAY)

FROM HARPO WITH LOVE (GUARDIAN)

ECHOES OF THE PAST [VOL. 1] (HARPIANO)

ECHOES & INTERLUDES [VOL.2] (HARPIANO)

PRODUCED, ARRANGED AND CONDUCTED:

THE BEST OF WYNTON KELLY (VEE JAY)

THE BOBBY VINTON SONGBOOK—"THE CASTAWAY STRINGS" (VEE JAY)

THE PETER, PAUL AND MARY SONGBOOK—"THE CASTAWAY STRINGS" (VEE JAY)

ARRANGED AND CONDUCTED:

HARPO—HARPO MARX (MERCURY)

HARPO AT WORK—HARPO MARX (MERCURY)

PLEASE DON'T EAT THE DAISIES—DORIS DAY (COLUMBIA)

ALEXANDRIA THE GREAT—LOREZ ALEXANDRIA (IMPULSE)

LOVE STROKES—GARY LEMEL/BILL MARX (CBS SIGNATURE)

HOW FAST FOREVER GOES—GARY LEMEL (HEADFIRST)

MOTION PICTURE SCORING

COMPOSED, CONDUCTED AND PRODUCED MUSIC FOR THE FOLLOWING FILMS:

WEEKEND PASS—(REVIEW PROD.)

HOLLYWOOD AFTER DARK—(JOHN HAYES PROD.)

COUNT YORGA, VAMPIRE!—(AIP)

THE RETURN OF COUNT YORGA—(AIP)

THE DEATHMASTER—(AIP)

SCREAM, BLACULA!—(AIP)

ACT OF VENGENCE—(AIP)

INVISIBLE STRANGLER—(Jordan-Lyon Prod.)

NO DEPOSIT, NO RETURN—(Golden Union Pictures)

MOVING UP—(AVCO Industries)

JOHNNY VIK—(Nauman Films)

TERROR HOUSE—(Far West Distributors)

MR. TOO MUCH—(Too Much Prod.)

BIG TROUBLE—(Columbia Pictures)

MURPHY'S ROMANCE—(Columbia Pictures)

WHO'S THAT GIRL?—(Warner Brothers)

FLAPJACK FLOOZIE—(Schillervision)

TELEVISION SCORING

Composed and conducted music for the following TV shows:

THE DONNA REED SHOW—(Desilu)

DAN RAVEN—(Desilu)

LOVE BOAT—(Aaron Spelling Prod.)

KEEPER OF THE WILD—(20TH CENTURY FOX)

FANTASY ISLAND—(SPELLING-GOLDBERG)

TELL ME A STORY—(WEINER GROUP CORP.)

STARSKY AND HUTCH—(SPELLING-GOLDBERG)

THE GRASS THAT NEVER BREAKS—(PBS-BALLET GRANT FROM NAT'L ENDOWMENT FOR THE ARTS)

THE TONIGHT SHOW—(NBC)

FROM HERE TO MATERNITY, 1986 (SCHILLERVISION)

THE UNKNOWN MARX BROTHERS, 1993 (PBS)

OTHER BOOKS BY BILL MARX . . . . .

INDEX